*Social and Economic Reform
in Ecuador*

# Social and Economic Reform in Ecuador

## Life and Work in Guayaquil

*Ronn F. Pineo*

University Press of Florida

Gainesville/Tallahassee/Tampa/Boca Raton

Pensacola/Orlando/Miami/Jacksonville

01 00 99 98 97 96 6 5 4 3 2 1

Library of Congress Cataloging-in-Publication Data
Pineo, Ronn F., 1954–
    Social and economic reform in Ecuador: life and work in Guayaquil  / Ronn F. Pineo.
        p.     cm.
    Includes bibligraphical references and index.
    ISBN 0-8130-1437-9 (alk. paper)
        1. Guayaquil (Ecuador)—Economic conditions.    2. Guayaquil (Ecuador)—Social
    conditions.    3. Urbanization—Ecuador—Guayaquil—History.    I. Title.
    HC203.G78P56    1996
    330.9866′32—dc20                                                                                      95-45919

The University Press of Florida is the scholarly publishing agency for the State University System of Florida, comprised of Florida A & M University, Florida Atlantic University, Florida International University, Florida State University, University of Central Florida, University of Florida, University of North Florida, University of South Florida, and University of West Florida.

University Press of Florida
15 Northwest 15th Street
Gainesville, FL 32611

*To Ardis and Tommy*

# Contents

# Figures, Maps, and Tables

## Figures

## Maps

## Tables

# Acknowledgments

The National Endowment for the Humanities, Towson State University, and the University of California, Irvine, all generously provided funding for this project.

I would also like to thank a few of the many people who have helped me. For their time, friendship, and support I will always be grateful to Jaime Rodríguez-O., David Rock, David Bushnell, James Baer, Julio Estrada Ycaza, Lois Roberts, Roger Davis, Juan Maiguashca, Carmen Aguilar Rendon, Esperanza Cardenas de Moreira, Delia Tello González, Cecilia Estrada de Ycaza, Antonieta Palacios, Emily Daugherty, Mark Whitman, Joe Moreland, Joyce Moreland, John Schebeck, Michael Martin, Rev. Paul Martin, Monica Martin, John Thomas Boyle, Charlene Boyle, Eddie O'Meara, Joyce O'Shaughnessy, Michael O'Meara, Jo O'Meara, Shelley J. Jensen, Michael Jensen, Jayne M. Pineo, Smith C. W. Pineo, Maryanne Pineo, Noel K. Pineo, Julie Pineo, Emily D. E. Pineo, Ronn Pineo (*père*), Claudia Pineo, Thomas O'Meara Pineo, and Ardis Ann O'Meara.

All photographs in this volume are from the collection of Julio Estrada Ycaza and are reproduced by permission of Cecilia Estrada de Ycaza.

# Introduction

Across Latin America the late nineteenth and early twentieth centuries brought exciting changes and new challenges. Although rising raw material exports generated riches, the concomitant process of rapid urbanization inexorably created heightened social strains. This dynamic tension is the theme of this book, which is a case study into one of the most central of modern historical issues, the difficult process of urban social reform.

Beginnings in most things count for a great deal, and for Latin America the period from 1870 to 1930 was an especially important one: it was the dawn of the modern urban age. As Latin America's leading urban historian, James Scobie, has noted, in the years before the 1870s the cities "generally . . . appeared small, poor and broken down," but "during the last decades of the nineteenth century, . . . the urban landscape of Latin America was completely transformed."[1]

During these years Latin American cities rebounded from their long post-independence economic slump, responding to export opportunities in the international economy. In Western Europe and the eastern United States, large markets opened up for Latin American raw materials: inputs for the spreading industrialization, Latin American copper, tin, rubber, cotton, nitrates, and wool; and, for the expanding European and U.S. consumer markets of middle-class employees and better-paid workers, Latin American coffee, sugar, wheat, beef, cacao, and tobacco.[2] As the value of Latin America's total exports steadily increased, cities developed as vital entrepots and processing centers for this rising trade and attracted ever-increasing numbers of immigrants and migrants, people who came in hope of finding a better life. The age of the modern Latin American city had begun.[3]

Remarkably, on this critical topic of Latin American urbanization history, very little has been accomplished. In the words of the leading scholars, works are "few and far between," and with so many gaps that the entire field must be judged "relatively unexplored."[4] Those urban histories that do exist are too often descriptive city biographies. The few studies that offer analysis almost invariably focus on narrow technical matters such as variable patterns of spatial development. And works from other disciplines, such as sociology, have only limited utility for those who frame historical questions.[5]

While there has been a great deal of attention given to the problems engendered by the massive urban growth in contemporary Latin America, scholars have interpreted these concerns as strictly a post–World War II phenomenon, the powerful immediacy of the present-day crises leading them to emphasize short-term causes. But while the extent of the present challenges must not be denied, their roots run deeper, stretching back to a critical period between 1870 and 1930.[6]

This crucial period presents further historiographical concerns. If the economic history of Latin America's export-led growth of the late nineteenth and early twentieth centuries has been the subject of serious study (Roberto Cortes-Conde and Stanley J. Stein provide an extensive discussion and guide to the literature in their 1977 publication *Latin America: A Guide to Economic History, 1830–1930*), the social history of Latin America for this era remains extremely underdeveloped.[7] Only a couple of historians have provided examples of what can be done and demonstrated the great value of a more inclusionary approach: most notably, Peter DeShazo, in his 1983 book *Urban Workers and Labor Unions in Chile, 1902–1927*, and June Hahner, in her 1986 work *Poverty and Politics: The Urban Poor in Brazil, 1870–1920*. Latin American urban social history for the late nineteenth and early twentieth centuries is thinnest of all.

We need works that offer a historical assessment of working-class life and living conditions in Latin American cities during the late nineteenth and early twentieth centuries. We need to know much more about the employment patterns, social conditions, and the politics of crime, education, and health care for urban Latin America during this key period.[8] The existing literature can offer only the roughest sense of conditions in turn-of-the-century cities and, more seriously, only a limited understanding of the difficult and complicated process of effectively responding to these conditions with needed social reforms.

Making comparisons, discerning patterns, and constructing theories is an especially weak area in the existing literature. Because urbanization has been more extensively studied for Europe and North America, theories drawn from that experience have often been employed in an effort to understand Latin America. This practice is unsound, for these theories are quite ill-suited to Latin American cities, cities which were historically less industrialized and far less politically inclusionary than those of the United States and western Europe.

Within Latin America, generally only the few great primary cities have received any attention at all; historians have given nearly no consideration to the many, the nonindustrial, nonprimary cities. Unfortunately, too many scholars have made the convenient assumption that the economic, political, and social patterns found in the few large cities must also hold for the many medium-sized ones.

For the nation of Ecuador, the entire field of social history remains in its absolute infancy. On Guayaquil for the late colonial to early independence era there is Michael Hamerly's 1973 book, *Historia social y económica de la antigua provincia de Guayaquil, 1763–1842,* but the late nineteenth and early twentieth centuries have yet to receive any real coverage.[9] Much of what has been written on Ecuador deals with the nation's political history and features partisan biographies of leaders and detailed treatments of Ecuador's boundary claims.[10] Historians of Ecuador, mostly *serranos* (from the highlands) working with archival resources from and about the sierra, have further concentrated their attention on Quito, the national capital, and have tended to ignore Guayaquil, despite the fact that Guayaquil is now more than four times the size of Quito. Indeed, for the whole field of Ecuadorian historiography there is much, much left to do.

In part the lack of study of Latin American social and urban history stems from the lack of source material. Several serious difficulties complicated the research task. As other historians exploring the social history of urban Latin America for this era have discovered to their dismay, the rich sources mined by scholars in Europe and the United States seldom exist in Latin America.[11]

This is especially true for Ecuador. Elsewhere in Latin America, in Argentina for example, scholars can make use of the "publications of the National Department of Labor [to] provide a broad-based documentation" about workers' social conditions.[12] But Ecuador, a smaller and economically less successful nation, could not always afford the costs of ordinary record-keeping. There are few synthetic sources that yield up convenient tabulations covering a series of years. To obtain information in Guayaquil about crime, health care, births, deaths, population, and other topics, one must dig the information out year by year. In addition, in Guayaquil many documents have been lost to fires (in 1896 and 1902), the ravages of the tropical environment, or have simply been thrown away. Some materials, while existent, are not organized or are inaccessible, locked away in storage rooms filled with various scattered papers.[13] Full runs of data are very difficult to construct. For the social historian of Latin America the work is never easy.

In this book I seek to address the major historiographical gaps in Latin American urban history, in Latin American social history, and in Ecuadorian history. I deal with three intertwining themes: the economic growth of coastal Ecuador that centered on the port of Guayaquil, the resulting social dilemmas of rapid urbanization, and the politics of city efforts to respond. One key contribution of this book will be a strong empirical account of basic conditions in Guayaquil, bringing together difficult-to-gather new data on critical aspects of the urban experience. I will focus especially on working men and women of Guayaquil, the people who day by day sought to deal with the implications of the rush of change. One of my major aims in this study is to offer a sense of what life was like for ordinary people in the city, to examine the conditions they confronted, and to understand their experiences, their work, their play, and their struggles—both individual and sometimes collective—to improve their lives. I will analyze the various working-class strategies and patterns of protest, which, along with other historical circumstances, shaped the possibilities for successful urban reform in Guayaquil.

In a departure from most investigations into the history of Latin American urbanization, this book is a study of a nonindustrial, nonprimary city. This is a new direction in Latin American urban social history, and my goal is to deepen our understanding of the complex historical process of urban social reform.

By exploring the genesis of modern Latin America's urbanization explosion, I seek to offer valuable perspective and hence greater insight into the severe urban dilemmas that are the challenge of the present. By studying ordinary people in everyday life, we can achieve a fuller and more complex understanding of our collective past, and a more democratic vision of history.

*Chapter One*

# Urbanization in a Nonindustrial, Nonprimary City
## A Case Study

Of Guayaquil frequent visitor Theodore Wolf commented at the turn of the century: "The change and improvement . . . is so considerable that anyone seeing the city 25 years ago, on his return today would scarcely know it."[1] In 1880 Guayaquil had been a city of roughly 170 city blocks, thirty major public buildings, and a population of 25,000. By 1920 it had grown to 700 blocks, ninety major public buildings, and more than 100,000 people (see table 1.1).

What happened in Guayaquil was taking place across Latin America during the late nineteenth and early twentieth centuries: rapid urbanization as part of a broader economic process of export expansion. The cities that grew fastest were those most engaged in a thriving international trade. Latin America's exports increased remarkably: Brazil's nearly doubled from 1869 to 1905, Argentina's rose eightfold from 1873 to 1910, and Mexico's increased tenfold from 1872 to 1910. Latin America urbanized. By 1900 Latin America counted thirteen cities with populations of 100,000 or more and some ninety-two that numbered in excess of 20,000.[2]

Guayaquil is an example of this general urban transformation. Some of what happened in Guayaquil was unique; much of what happened was not. To learn from this case study, we must be able to distinguish between the two.

### Major Themes and Arguments

Chapter 2, "Economic Geography: Guayaquil, the Guayas River Basin, and the Exigencies of Cacao," explores how geography set the parameters of the possible. In it we examine the setting for this case study, considering how the

**Table 1.1.** Population, city blocks, and major buildings in Guayaquil, selected years, 1764–1950

| Year | Population | City blocks | Major buildings |
|------|-----------|-------------|-----------------|
| 1764 | 4,914 | — | — |
| 1820 | 13,000 | 80 | — |
| 1840 | 13,093 | — | — |
| 1843 | 14,740 | — | — |
| 1848 | 14,000 | — | — |
| 1857 | 23,207 | — | — |
| 1877 | 26,000 | — | — |
| 1880 | 25,866 | 169 | — |
| 1882 | 36,000 | 182 | — |
| 1887 | 43,460 | — | 11 |
| 1890 | 44,772 | — | 16 |
| 1892 | 45,000 | — | — |
| 1894 | 50,000 | — | — |
| 1897 | 51,000 | — | — |
| 1899 | 60,483 | — | — |
| 1903 | 70,000 | 417 | — |
| 1904 | — | — | 26 |
| 1905 | 81,650 | — | 28 |
| 1908 | 80,000 | — | — |
| 1910 | 82,000 | — | — |
| 1919 | 91,842 | — | — |
| 1920 | 100,000 | 700 | 91 |
| 1925 | 120,000 | — | — |
| 1950 | 266,000 | — | — |

*Sources:* GG, *Informe, 1877*, 2–4, *1907*; PCC, *Informe, 1887*; Matamoros Jara, *Almanaque de Guayaquil*, 64; Linke, *Ecuador*, 4–8; Estrada Ycaza, *El hospital*, 58, 142; Gallegos Naranjo, *1883 almanaque*, 201; IP, *Informe, 1890*, 8, 14–17, *1903*, 4, 16; Quintero López, *El mito del populismo*, 360; L. F. Carbo, *El Ecuador en Chicago*, 43–47; Estrada Ycaza, *Regionalismo y migración*, 265; IP, *Boletín de información, 1904*, 64–65, *1905*, 133; MI, *Anexos al informe, 1910*, 16; MIP, *Informe, 1910*; SS, *Informe, 1911*; Enock, *Ecuador*, 243; *América libre, 1925 almanaque*, 6–10.

natural advantages of the port of Guayaquil and its hinterland, in both transport and in agricultural production, offered the necessary preconditions for economic growth. We also examine how the requirements of cacao production helped shape coastal land ownership patterns and the relations of production.

Geography also defines the type of export, and exports can vary greatly in their exigencies. Exports requiring extensive processing prior to shipment could in some cases stimulate industrial development. Agricultural exports that require very small capital investments in production could encourage the formation of a middle class of medium-sized growers.

Ecuador exported cacao, and cacao needs very little treatment or refinement prior to shipping. In Ecuador, the emerging cacao plantations required only modest amounts of capital. Still, ownership was beyond the means of most Ecuadorians, even if it was within the reach of the preexisting domestic coastal elite. Large infusions of foreign capital were not needed to grow cacao in Ecuador.

Upriver from Guayaquil, the coastal cacao growers soon eliminated smaller competitors, gained control of the best land (that with rich soil and access to river transportation), and monopolized the existing marketing networks. These large estates employed relatively few workers, for in cacao production, labor demand is seasonal and limited. Growers filled their nominal demand for workers from the vast pool of migrants who streamed down from the impoverished highlands.

Chapter 3, "The Performance of a Primary Product Export: Cacao and the Dimensions of Economic Change," examines the structure and prosperity of Guayaquil's cacao export economy. In large measure, the nature and the performance of the economy determined the possibilities for urban social reform in Latin America. That is, certain economic circumstances created a more advantageous situation for responding to the social dilemmas of rapid urbanization. Economic prosperity, in industrialized or highly successful primary-product exporting cities, meant more wealth, employment and investment opportunities, and, most importantly, more tax revenue. Economic success also brought foreign investment and loans that added further to the riches of the local economy. And a diversified export pattern provided an added advantage, protecting the economy from inevitable price shifts and boom/bust cycles in international markets. Cities without these economic advantages—cities like Guayaquil—could less afford the costs of reform.

During the late nineteenth century, economic change and urbanization generated new patterns of politics in Latin America. Old notions of limited government began to give way to calls for a more active state, one more aggressively involved in improving the urban environment. In part this new perspective resulted naturally from increased government revenues from foreign commerce, funds that made it possible for the state to be much more active. At the same time, the new prosperity brought by rising exports triggered a significant political change in much of Latin America. The locus of political power began to shift away from the countryside and toward the city. Previously, in the chaotic years following independence, tough, charismatic, rural strongmen had come to dominate national politics in much of Latin America, and their endless personal wrangling had often left the young republics in a state of perpetual disorder. But by the late nineteenth century, political stability, requisite for continued economic growth, had become a more urgent concern. As states employed their increased resources to centralize and expand the forces of repression, the achievement of stability at last became possible. Cities assumed a more central role in the economy, and the emerging urban elite, more prosperous and numerous than ever before, successfully ended the disruptive and corrupt governance of the old rural caudillos.

In Ecuadorian national politics, however, this process was less complete. Divided in half by some of the world's most awe-inspiring mountains, the towering Andes, Ecuador is a country of profound local differences and an intense sense of regionalism. The locally based elites in each zone—the traditional, autarkic, landed oligarchy of various districts in the sierra, and the nonforeign merchants and great estate owners of the coast—worked diligently to protect their own interests and, if possible, to capture the national government and use its power and resources to advance those interests. Bitter personal rivalries between ambitious caudillos—rival strongmen who exploited the regional tensions to advance their own opportunistic desires for plunder and the spoils of office—contributed to the atmosphere of violence. Endless, expensive civil war resulted.

Guayaquil's principal complaints were that taxes on its cacao trade were the only important source of government revenue, and that this money had to pay the mounting bills of the national government in Quito before the needs of Guayaquil might be considered. The political realities imposed by Ecuador's regionalism significantly restricted efforts by the local elites in Guayaquil to oversee the city's progress.

Other factors also limited the fiscal resources available to the municipality of Guayaquil. In Ecuador, tax collection was haphazard at best, and the poorly paid officials all too easy to bribe. What money did arrive in government coffers often went to pork-barrel projects set up to reward cronies, to poorly conceived and coordinated public works projects, or to the military. Chapter 4, "The Political Economy of Regionalism: The Fiscal Context," surveys the political context for elite governance over the growth of Guayaquil.

As its economy bloomed, Guayaquil became the largest and richest city in Ecuador. Planters and merchants built great fortunes, while impoverished Indian migrants from the highlands came down to the coast with hopes of finding a better life. Chapter 5, "The People of Guayaquil: Daily Lives of the Poor and Rich," details the demographic dimensions of this change: the gender ratio, age, ethnicity, regional origins, and occupations of the city's population. It also studies the changing composition of the Guayaquil elite—a relative handful of merchants, growers, and their families who controlled most of the rising cacao riches—and Guayaquil's social history, including recreation and day-to-day life in the city.

Between 1870 to 1925 Guayaquil took steps to deal with the crush of new demands imposed by breakneck population growth—building water and sewer lines, paving downtown streets, opening schools, adding police officers, dedicating new health facilities. These civic efforts were not without effect, yet many observers, including government officials, physicians, foreign dignitaries, and newspaper editors, pointed out massive and persistent problems. School inspectors lamented the woeful state of education. Citizens complained of appallingly low standards of police professionalism. Fires repeatedly raged through the city. And Guayaquil remained remarkably filthy, with a dreaded renown as a most disease-infested port. In the eyes of many in the community, city services failed to meet growing needs.

In part this record can be explained by the confluence of imposing local circumstances. The equatorial climate provided a flourishing environment for disease, and the unacclimated migrants from the highlands who accounted for much of the increase in the city's population proved all too easy prey. Busy dockside activity placed Guayaquil at constant risk of infection with epidemics from all over the globe. The population multiplied from about 25,000 in 1870 to 125,000 in 1925; it swiftly overloaded existing and even new services.

Chapter 6, "Life in Guayaquil: Servicing a Growing City," and chapter 7, "Disease, Health Care, and Death in Guayaquil," provide details on the provisioning of urban social services. Chapter 6 focuses on the urban environment of Guayaquil during this era of rapid growth as evidenced, for example, in the social patterns of crime, which differed from those of other cities of the era, in the educational opportunities that awaited migrants to the city, and in residents' chances for realizing the common dream of upward social mobility. Chapter 7 profiles the city's sanitation, public health, medical care, disease, and mortality.

Historians often have given workers and their politics but passing notice. Chapter 8, "Collective Popular Action: Unions, the Collapse of the Cacao Economy, and the General Strike of 1922," concentrates on workers and the collective strategies that ordinary women and men adopted to deal with the challenges of making a life in Guayaquil. Most people took action as individuals, trying to succeed within the system or forging ties with an influential patron. On occasion, and despite the odds, some promoted community, workplace, or class-based actions by forming or joining mutual-aid groups, trade associations, and unions. The export economy collapsed in 1922, and, in a stunning and singular social episode, people adopted the strategy of mass action, staging a collective and spontaneous insurgency. Chapter 8 analyzes this nexus of conditions, worker response, reform politics, the shifting patterns of worker action, and the limits of their successes. Finally, chapter 9, "Reflections on the Possibilities of Urban Social Reform: Lessons from the Guayaquil Experience," summarizes the principal dilemmas of reform during rapid urbanization.

# Chapter Two

---

# Economic Geography
## Guayaquil, the Guayas River Basin, and the Exigencies of Cacao

Guayaquil and the adjacent Guayas River Basin enjoyed several natural advantages for the expansion of cacao export agriculture: a well-protected port, excellent soil properties, suitable climate, and easy river transportation. Together, geography and the exigencies of cacao cultivation helped give shape to local patterns of land tenure and labor; cacao particularly influenced the economic and social patterns of production that developed in Guayaquil's upriver regions.

### Soil, Climate, and Transport

Blessed with a superb natural harbor and fertile conditions for growing cacao, Guayaquil and the surrounding area were in an ideal position to respond to the strong pull of new commercial opportunities in the world market during the late nineteenth and the early twentieth centuries.

Ocean transport into and around Guayaquil benefits from several factors. The waters of the Gulf of Guayaquil, the largest gulf between Panamá and Valparaíso, Chile, are generally calm and fog-free. Traveling north from the gulf, most nineteenth-century vessels of this age found the thirty-mile-long river channel into Guayaquil deep and wide enough to accommodate them.

Guayaquil took advantage, too, of a particularly good fluvial network, that of the Daule (160 miles in length) and Babahoyo (110 miles) rivers, which converge to form the Río Guayas. This water transportation system was no small advantage; to this day it costs less to ship goods by water than to haul them across land. Daily tidal changes make the Guayas a river that actually flows in both directions, at currents of five miles per hour coming and going

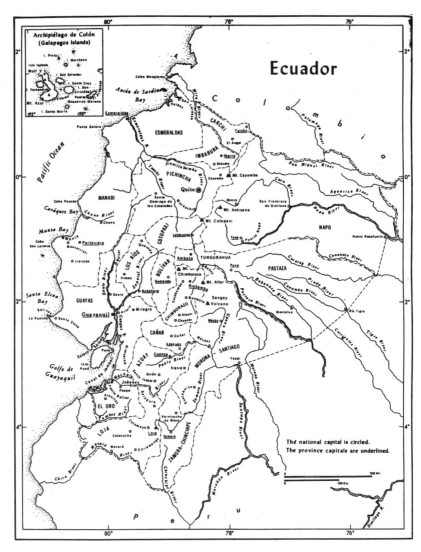

Ecuador. Reproduced and adapted from Cathryn L. Lombardi and John V. Lombardi, with K. Lynn Stoner, *Latin American History: A Teaching Atlas* (Madison, Wisc.: Conference on Latin American History, University of Wisconsin Press, 1983).

and that shift every twelve hours. The port of Guayaquil stands at the mouth of the 25,000-square-mile Guayas River valley, the largest river basin on the Pacific coast of Latin America. The flat basin forms a natural transportation grid of rivers that branch off and link up in a convenient series of shortcuts (such as the Pila River between the Vinces and the Daule rivers) that minimize backtracking. By 1841 steam-powered craft began to navigate upstream of Guayaquil, and by the end of the century these vessels worked right up to the Andean foothills along the many small rivers that flow into the Guayas (the Vinces, Santa Rosa, Machala, Balao, Naranjal, Yaguachi, Bodegas, and Baba). By 1910 the forty-six swift, steam-powered river craft that operated out of Guayaquil had reduced travel times by two-thirds. Barges penetrated as far inland as Quevado. Balsas, a smaller type of craft used since precolonial times, worked the lesser tributaries. The rivers served as highways to funnel cacao into Guayaquil.

Weather conditions on the Ecuadorian littoral help create good growing conditions, particularly for cacao. The Andes and the cold Humboldt Current of the Pacific Ocean largely determine the rainfall and temperature patterns. The Humboldt Current, bringing chilly Antarctic waters up South America's Pacific Coast, directly affects rainfall; its waters draw moisture out of the air and leave adjacent regions without rainfall. Coastal areas of Chile and Peru swept by the Humboldt Current are among the driest places on the globe. When the Humboldt reaches Ecuador, though, it splits into two branches. The main part passes well out into the ocean, but a smaller stream cuts closer to shore for most of the year. The nearer spur leaves the southern coast of Ecuador dry, though not as arid as the Peruvian or northern Chilean coasts. From January to May a warm countercurrent from the north usually arrives to push Ecuador's Humboldt branch out to sea, thus making the land colder than the sea and bringing rain to southern coastal Ecuador.

Annual rainfall averages twenty-two inches in Guayaquil and increases as one approaches the base of the Andes Mountains, where seventy-five inches of rain soak portions of the foothills each year. The cacao-producing Guayas Basin is hot and wet. It receives somewhat more than forty inches of rain a year, and even during the drier summer months, June through November, is covered by a damp mist in the mornings. Guayaquil's average annual temperature is 81 degrees Fahrenheit, under ever-present cloud cover. It seldom gets colder than 66 degrees Fahrenheit or warmer than 95. It is generally a bit warmer upriver and in the hills approaching the mountains.

The coastal plain of Ecuador has some of the best soil in the world. The rich alluvium of the Santo Domingo-Bucay belt washed down from the Andes over the ages to blanket the littoral, which, at 400 miles in length and 50 to 150 miles in width, comprises about one-quarter of the country. Its soil has fine moisture-holding properties and produces exceptional crop yields.[1]

In sum, the ample but not excessive rainfall, warm but not oppressive temperatures, thick layer of black Andean alluvium, outstanding fluvial network, and fine river port blessed the coastal region around Guayaquil with an impressive array of natural economic advantages for agro-export.

## A Survey of the Outlying Area

All the coastal provinces, Los Ríos, Guayas, El Oro, Manabí, and Esmeraldas, produced significant quantities of cacao. In 1900 there were some 4,827 large cacao estates in the coastal region as a whole that together supported over 58 million cacao trees. Los Ríos led the provinces in cacao production, with its 1,594 large cacao plantations and some 31 million trees. It was followed by Guayas, with 546 estates and 15 million trees; El Oro, with 977 estates with 7 million trees; Manabí, with 1,440 estates and 7 million trees; and Esmeraldas, with 270 cacao estates and 236,000 trees.[2]

In Los Ríos cacao was king. This province, north of Guayaquil in the fertile Guayas Basin, in 1900 produced nearly half the nation's crop of cacao, 230,000 of Ecuador's total 472,000 quintals. In 1900, Los Ríos had eleven parishes with more than one million cacao trees, while the second leading cacao province, Guayas, had three parishes with that number of cacao trees. (In Ecuador each province in broken into cantons, each canton into parishes, and each parish into wards.) Indeed, of the fifteen parishes in the province of Los Ríos, only four did not have at least a million cacao trees. The orchards of one parish alone, Vinces, totaled over 5.9 million cacao trees, making it the single richest parish for the production of cacao in all of Ecuador. Ownership of the large estates was concentrated among a few growers: in 1904 twenty-six families held 59 percent of all Los Ríos property (by value); 6 percent held 54 percent of the land value. By the 1920s, Los Ríos had 2,435 large estates with 70 million trees, more than double its total twenty years prior. Los Ríos had 74 percent of Ecuador's cacao trees by the 1920s on properties worth nearly 60 million *sucres*.[3]

Los Ríos province, approximately 3,500 square miles and with a 1909 population of about 60,000, also produced sugar cane, coffee, rice, rubber, tobacco, cinnamon, and cattle. The town of Babahoyo, actually little more than a line of bamboo huts along the river of the same name, served as a transfer point from boat to mule for the limited trade between the coast and the sierra.[4]

Guayas province, covering approximately 13,350 square miles, divides into two principal geographic zones. The arid western quarter falls chiefly within the canton of Santa Elena, one of the province's four (and later five) cantons. The eastern portion of Guayas province is wetter and more fertile.

Too dry to support commercial agricultural activity, Santa Elena canton did at least offer salt and oil production. Local handicraft workers also wove straw into hats (misnamed "Panamá hats," because Panamá canal construction crews adopted them as standard wear). Eastern Santa Elena canton had some cattle ranches and produced *tagua*, or "vegetable ivory," used to make buttons. Of Guayas' four cantons in 1909, Santa Elena had the smallest population, 11,000 of the 231,000 in the province.[5]

The canton of Guayaquil was much larger than the city itself. In fact, in 1909 the canton had thirteen rural parishes and only five urban ones. Guayaquil canton, located in the center of Guayas province along the Rio Guayas and its saltwater estuaries, sustained a variety of economic activities: sugar, plantain, rice, and coffee production; timber; cattle ranching; and fishing. There was some mining as well; in the city there was a gypsum quarry.[6] And Guayaquil canton was one of the richest cacao-producing zones on the coast. Toward the eastern part of the canton, especially into Naranjal and Balao parishes, cacao became by far the most important crop. In 1900, Naranjal parish had eighty-five large cacao estates with 3.4 million cacao trees; Balao parish had thirty-six cacao estates with a total of 5.8 million trees. The massive Tenguel estate in Balao parish, the largest cacao plantation in Ecuador, had 2 million cacao trees, and produced about 500 tons of cacao annually.

The canton of Daule, in northern Guayas province, had 65,200 inhabitants in 1909 and produced Ecuador's best cigar tobacco, as well as sugar, oranges, lemons, coffee, cattle, corn, various vegetables and tropical fruits, and, of course, cacao. At the turn of the century, Las Ramas parish, along the Vinces River, had ninety-three major cacao estates with a total of 1.3 million cacao trees.

In eastern Guayas, the canton of Yaguachi, with a 1909 population of 25,000, also grew cacao, with the thickest concentrations in the northern area. Other important products included sugar, rice, coffee, pineapples, plantains, and cattle. Yaguachi had large mills for processing sugar cane into refined sugar and *aguardiente* liquor. Eighty percent, 93,000 of 117,000 quintals, of processed sugar produced in Ecuador in 1900 came from the seven major sugar mills of Yaguachi canton.[7]

The three other coastal provinces, Manabí, El Oro, and Esmeraldas, produced cacao in somewhat smaller amounts. Manabí lies in the central Pacific coastal region of Ecuador (covering approximately 13,000 square miles and with a 1909 population of 120,000). In 1900 its 1,440 cacao estates (with 6.5 million trees) yielded about 40,000 quintals of cacao, or 9 percent of

Ecuador's total. In Manabí cacao grew primarily in Chone parish, where 612 cacao estates had a total of nearly 3.3 million trees. Exploitation of wild tagua and wild rubber, which flourished in the coastal jungle, added to local enterprise in Manabí. Estate owners typically diversified their activities. For example, the La Clemencia hacienda owned by Colonel Juan C. Alvarez, had 100,000 cacao trees, 20,000 rubber trees, 2,000 coffee trees, and 100 cattle in 1909. The hacienda was valued at about 100,000 sucres. However, like other rural landowners, Alvarez was capital poor; in 1909 his debts totaled over 5,000 sucres.[8]

Chone parish, and the other cacao-growing districts of Manabí, did not export their harvests through Guayaquil; most rivers in this region run westward to the Pacific Ocean and away from the Guayas river basin. Chone parish sent its cacao down the river of the same name to the port of Bahía de Caráquez and from there directly to European markets.

The province of El Oro, on the southern Pacific coast of Ecuador below Guayas province, had a 1909 population of 45,000 and counted 977 cacao estates with 6.7 million cacao trees. El Oro produced 15 percent (70,000 quintals) of Ecuador's cacao harvest at the turn of the century. The cacao of this region was generally considered to be of inferior quality, especially when judged against the aromatic beans of Los Ríos. El Oro supported economic activity beyond cacao production: in Zaruma there was gold, and elsewhere farmers grew coffee, sugar cane, and tobacco. The best cacao-producing parishes in El Oro were Guabo parish in Machala canton, with 138 cacao estates and 2.7 million trees, and Pasaje parish in Pasaje canton, with 652 cacao estates and 4.6 million cacao trees in 1900. Growers in El Oro prior to 1899 sent their cacao to Guayaquil, but in that year the new Puerto Bolívar opened near the city of Machala. Export houses set up shop, and international steamers began to stop in. Like Manabí, then, El Oro produced a fair amount of cacao but did not use the port of Guayaquil.

The province of Esmeraldas, on the northern Pacific coast of Ecuador, produced small amounts of cacao. In 1900 it had 270 estates and 260,000 cacao trees. Mostly, though, Esmeraldas remained rich in potential. The province had but 20,000 people, most of whom lived as subsistence farmers. A few grew tobacco, while others harvested the wild rubber or tagua of the forests. Cacao was not especially important to the province. What cacao its producers grew, they shipped through the port town of Esmeraldas.

## Land Tenure and Relations of Production in Cacao

During the colonial era, fertile, vacant lands were available everywhere on the coast. The cacao plantations were of modest size, and there were also countless small subsistence farmers. However, during the later colonial period and into the nineteenth century, some larger farms began to appear. Inevitably, the larger and more successful cacao growers began to displace the small and medium-sized holders, and by the 1880s vast estates began to control more and more land. The best of these nestled along the shores of the many navigable rivers above Guayaquil, giving them the advantages of access to cheap water transport and control of the most highly prized farm land, the lush, silted banks. The large-scale planters also monopolized control of the steam-powered river transport into each district. Cacao operations depended on cheap river transport; if the adjacent river shifted its banks, as could often happen, a hacienda might have to be abandoned because it no longer had access to water transportation.

The large landowners employed their economic strength and their control over local governments to develop their estates. A landowner could appeal to authorities, in both the colonial and national periods, for the right to occupy vacant lands. If the land already had occupants, they often were uprooted and expelled. After 1896, "vacant" land was no longer free, although it still could be purchased from the government for four sucres per hectare. Few bothered to pay.[9] Vaguely drawn estate boundaries made it easy to illegally enlarge one's holdings by encroaching on those of neighbors. If encroachment failed, one could add holdings through actual purchase. Acquiring land by purchase grew increasingly common by the late nineteenth century and hastened the dissolution of most of the remaining small and medium-sized farms. Some larger growers also lent money on smaller holdings, then seized the land when borrowers defaulted. During the boom years, great estates dominated cacao country. Besides holding the best land and access to transportation, large-scale planters also controlled key sources of credit and the critical marketing links.

As the cacao frontier rapidly pushed into the hill country of the coast (especially after the 1880s introduction of the heartier Venezuelan variety of cacao), growers continually complained of labor shortages, especially during the peak harvest periods of December and from April through June. Great estate owners turned for workers to the vast pool of internal migrants who had fled the crowded and impoverished sierra, especially the southern sierra.

Probably the most important cause of internal migration to the coast and to Guayaquil was the "push" effect of rural poverty. In the sierra, land was scarce and labor relatively plentiful. Already in the eighteenth century, during the sierra's long economic decline, migration to the coast had become commonplace. Many peasants lost their farms, as large haciendas emerged

Cacao drying in front of the hacienda La Maravilla, upriver in Babahoyo, ca. 1890.

and land seizures became more frequent. A surge of Indian rebellions accompanied; whereas few such uprisings took place in the seventeenth century, there were eight major outbreaks in the sierra in the eighteenth century.

Beginning in the early nineteenth century, the tempo of migration accelerated.[10] Migrants from the sierra left conditions of landlessness and forced labor.[11] In order to obtain access to a small parcel of land (*huasipungo*), Indian families had to consent to provide agricultural labor and to serve as domestic servants for a hacienda owner. In return, the Indians had the right to use the owner's lands to collect wood and straw, or to graze such few animals as they might have. The owner paid wages for labor, and typically supplied Indians with advances of food, clothing, animals, and cash. Most Indian families quickly lapsed into debt and legally surrendered their freedom of movement until they could retire their obligations. They seldom broke free of those obligations. Thus restricted, Indians suffered various abuses, either at the hands of the hacienda owner, or, more commonly, from foremen, local police, or even the local clergy. *Hacendados*, the landowners, got involved "in the most intimate activities, such as the [Indians'] spouse selection, [and the choosing of] the names and occupations of their children."[12] Willfulness by workers met with corporal punishment by the landowner or public officials. Said one visitor, "The minor Government officials do as they please in the remote districts, and maltreat and extort all they can out of the down-trodden Indians, who very seldom retaliate."[13] In some outlying areas there were no rural police, leaving law enforcement totally at the landowners' discretion. Legislative decrees designed to end this system of debt peonage, such as the ban on *concertaje* (forced labor) in 1918, did little to actually halt the practice.

U.S. travelers often drew the obvious parallel to the conditions of antebellum Southern slaves they had seen. "Poorly fed [,] ill clad, . . . ignorant . . . [,] superstitious [,]" and living in "scualor and poverty," the "servility [of Ecuador's highland residents was] . . . positively painful to behold," said one.[14] Beyond these conditions, and to Indians perhaps most galling, they were obligated to pay heavy taxes. There was ample reason to flee the highlands. Perhaps only the most fatalistic or unambitious stayed behind. Some peasants escaped into psychological withdrawal or alcoholism; many escaped to the coast.

Seasonal migrations had long been part of the ordinary routine even within the sierra, where workers divided their time between plots in the mountains and in the valleys. Migrants to the coast typically first came as seasonal laborers to the cacao-producing regions. Perhaps lured by the higher wages, the absence of heavy taxes, and relative freedom of the coast, and driven by the dull, endless, and unrewarding routine of sierra penury, some workers ultimately decided to leave their traditional homelands in the mountains and move their families permanently to the coast. As César Cisneros Cisneros described this process, "some Indian heads of families moved to the Coast provinces, . . . especially to. . . [Los] Ríos. . . . Above all, the higher salaries cause[d] this seasonal movement which happen[ed] year after year. Many of them decide[d] to change their residence. A few months later they [would] move their families and become day laborers in the haciendas of the littoral."[15]

The great cacao estate owners were eager to control labor, and they tried several strategies to ensure a sufficient work force on hand for the critical harvest periods. Some growers experimented with paying off the debts of sierra workers and providing them free transportation to the coast. Growers also sought to tie workers to haciendas by a system of debt peonage, granting cash advances and allowing purchases on credit—at a sharp markup—at the hacienda store. The debts had to be paid off before one could leave the hacienda, and accrued debts passed to one's heirs. The growers secured antivagrancy laws and other legal measures to restrict the freedom of coastal workers. For example, in the 1860s the province of Los Ríos passed a law requiring all farm hands to purchase a pass from the government to certify that they did not owe debts to any hacienda owner.

Yet for all of these efforts, a system of purely coerced labor did not emerge. In the end, the owners found that the only sure way to assure an adequate work force on hand at harvest time was to offer sufficiently attractive wages. So they did, and workers could earn enough money in two days to get along for a week. Each family also received a small plot to raise their own food. Moreover, planter efforts to ensnare their employees in a web of debt actually proved to be a benefit to workers in many cases. Rival growers, desperate for field hands, constantly pilfered workers from other estates by paying off workers' debts, or more typically, by enticing them to skip out on their existing obligations with offers of fresh and yet more generous advances. If one did happen to fall into the clutches of an overly demanding hacendado, it was easy to get away. Owners complained endlessly about runaways who left a string of debts trailing behind.

So migrants streamed down from the sierra in ever larger numbers, coming to take advantage of the higher wages and relative freedom of the coast. Coastal mestizos and Indians did not have to pay the onerous tribute burdens as did highland Indians. Coastal hacienda owners also obtained laws that exempted cacao workers from impressment into road gangs or, worse, into the army.

Most of the employees on the cacao estates labored as *jornaleros,* or day workers. While haciendas harvested some cacao all year, most jornaleros and their families worked for the landowner only during the two principal cacao fruitage seasons. Typically, the entire family labored together in getting out the harvest. Men used a *garabato,* a long pole with a curved piece of metal on the end, to reach up into the trees and lop off the cacao pods, or *mazorcas.* The women and children gathered the cacao, and began preparing it to dry by opening the pods.[16] Male workers then spread the cacao beans out in the sun on bamboo to dry. At night they covered the beans with banana leaves to protect them from moisture. After they dried and partially fermented the cacao, the men loaded it aboard small steam-powered craft for shipment down river to Guayaquil. A small group of families might be asked to stay on after the harvest to maintain the cacao orchards, tend other crops such as tobacco, rice, or sugar, or see after the livestock.

Most migrants from the sierra first took jobs as jornaleros, but some soon improved their situation. If one had learned enough about cacao and was mature and responsible enough, he might after a few seasons obtain a position as a producer, or *sembrador.* To get a contract, one typically had to be married and have a family, for the entire family would be expected to work. Sembradores received a plot of virgin land from the landowner on which, after clearing and burning the tropical growth, they planted seedlings supplied by the hacendado. Next to the young plants the workers placed faster growing banana trees, whose leaves would protect the cacao seedlings from scorching tropical rays. Between rows, the families planted their subsistence food crops, yucca, corn, and beans. After four or five years, when the cacao trees reached maturity and began to offer their first harvest, the sembrador family turned the land back to the owner, the sembrador usually receiving a nominal fee of twenty to thirty cents for each healthy tree. After completion of a contract, the sembrador generally sought a new one or, if the family had acquired no debts, they might move on to another hacienda.

Certainly some coastal dwellers, especially the independent-minded *montuvios*, the miscegenated descendants of slaves, preferred autonomy and isolation to working on the haciendas. Still, it seems that most people were drawn to the haciendas by the wages, cash advances, and various legal exemptions hacienda employment provided. Perhaps some chose hacienda life because they did not care to be alone.

But estate owners employed surprisingly few permanent workers. For example, in 1893, Mercedes Oragueva, widow and owner of Suya Grande, hired twenty peons and one mayordomo to tend her 100,000 trees; María Saenz's El Rosan, with 500,000 trees, employed one administrator, one mayordomo, and 108 peons; Pechichal, owned by José Miguel Ordoñez, with 230,000 trees, employed 150 *"peones del interior"*; José Ramon Ramos's Balao Chiquito, with 500,000 trees, employed 100 peons; and the estate of Jacinto Caamaño, Tengual, with one million trees, employed 300 peons. The situation remained the same over time. In 1922 in Balao parish, Guayaquil canton, the fourteen greatest estates had an average workforce of 138 laborers.[17]

In sum, favorable geography made profitable cacao production possible, and this, in turn, made the city of Guayaquil possible. The economic progress of the port of Guayaquil depended on the cacao grown upriver, especially in Los Ríos Province. The region's considerable natural advantages in both production and transport were crucial to the area's demographic and economic expansion. It was the exigencies of growing cacao in Ecuador that gave shape to the principal land ownership and labor patterns: large estates clustered along the rivers, and a labor system developed of relatively well-paid but only seasonally employed free wage workers.

*Chapter Three*

---

# The Performance of a Primary Product Export

## Cacao and the Dimensions of Economic Change

During much of the colonial period, Guayaquil's economic role had been that of Spain's ship building and ship repair center on the Pacific coast of the Indies. Guayaquil continued in this capacity until the 1700s, when larger European-made vessels began to arrive in Pacific coast waters from around Drakes' Passage.[1] By that time, though, cacao exports had increased in importance for coastal Ecuador, which sent most of its shipments up the coast to New Spain. The crown made efforts to restrict such trade, but Venezuela, the main legal supplier of cacao to New Spain, could not meet the demand. Hence a lively cacao smuggling trade developed out of Guayaquil. By the eighteenth century, Guayaquil shipped contraband cacao to northern Europe as well, and the port of Guayaquil emerged as a colonial smugglers' emporium. The loosening of trade restrictions under the Bourbon kings of the late eighteenth century ultimately brought the legalization of the cacao trade, and in the early 1800s cacao made up half of all exports from the colonial province of Guayaquil and brought in four times more money than the district had realized from cacao exports only thirty-five years earlier.[2]

For most of the Latin America colonies, the struggles to gain independence from Spain had proved quite injurious to their economic wellbeing. Sometimes prosperous but always fragile, these economies could not withstand the social chaos and destruction of the many years of combat. Silver, the motor of much of the colonial Spanish-American economy, suffered severe losses. Miners became soldiers; the abandoned mines flooded and collapsed. Troops swept back and forth across the food-producing heartland, seizing crops and demolishing agricultural infrastructure. Residents with capital fled. Most of the newly created republics began life with devastated economies and vast war debts.[3]

Global trade tripled during the first half of the nineteenth century, yet Latin America did not generally participate in this expansion. Investors, notably British, showed early interest in Latin America and ventured capital in the young republics. But when their investments quickly floundered in the war-ravaged economic environment of Latin America, the inflow of capital halted abruptly. For much of Latin America, the years 1820 to 1870 were a time of continued, long-term economic depression and isolation from world markets.

### The Rise of the Latin American Export Economies

During the second half of the nineteenth century, the world economy underwent substantial transformations as industrialization spread beyond Great Britain into France, Germany, and the United States. As the nineteenth century progressed, Great Britain enjoyed success, particularly in exporting textiles to the rest of the world. This achievement created a ready pool of available capital for the British. They sought investment opportunities. Tentatively at first, and then with greater enthusiasm, the British once again embraced Latin America. Capital from Great Britain and other industrial nations started flowing into Latin America, funding public works, utilities, mining operations, and the building of railways.[4]

By the latter half of the nineteenth century, industrialization had augmented the buying power of many European families. European consumers could now afford new products for their homes and tables. At the same time, Europe experienced rapid population growth as the death rate fell but the fertility rate did not. Aggregate demand increased for such items from Latin America as coffee, beef, grain, sugar, and chocolate. Industry and modern agriculture in Europe and the United States heightened the demand for tin, copper, nitrates (used as a fertilizer and in making gunpowder), rubber, and cotton. Latin America responded to feed these new appetites.

The industrial age also generated numerous inventions that facilitated raw-material production and that effectively drew Latin America closer to the centers of world commerce. New technologies made it possible to farm previously unused land and to cheaply ship fresh produce to Europe. Shipping costs fell by two-thirds from 1870 to 1900;[5] steamships with iron hulls greatly reduced travel times as well as transit costs. Railroads sped products to port, and refrigeration kept meat fresh during the trip to Europe. Modern windmills enabled settlers to draw groundwater in areas like the Argentine Pampas that did not have river water. Repeating rifles helped drive away natives. Later, the use of barbed wire kept cattle and sheep from trampling crops. Steel plows cut through unyielding virgin sod. With the array of technological innovations Latin America joined a world economy larger and more interconnected than any that had come before.

For Guayaquil and the surrounding region, independence—in 1820—and its aftermath had not brought economic decline. Indeed, after independence, the region saw exports rise: in the 1830s and 1840s Guayaquil became one of the larger suppliers of cacao to the world market. But the economic growth of the late nineteenth century far exceeded that of earlier periods.[6]

The changes in the world economy during the late nineteenth century drove the transformation of Guayaquil and the adjacent cacao-producing region. With cacao, the increased buying power of consumers in the industrial economies (coupled with a singularly pleasant discovery—that of combining milk with chocolate by the Swiss in the 1860s) dramatically whetted global desires for Ecuador's export crop. In the United States, for example, the number of chocolate factories rose from 949 in 1869 to 2,391 in 1914. By the 1880s Ecuador supplied about two thirds of the world's cacao.[7]

## The Cacao Economy

If cacao greatly influenced the economic life of Ecuador, it dominated that of Guayaquil.[8] The value of Ecuador's cacao sales rose over 700 percent from the 1870s to the 1920s (see table 3.1), averaging 2.9 million pesos a year in the 1870s and reaching 36 million sucres a year in the 1920s. (Ecuador changed the name of its national currency from peso to sucre in 1884.) Cacao accounted for about three-quarters of Ecuador's total exports in those years, nearly all of it shipped from Guayaquil (see tables 3.2, 3.3, and 3.4). As a reflection of this increase, port traffic rose considerably: 149 oceangoing vessels called in 1869; by 1922 over 400 came. Already by the 1880s *lanchas* (small boats) had to be used to serve the deeper-drafting vessels that began to call in port. And the city built more piers: there were fifteen in 1887; nine years later, in 1896, there were thirty-seven.[9] Overall, total port tonnage expanded between 1869 and 1922 from 63,000 to more than 400,000.

Guayaquil handled at least 80 percent of Ecuador's total export trade during this era (see table 3.2) and 90 percent or more of the country's cacao exports. Ecuadorian exports of this era were, in the main part, Guayaquil's exports (see table 3.3). Cacao filled the city. Workers spread the beans out to dry, "and everywhere along the river front the pleasant aroma of cocoa . . . perfume[d] the streets."[10]

The strong performance of cacao exports depended on new-found buyers. Earlier, from 1836 to 1853, Ecuador shipped most of its cacao to Spain

The port of Guayaquil, 1921.

(see table 3.5).[11] During those years, Ecuador shipped about as much cacao to Chile, Mexico, and Peru as it did to the developed nations of Europe. But by mid-century the pattern changed. Spain became a minor trading partner, replaced by France and, to a lesser degree, Germany. After 1889, the French clearly emerged as the leading purchasers of all Ecuadorian products. Germans were the second leading buyers of Ecuadorian exports before the turn of the century. After 1900 the United States became the second leading destination for Ecuador's cacao. During Ecuador's cacao boom years, the French purchased most of its exports, including well over half of Guayaquil's cacao

**Table 3.1.** Value of Ecuador's cacao exports, 1852–1929, by decade and as a percentage of total exports (value in 1,000s of sucres—pesos before 1884)

| Year | Yearly average | % change | % of all exports |
| --- | --- | --- | --- |
| 1852–59[a] | 1,248 | — | 53 |
| 1860–69 | 2,476 | 98 | 59 |
| 1870–79 | 2,900 | 17 | 70 |
| 1880–89 | 4,744 | 64 | 68 |
| 1890–99 | 8,381 | 77 | 66 |
| 1900–9 | 13,243 | 58 | 64 |
| 1910–19 | 20,399 | 54 | 66 |
| 1920–29 | 28,356 | 72 | 48 |

*Sources:* V. E. Estrada, *Balanza económica;* L. A. Rodríguez, *Search for Public Policy,* 178, 180, 192, 193.
[a]Figures for 1850 and 1851 are not available.

**Table 3.2.** Guayaquil's share of Ecuador's total exports, selected years, 1868–1921 (value in 1,000s of sucres—pesos before 1884)

| Year | Guayaquil's exports | Ecuador's total exports | Guayaquil's share (%) |
|------|---------------------|-------------------------|------------------------|
| 1868 | 3,356 | 4,149[a] | 81[a] |
| 1869 | 3,706 | 4,500 | 82 |
| 1870 | 4,169 | 5,440 | 77 |
| 1886 | 8,297 | — | — |
| 1900 | 12,455 | 15,419 | 81 |
| 1902 | 15,000 | 18,000 | 83 |
| 1903 | 15,384 | 18,626 | 83 |
| 1904 | 18,411 | 23,284 | 79 |
| 1905 | 14,149 | 18,566 | 76 |
| 1907 | 18,280 | 22,907 | 80 |
| 1908 | 23,442 | 26,559 | 88 |
| 1909 | 19,508 | 24,879 | 78 |
| 1912 | 23,084 | 28,168 | 82 |
| 1913 | 25,193 | 32,488 | 78 |
| 1918 | 23,539 | 27,500 | 86 |
| 1919 | 33,934 | 43,221 | 79 |
| 1920 | 38,261 | 49,892 | 77 |
| 1921 | 26,446 | 33,969 | 78 |

*Sources:* USCD, Charles Weile, "Report," 9 February 1870; George P. Bragdon, "End of Year Report," 30 September 1870; Martin Reinberg, "Report of [sic] Ecuador and Commerce of Guayaquil for 1886," 10 March 1887; MH, *Exposición, 1871;* V. E. Estrada, *Balanza económica;* CCm, *Memoria, 1900, 1902, 1903, 1904, 1905, 1907, 1908, 1913, 1919, 1921; El Ecuador: guía,* 895.
[a]Estimate.

in 1908. Cacao made up 93 percent of French purchases from Ecuador in 1900. While Spain's percentage was even higher (99 percent of its purchases from Ecuador were of cacao), by 1900 Spain was no longer an important trading partner. For the United States, a major buyer of Ecuadorian products, cacao made up only half of its purchases in 1900. Rubber, which grew wild along the coast, made up nearly one-quarter of American purchases from Ecuador in 1900; in the 1870s and 1880s the United States had bought more rubber than cacao from Ecuador. Germany bought almost as much tagua, which also grew wild on the coast, as it did cacao.[12]

This pattern (see table 3.6) held until World War I disrupted international commerce and virtually closed off European markets. The United States picked up much of the slack; its purchases of Ecuadorian exports jumped from 7.7 million sucres in 1908 to more than 26 million sucres in 1917; the U.S. share of Ecuador's exports grew from less than one-third to more than three-fourths of all sales. After the war, German and French markets revived, at least until the cacao economy collapsed in the 1920s.

**Table 3.3.** Value of Guayaquil's cacao exports as a percentage of Ecuador's total cacao exports, selected years, 1869–1921 (value in 1,000s of sucres—pesos before 1884)

| Year | Guayaquil's cacao exports | Ecuador's cacao exports | Guayaquil's share (%) |
|------|---------------------------|-------------------------|-----------------------|
| 1869 | 1,818[a] | 2,476[a] | 73[a] |
| 1886 | 6,505 | — | — |
| 1903 | 11,268 | 12,195 | 92 |
| 1904 | 13,537 | 15,249 | 89 |
| 1905 | 9,544 | 10,916 | 87 |
| 1906 | 10,171 | 12,198 | 83 |
| 1907 | 12,528 | 13,478 | 93 |
| 1908 | 16,670 | 17,737 | 94 |
| 1909 | 13,071[a] | 14,523 | 90[a] |
| 1913 | 19,104 | 20,531 | 93 |
| 1915 | 19,938 | 21,439[a] | 93[a] |
| 1916 | 23,607 | 26,236 | 90 |
| 1917 | 19,894 | 21,947 | 91 |
| 1918 | 16,032 | 17,116 | 94 |
| 1919 | 26,697 | 29,491 | 91 |
| 1920 | 31,819 | 35,573 | 90 |
| 1921 | 19,376 | 20,363 | 95 |

*Sources:* USCD, Charles Weile, "Report," 9 February 1870; George P. Bragdon, "End of Year Report," 30 September 30, 1870; Martin Reinberg, "Report of [sic] Ecuador and Commerce of Guayaquil For 1886," 10 March 1887; V. E. Estrada, *Balanza económica;* CCm, *Memoria, 1903, 1904, 1905, 1907, 1908, 1913, 1919, 1921; El Ecuador: guía,* 895; L. A. Rodríguez, *Search for Public Policy,* 191.
[a]Estimate.

## Imports

Imports showed a different pattern in which the British made effective use of their nearly monopolistic control over shipping along South America's Pacific coast. Until the 1880s, only Great Britain ran commercial steamers into Guayaquil, and the British continued to hold a formidable shipping advantage until World War I halted normal trade (see table 3.7). Would-be foreign competitors complained, as did Guayaquil merchants who had no choice but to rely upon British shipping. The British Steam Navigation Company "monopolized the carrying trade," the United States Consul in Guayaquil noted with a touch of envy. Twice, in 1871 and in 1879, thirty leading merchants in Guayaquil wrote to the company to express discontent with the poor service they received. The British, Guayaquil merchants complained, were aloof, careless, and at times, dishonest. But the British cared little. "After all," the British Foreign Office declared, "Ecuador is a very small minnow." The Pacific Steam Navigation Company gave preference to British freight and showed a studied indifference to the theft of non-British cargo.[13]

**Table 3.4.** Cacao as a percentage of Guayaquil's total exports, selected years, 1856–1921 (value in 1,000s of sucres—pesos before 1884)

| Year | Cacao exports | Total exports | % cacao |
|---|---|---|---|
| 1856–57 | 1,825 | 2,715 | 67 |
| 1869 | 1,818[a] | 3,706 | 49[a] |
| 1870 | 2,383 | 5,296[a] | 45 |
| 1871 | 1,823 | 4,051[a] | 45 |
| 1872 | 2,302 | 4,263[a] | 54 |
| 1873 | 3,274 | 5,846[a] | 56 |
| 1874 | 3,029 | 4,808[a] | 63 |
| 1877 | 2,632 | 3,463[a] | 76 |
| 1879 | 6,194 | — | — |
| 1884 | 3,782 | 5,908[a] | 64 |
| 1885 | 4,029 | 4,854[a] | 83 |
| 1886 | 6,505 | 8,297 | 78 |
| 1889 | 5,621 | 7,917[a] | 71 |
| 1890 | 6,571 | 9,807[a] | 67 |
| 1891 | 4,233 | 6,225[a] | 68 |
| 1892 | 7,307 | 10,292[a] | 71 |
| 1893 | 9,766 | 12,208[a] | 80 |
| 1903 | 11,268 | 15,384 | 73 |
| 1904 | 13,537 | 18,411 | 74 |
| 1905 | 9,544 | 14,149 | 68 |
| 1908 | 16,670 | 23,442 | 71 |
| 1909 | 13,071[a] | 19,508 | 67[a] |
| 1912 | — | 23,084 | — |
| 1913 | 19,104 | 25,193 | 75 |
| 1918 | 16,032 | 23,539 | 68 |
| 1919 | 26,697 | 33,934 | 79 |
| 1920 | 31,819 | 38,261 | 73 |

*Sources:* Hamerly, "Quantifying the Nineteenth Century," 147–48; MH, *Exposición, 1857;* USCD, Martin Reinberg, "Report of [*sic*] Ecuador and Commerce of Guayaquil For the year 1886," 10 March 1887; and adapted from tables 3.2 and 3.3.
[a]Estimate.

Guayaquil's rising commerce after 1870 was outgrowing the British shipping monopoly, but when rival carrying lines appeared, such as the U.S.-based Ward Line during World War I, Pacific Navigation would operate at a loss until the challenger went under. Pacific Navigation would recoup its losses by introducing steep new charges.[14]

Clearly, control of shipping gave the British trade benefits. But the British had another advantage. They offered import items to Guayaquil on far better terms than did other traders. While U.S. companies demanded cash payment within thirty days, British firms often allowed six months of credit to

**Table 3.5.** Destinations of Ecuador's exports, selected years, 1889–1922 (value in 1,000s of sucres)

| Year | France | United States | Great Britain | Germany | Spain | Other | Total |
|------|--------|---------------|---------------|---------|-------|-------|-------|
| 1889 | 1,945 | 731 | 1,275 | 1,222 | 1,672 | 1,065 | 7,910 |
| | (25%) | (9%) | (16%) | (15%) | (21%) | (13%) | |
| 1890 | 2,280 | 931 | 1,730 | 1,404 | 1,842 | 1,575 | 9,762 |
| | (23%) | (10%) | (18%) | (14%) | (19%) | (16%) | |
| 1891 | 2,493 | 999 | 936 | 1,092 | 599 | 1,233 | 7,352 |
| | (34%) | (14%) | (13%) | (15%) | (8%) | (17%) | |
| 1893 | 5,603 | 1,499 | 1,706 | 2,514 | 1,309 | 1,811 | 14,442 |
| | (39%) | (10%) | (12%) | (17%) | (9%) | (13%) | |
| 1897 | 2,563 | 1,613 | 1,072 | 2,033 | 758 | 708 | 8,747 |
| | (29%) | (18%) | (12%) | (23%) | (9%) | (8%) | |
| 1898 | 4,901 | 2,393 | 2,637 | 2,665 | 1,078 | 612 | 14,286 |
| | (34%) | (17%) | (18%) | (19%) | (8%) | (4%) | |
| 1899 | 5,645 | 2,687 | 2,163 | 3,785 | 1,459 | 818 | 16,557 |
| | (34%) | (21%) | (17%) | (16%) | (6%) | (6%) | |
| 1900 | 5,488 | 3,244 | 2,653 | 2,439 | 924 | 924 | 15,672 |
| | (35%) | (21%) | (17%) | (16%) | (6%) | (6%) | |
| 1901 | 6,694 | 2,785 | 2,143 | 2,036 | 1,363 | 1,302 | 16,323 |
| | (41%) | (17%) | (13%) | (12%) | (8%) | (8%) | |
| 1902 | 7,041 | 4,371 | 2,026 | 1,853 | 1,341 | 1,474 | 18,106 |
| | (39%) | (24%) | (11%) | (10%) | (7%) | (8%) | |
| 1903 | 4,915 | 4,806 | 2,328 | 3,308 | 1,206 | 2,063 | 18,626 |
| | (26%) | (26%) | (12%) | (18%) | (6%) | (11%) | |
| 1904 | 7,808 | 5,234 | 1,899 | 4,346 | 1,150 | 2,847 | 23,284 |
| | (34%) | (22%) | (8%) | (19%) | (5%) | (12%) | |
| 1905 | 6,254 | 5,071 | 1,116 | 2,862 | 348 | 2,913 | 18,564 |
| | (34%) | (27%) | (6%) | (15%) | (2%) | (16%) | |
| 1906 | 6,808 | 6,843 | 1,283 | 3,596 | 1,005 | 2,430 | 21,965 |
| | (31%) | (31%) | (6%) | (16%) | (5%) | (11%) | |
| 1907 | 8,093 | 6,015 | 2,329 | 2,967 | 716 | 2,787 | 22,907 |
| | (35%) | (26%) | (10%) | (13%) | (3%) | (12%) | |
| 1908[a] | 10,100 | 7,700 | 3,500 | 2,000 | 1,600 | 1,700 | 26,600 |
| | (38%) | (29%) | (13%) | (8%) | (6%) | (6%) | |
| 1909 | 8,922 | 6,832 | 2,498 | 3,156 | 585 | 2,887 | 24,879 |
| | (36%) | (28%) | (10%) | (13%) | (2%) | (12%) | |
| 1910 | 9,847 | 8,399 | 2,339 | 4,617 | 822 | 2,038 | 28,062 |
| | (35%) | (30%) | (8%) | (17%) | (3%) | (7%) | |
| 1911 | 9,321 | 6,555 | 2,026 | 4,397 | 950 | 2,866 | 26,116 |
| | (36%) | (25%) | (8%) | (17%) | (4%) | (11%) | |
| 1912 | 8,430 | 8,143 | 4,199 | 3,134 | 872 | 3,390 | 28,168 |
| | (30%) | (29%) | (15%) | (11%) | (3%) | (12%) | |
| 1913 | 11,075 | 7,729 | 3,336 | 5,406 | 1,378 | 3,564 | 32,488 |
| | (34%) | (24%) | (10%) | (17%) | (4%) | (11%) | |

**Table 3.5.** continued

| Year | France | United States | Great Britain | Germany | Spain | Other | Total |
|------|--------|---------------|---------------|---------|-------|-------|-------|
| 1915 | 2,400 | 11,700 | 5,500 | — | 1,200 | 5,733 | 26,533 |
|      | (9%) | (44%) | (21%) | | (5%) | (22%) | |
| 1916 | 4,500 | 17,600 | 7,300 | — | 1,500 | 5,252 | 36,152 |
|      | (12%) | (49%) | (20%) | | (4%) | (15%) | |
| 1917 | 2,977 | 26,280 | 224 | — | 1,405 | 2,672 | 33,558 |
|      | (9%) | (78%) | (1%) | | (4%) | (8%) | |
| 1918 | — | 21,400 | 2,000 | — | 700 | 3,400 | 27,500 |
|      | | (78%) | (7%) | | (3%) | (12%) | |
| 1919 | 8,600 | 20,800 | 7,300 | — | 1,400 | 5,121 | 43,221 |
|      | (20%) | (48%) | (17%) | | (3%) | (12%) | |
| 1920 | 1,781 | 27,561 | 8,725 | 1,791 | 863 | 9,171 | 49,892 |
|      | (4%) | (55%) | (18%) | (4%) | (2%) | (18%) | |
| 1921 | 2,798 | 10,663 | 1,080 | 10,076 | 2,476 | 6,876 | 33,969 |
|      | (8%) | (31%) | (3%) | (30%) | (7%) | (20%) | |
| 1922 | n/a | 30,343 | 2,999 | n/a | n/a | n/a | 46,107 |
|      | | (66%) | (7%) | | | | |

*Sources:* GG, *Informe, 1901;* CCm, *Memoria, 1902, 1903, 1904, 1905, 1908, 1913, 1919, 1921;* El Ecuador: *guía,* 955–63; *América libre,* 277–83; GBFO, R. C. Mitchell, "Report on the Economic and Financial Conditions in Ecuador, September, 1923," 25 September 1923; "Report," 3 September 1924; "Report on British Trade with Ecuador," 9 December 1924.
[a]Estimate.
— = less than 1%

Guayaquil importers. But the British could not maintain their advantageous position forever. In the 1920s, Dutch and German steamers, using the newly opened Panamá Canal (completed in 1915 but not fully operational until after World War I), began at last to seriously challenge British shipping supremacy along the southern Pacific coast.[15]

Imports kept pace with the bustling export trade. From 1889 to 1899 Ecuador averaged 10 million sucres a year in imports; from 1900 to 1909, 16 million; from 1910 to 1919, 19 million sucres; and in 1920 imports reached their highest level, more than 43 million sucres. Guayaquil dominated Ecuador's import trade to an even greater extent than it controlled the nation's export trade. Guayaquil's share of Ecuador's imports did not fall below 91 percent, and at times reached as high as 95 percent.[16]

Great Britain supplied from one-quarter to more than one-third of Ecuador's imports prior to World War I (see table 3.8). Earlier, the French had provided as much as a quarter of Ecuador's imports, but after 1900 their position swiftly declined. By World War I the French supplied less than a tenth of all imports; during the war they sold even less. Likewise, the Germans provided only about one-sixth of all imports before World War I and during

**Table 3.6.** Destinations of cacao exports from Ecuador, selected years, 1856–1877, Guayaquil only 1869–1921 (value in 1,000s of sucres—pesos before 1884)

| Location | 1856 | 1857 | 1858 | 1861 | 1862 | 1863 | 1864 | 1865 | 1866 | 1867 |
|---|---|---|---|---|---|---|---|---|---|---|
| Spain | 40% | 63% | 38% | 60% | 61% | 71% | 74% | 72% | 57% | 58% |
| Great Britain | 16% | 18% | 22% | 18% | 20% | 6% | 6% | 11% | 4% | 10% |
| France | 15% | 3% | 16% | 17% | 9% | 11% | 3% | 5% | 22% | 8% |
| United States | 6% | 0% | 0% | 0% | 0% | 0% | 0% | 0% | 0% | 0% |
| Germany | 7% | 8% | 6% | 5% | 5% | 7% | 8% | 4% | 13% | 17% |

| Location | 1868 | 1869 | 1870 | 1871 | 1872 | 1873 | 1874 | 1875 | 1876 | 1877 |
|---|---|---|---|---|---|---|---|---|---|---|
| Spain | 35% | 49% | 51% | 38% | 41% | 32% | 28% | 71% | 59% | 44% |
| Great Britain | 19% | 17% | 17% | 32% | 21% | 15% | 24% | 6% | 7% | 22% |
| France | 21% | 8% | 11% | 6% | 0% | 0% | 0% | 0% | 0% | 0% |
| United States | 0% | 0% | 0% | 0% | 4% | 4% | 2% | 7% | 14% | 21% |
| Germany | 16% | 19% | 15% | 17% | 33% | 37% | 23% | 4% | 9% | 0% |

**Table 3.6.** continued

| Year | France | United States | Great Britain | Germany | Spain | Other | Total |
|------|--------|---------------|---------------|---------|-------|-------|-------|
| 1869 | 223 (13%) | 78 (5%) | 291 (16%) | 286 (16%) | 655 (38%) | 209 (12%) | 1,742 |
| 1903 | 4,205 (37%) | 2,138 (19%) | 1,173 (10%) | 1,761 (16%) | 1,200 (11%) | 791 (7%) | 11,268 |
| 1904 | 6,282 (46%) | 1,845 (14%) | 1,288 (10%) | 2,458 (18%) | 1,110 (8%) | 554 (4%) | 13,537 |
| 1905 | 5,054 (53%) | 1,456 (15%) | 443 (5%) | 1,224 (13%) | 833 (9%) | 534 (6%) | 9,544 |
| 1908 | 9,585 (57%) | 2,792 (17%) | 1,614 (10%) | 681 (4%) | 1,466 (9%) | 532 (3%) | 16,670 |
| 1913 | 9,820 (51%) | 4,374 (23%) | 650 (3%) | 1,995 (10%) | 1,211 (6%) | 1,055 (6%) | 19,104 |
| 1919 | 7,420 (28%) | 12,628 (47%) | 3,908 (15%) | — | 1,286 (5%) | 1,455 (5%) | 26,697 |
| 1921 | 1,395 (7%) | 6,566 (34%) | 354 (2%) | 6,815 (35%) | 1,235 (6%) | 3,011 (16%) | 19,376 |

Sources: *Revista del banco crédito y hipotecario*, 1 September 1878, cited in unpublished research notes of Julio Estrada Ycaza; USCD, Charles Weile, "Report," 9 February 1870; CCm, *Memoria*, 1903, 1904, 1905, 1908, 1913, 1919, 1921.
— = less than 1%

**Table 3.7.** Oceangoing vessels into Guayaquil, selected years, 1869–1923 (by nation of origin)

| Year | Britain | Germany | Ecuador | Peru | France | Chile | Other | Total |
|------|---------|---------|---------|------|--------|-------|-------|-------|
| 1869 | 61 | 18 | 20 | 24 | 10 | n/a | 16 | 149 |
| | (41%) | (12%) | (13%) | (16%) | (7%) | | (11%) | |
| 1870[a] | 73 | 25 | 8 | 4 | 9 | n/a | 16 | 135 |
| | (54%) | (19%) | (6%) | (3%) | (7%) | | (12%) | |
| 1871 | 74 | 10 | — | — | 4 | — | — | 95 |
| | (78%) | (11%) | | | (4%) | | | |
| 1872 | 78 | 17 | — | — | 22 | — | — | 103 |
| | (76%) | (17%) | | | (21%) | | | |
| 1873 | 73 | 16 | — | — | 30 | — | — | 123 |
| | (59%) | (13%) | | | (24%) | | | |
| 1874 | 76 | 13 | — | — | 5 | — | — | 96 |
| | (79%) | (14%) | | | (5%) | | | |
| 1877 | 73 | 10 | — | — | 5 | — | — | 86 |
| 1878 | 104 | 16 | 28 | 32 | 7 | n/a | 12 | 199 |
| | (52%) | (8%) | (14%) | (16%) | (4%) | | (6%) | |
| 1879 | 121 | 19 | 33 | 18 | 9 | n/a | 28 | 228 |
| | (53%) | (8%) | (23%) | (1%) | (5%) | | (10%) | |
| 1886[a] | 116 | 16 | 26 | n/a | n/a | n/a | 25 | 183 |
| | (63%) | (9%) | (14%) | | | | (14%) | |
| 1897 | 102 | 32 | 0 | 0 | 0 | 52 | 11 | 197 |
| | (52%) | (16%) | | | | (26%) | (6%) | |
| 1898 | 111 | 24 | 0 | 0 | 3 | 53 | 16 | 207 |
| | (54%) | (12%) | | | (1%) | (26%) | (8%) | |
| 1903[a] | 87 | 29 | 3 | 5 | 0 | n/a | 37 | 161 |
| | (54%) | (18%) | (2%) | (3%) | | | (23%) | |
| 1905 | — | — | — | — | — | — | — | 211 |
| 1907 | — | — | — | — | — | — | — | 240 |
| 1922–23 | 67 | 37 | n/a | 43 | 12 | 55 | 104 | 324 |
| | (21%) | (11%) | | (13%) | (4%) | (17%) | (32%) | |

*Sources:* USCD, Weile, "Year Review," 9 February 1870; Bragdon, "Year Report," 30 September 1870; Eder, "Commerce," 15 March 1879; McLean, "Report," 24 January 1880; Reinberg, "Report," 10 March 1887; Gallegos Naranjo, *1883 almanaque;* IP, *Informe, 1897, 1898, 1903;* CCm, *Memoria, 1905, 1907;* GBFO, Mitchell, "Report," 25 September 1923; Chiriboga, *Jornaleros,* 47.
*Note:* In 1903, China = 24 (15% [est.]). In 1922–23, United States = 38 (12%).
[a]Estimate.

the war stopped exporting to Ecuador almost entirely. Throughout this era, neither the French nor the Germans could challenge British control of the import trade.

Increasingly, however, the United States offered the British some competition. Whereas in the 1880s the United States had provided only about half

**Table 3.8.** Origins of Ecuador's imports, selected years, 1853–1923 (value in 1,000s of sucres—pesos before 1884)

| Year | Great Britain | United States | France | Germany | Peru | Other | Total |
|---|---|---|---|---|---|---|---|
| 1853 | n/a | n/a | n/a | n/a | n/a | n/a | 2,113 |
| 1854 | n/a | n/a | n/a | n/a | n/a | n/a | 1,915 |
| 1855 | n/a | n/a | n/a | n/a | n/a | n/a | 1,938 |
| 1856 | n/a | n/a | n/a | n/a | n/a | n/a | 2,487 |
| 1857 | n/a | n/a | n/a | n/a | n/a | n/a | 3,595 |
| 1878 | n/a | 1,088 | n/a | n/a | n/a | n/a | n/a |
| 1889 | 2,351 | 1,378 | 1,989 | 1,331 | 740 | 1,893 | 9,682 |
|  | (24%) | (14%) | (21%) | (14%) | (8%) | (20%) |  |
| 1890 | 2,672 | 1,608 | 2,464 | 1,319 | 931 | 1,022 | 10,016 |
|  | (27%) | (16%) | (25%) | (13%) | (9%) | (10%) |  |
| 1891 | 1,829 | 1,496 | 1,781 | 1,042 | 512 | 581 | 7,241 |
|  | (25%) | (21%) | (25%) | (14%) | (7%) | (8%) |  |
| 1893 | 3,054 | 2,005 | 2,082 | 1,688 | 630 | 1,063 | 10,522 |
|  | (29%) | (19%) | (20%) | (16%) | (6%) | (10%) |  |
| 1897 | 5,195 | 2,336 | 2,261 | 2,385 | 1,217 | 2,135 | 15,529 |
|  | (33%) | (15%) | (15%) | (15%) | (8%) | (14%) |  |
| 1898 | 2,578 | 2,600 | 998 | 1,371 | 748 | 1,575 | 9,870 |
|  | (26%) | (26%) | (10%) | (14%) | (8%) | (16%) |  |
| 1900 | 3,975 | 3,430 | 1,241 | 2,577 | 495 | 1,699 | 13,417 |
|  | (30%) | (26%) | (9%) | (19%) | (4%) | (13%) |  |
| 1901 | 3,575 | 3,966 | 1,996 | 2,713 | 794 | 2,082 | 15,126 |
|  | (24%) | (26%) | (13%) | (18%) | (5%) | (14%) |  |
| 1902 | 5,751 | 2,983 | 1,588 | 2,086 | 510 | 1,524 | 14,442 |
|  | (40%) | (21%) | (11%) | (14%) | (4%) | (11%) |  |
| 1903 | 3,197 | 2,797 | 1,012 | 2,000 | 500 | 1,563 | 11,069 |
|  | (29%) | (25%) | (9%) | (18%) | (5%) | (14%) |  |
| 1904 | 4,010 | 4,898 | 1,235 | 2,985 | 360 | 1,850 | 15,338 |
|  | (26%) | (32%) | (8%) | (19%) | (2%) | (12%) |  |
| 1905 | 4,559 | 4,542 | 1,119 | 3,102 | 474 | 1,939 | 15,734 |
|  | (29%) | (29%) | (7%) | (20%) | (3%) | (12%) |  |
| 1906 | 5,540 | 4,657 | 1,276 | 3,095 | 206 | 2,238 | 17,012 |
|  | (33%) | (27%) | (8%) | (18%) | (1%) | (13%) |  |
| 1907 | 7,047 | 4,698 | 1,197 | 3,601 | 294 | 2,863 | 19,700 |
|  | (36%) | (24%) | (6%) | (18%) | (2%) | (15%) |  |
| 1908 | 7,177 | 4,098 | 1,477 | 4,298 | 730 | 2,775 | 20,555 |
|  | (35%) | (20%) | (7%) | (21%) | (4%) | (14%) |  |
| 1909 | 6,282 | 4,796 | 1,221 | 3,347 | 226 | 2,832 | 18,704 |
|  | (34%) | (26%) | (7%) | (18%) | (1%) | (15%) |  |
| 1910 | 5,053 | 4,629 | 1,081 | 3,232 | 123 | 2,359 | 16,477 |
|  | (31%) | (28%) | (7%) | (20%) | (1%) | (14%) |  |
| 1911 | 5,827 | 5,325 | 1,470 | 4,900 | 566 | 5,152 | 23,240 |
|  | (25%) | (23%) | (6%) | (21%) | (2%) | (22%) |  |

**Table 3.8.** continued

| Year | Great Britain | United States | France | Germany | Peru | Other | Total |
|---|---|---|---|---|---|---|---|
| 1912 | 6,293 | 5,528 | 1,268 | 4,332 | 363 | 3,522 | 21,306 |
| | (30%) | (26%) | (6%) | (20%) | (2%) | (17%) | |
| 1913 | 5,391 | 6,381 | 849 | 3,216 | 330 | 2,005 | 18,182 |
| | (30%) | (35%) | (5%) | (18%) | (2%) | (11%) | |
| 1915 | 6,700 | 6,600 | 500 | — | 600 | 2,910 | 17,310 |
| | (39%) | (38%) | (3%) | (3%) | (17%) | | |
| 1916 | 4,900 | 11,000 | 800 | — | 300 | 2,798 | 19,198 |
| | (26%) | (57%) | (4%) | (2%) | (11%) | | |
| 1917 | 5,048 | 12,206 | 668 | — | 524 | 2,494 | 20,940 |
| | (24%) | (58%) | (3%) | (3%) | (12%) | | |
| 1918 | 3,900 | 9,500 | 300 | — | 500 | 2,491 | 16,691 |
| | (23%) | (57%) | (2%) | (3%) | (15%) | | |
| 1919 | 3,200 | 16,800 | 600 | — | 600 | 2,808 | 24,008 |
| | (13%) | (70%) | (2%) | (2%) | (12%) | | |
| 1920 | 9,834 | 25,424 | 1,395 | 1,123 | 965 | 4,754 | 43,495 |
| | (23%) | (59%) | (3%) | (3%) | (2%) | (11%) | |
| 1921 | 7,046 | 8,925 | 1,644 | 1,879 | 936 | 3,056 | 23,486 |
| | (30%) | (38%) | (7%) | (8%) | (4%) | (13%) | |
| 1922 | 9,543 | 17,937 | n/a | n/a | n/a | n/a | 33,586 |
| | (26%) | (49%) | | | | | |
| 1923 | n/a | 21,073 | n/a | n/a | n/a | n/a | 36,805 |
| | | (57%) | | | | | |

*Sources:* USCD, Wile, "Report," 9 February 1873, Eder, "Report on Commerce in Ecuador in 1878," 15 March 1879; GG, *Informe*, 1901; CCm, *Memoria*, 1902, 1904, 1907, 1908, 1913, 1919, 1921; *América libre*, 277; GBFO, R. C. Mitchell, "Report on the Economic and Financial Conditions in Ecuador September, 1923," 25 September 1923, "Report on British Trade with Ecuador," 9 December 1924; Ayala Mora, *Época republicana*, 126.
[a]Estimate
— = less than 1%

as many imports to Ecuador as did Great Britain, by the 1890s they competed evenly, each providing one-quarter to a third of Ecuador's imports. World War I ended the equilibrium and accelerated the United States' ascendancy in imports. During the war, the share of U.S. imports soared to 70 percent. After World War I, the United States continued as Ecuador's chief supplier at more than half of all foreign goods. By then the British could only comfort themselves with empty bromides: "the demand is principally for a cheap article."[17] Perhaps, but the demand was principally for U.S.-made ones.

Guayaquil's burgeoning population came to depend upon imported food: potatoes from Chile, butter and flour from California, lard from the eastern United States, rice from Asia or Peru, and vegetables and refined sugar from Peru. Indeed, food and inexpensive cloth were the leading imports, despite the fact that the sierra had an abundance of both. Total rice imports rose from 3,996 quintals in 1880 to 175,161 by 1911; those of wheat rose from 48,125 quintals in 1880 to 145,923 in 1911. Guayaquil had to rely on those imports to sustain its growing population, for the city and region proved incapable of providing for their own needs. The city used the money it earned from cacao and other exports to import products for its own consumption.[18]

A possible alternative to this heavy reliance on imported food, bringing in products grown in the highland provinces, was not viable, because the formidable Andes and an underdeveloped overland transportation network to them greatly restricted trade with the highlands. Transportation costs made it difficult for food from the sierra provinces of Chimborazo and Tunguragua to compete against imports in Guayaquil.[19] Shipment costs likewise drove up the cost of imports to the interior, generally forcing *serranos*, the mountain dwellers, to make do with their own products.

Asses provided the chief means of transport into the mountains, but even in good weather and the best of circumstances, the journey to Quito could take two weeks, with few hotels or boarding houses along the way. Ecuador had built a road in the highlands in the 1870s, but by 1885 it was of little use. As one traveler noted, "long neglect" had left "no other road than a meandering, never worked mule path" for much of the way. Thirteen years later, in 1898, the situation was no better, as another hapless sojourner glumly reported: "there is not even a wagon road from . . . [Quito] to the coast." The highway, known as the "Vía Flores," was passable for only three to six months each year and closed the rest of the time due to heavy rains.[20]

After the completion of a national railway in 1909 (a breathtaking engineering feat, if a stunningly expensive one) transportation costs still remained prohibitive. Limited rolling stock, the need for frequent repairs all along the line, and high operating costs plagued the railway from its inception. The railway rarely operated at a profit.[21] Accordingly, in Guayaquil, sierra foods—onions, potatoes, vegetables—could not compete with cheaper foreign imports. Highland Ecuador sold few products to outsiders and bought few items from without; all the while the prosperous economy of the coast bounded ahead. Guayaquil developed few economic ties with the populous mountain valleys of the interior.[22]

Guayaquil paralleled other South American cities in the growth of its commerce in the late nineteenth century. In Chilean ports, to take one example, net registered tonnage doubled from 1879 and 1887 and quadruped from 1888 to 1912.[23] However, among the various emerging Latin American export economies, Ecuador did exhibit some unusual patterns in its success. During the first half of the nineteenth century, much of Latin America was out of step with upward trends in the world economy. The Guayaquil area was an exception; it was out of step with downward trends among Latin American economies. In the second half of the nineteenth century, most of Latin America exported to Great Britain. Toward the end of the century, Germany and the United States challenged the British in world trade, but the French lagged behind. Ecuador's strong export link with France, instead of Great Britain, made it then a somewhat rarer example of dependent monoculture for that era. But in the main, Ecuador was like the rest of Latin America. The dramatic upswing in the international economy during the second half of the nineteenth century pulled nearly all of Latin America into line with world trends. Ecuador, especially Guayaquil, joined in.

# Chapter Four

# The Political Economy of Regionalism
## The Fiscal Context

The prospering cacao export trade reconfigured the regional distribution of economic power in Ecuador, thereby generating new patterns of national politics. Historians of Ecuador have typically divided the nation's political history for the late nineteenth and early twentieth centuries into five periods. From 1860 to 1875 (period one), pro-Church conservative Gabriel García Moreno controlled the national government, quieting opponents with repression, smashing all those who rose up against him. In the eyes of his supporters, García Moreno deserved credit for bringing stability to the young nation. But not all shared this view, and in 1875 one disturbed critic murdered the president on the steps of the capital. By 1876 General Ignacio Veintemilla had emerged as the nation's new strongman, a position he defended until 1883, when he was driven from office by force of arms (period two, 1876–1883). The third period, 1884 to 1895, brought three elected leaders to the fore: José María Plácido Caamaño (1884–88), Antonio Flores Jijón (1888–92), and Luís Cordero (1892–95). Ecuadorian political historians term this the "Progressive Era" because political power three times changed hands via elections (with two consecutive presidents completing their terms in office) and because some trappings of modernity began to make their appearance in Ecuador.

From 1895 to 1925, the Liberal Party governed Ecuador. The fourth period, 1895–1916, was a time of frequent civil wars. These swirled around the personal ambitions of two generals, Eloy Alfaro (president 1895–1901, 1906–11) and Leonidas Plaza Gutiérrez (president 1901–6, 1912–16). General Alfaro led the Liberals to victory in the civil war of 1895. In 1901, Plaza followed Alfaro in office; this despite Alfaro's best efforts. In 1906 Plaza named a successor (not Alfaro) and left the country. Alfaro changed that plan when he again seized office by force. In 1911 Alfaro attempted to stay in office, which triggered an especially bloody civil war. By 1912 Ecuador drifted into anarchy, but the wars ended by 1916. Alfaro and his top supporters were murdered in a most gruesome and very public manner in Quito.

The fifth period, 1916–25, proved more peaceful, as General Plaza turned the national government over to civilians. Three elected presidents of a mildly reformist bent governed: Alfredo Baquerizo Moreno (1916–20), José Luís Tamayo (1920–24), and Gonzalo Cordova (1924–25). These leaders were "liberal" inasmuch as they encouraged the expansion of public works projects, introduced civil marriage and divorce, and seized Church lands. In 1925, however, Ecuador returned to form, when yet another military coup took place and President Cordova was removed from office.[1]

Until recently, most scholars of Ecuadorian politics have seen the 1895 triumph of the Liberal Party as a watershed: the removal from national power of the traditional sierra land-owning elite and the unambiguous implementation of liberal reforms (such as public works projects, civil marriage, and secularization of education) under the leadership of an emerging coastal elite dominated by banking and commercial interests. To this view, 1895 marked the triumph of a plutocratic "agromercantile bourgeoisie."[2] Many scholars—Agustín Cueva, Manuel Chiriboga, and Rafael Quintero López, among others—have taken this position, arguing that 1895 brought, in various formulations, the agro-export, commercial, or banking elite of the coast to national dominance.[3] However, Osvaldo Hurtado (1985) broke with this traditional view, for although he too saw the rise of a "bankocracy" during the Liberal Era, he went on to stress that political parties in Ecuador have actually been much less important than have "caudillos." Hurtado concluded that, "periodization schemes that pretend to divide the political history of Ecuador into Conservative and Liberal are not altogether accurate."[4] Linda Alexander Rodríguez took this understanding further, demonstrating in her work, *The Search for Public Policy* (1984), that "the Liberals had not fundamentally altered government policies. Rather they expanded tendencies [of using the state to foster reform] already well articulated in Ecuador. They differed from earlier regimes primarily in their access to greater revenues from cacao exports."[5] Rodríguez showed that what was different about the "Liberal Era" was not so much novel actions or ideology; mostly, they just had more money to spend.

### Ecuador's Political Culture

Commensurate with its expanded economic role, coastal Ecuador now seized a larger share in the distribution of national political power. However, this did not mean that coastal hegemony ensued. Instead, regional politics remained, and within this system Guayaquil and the coast faced a variety of continuing political frustrations.

The larger context for Guayaquil's politics lay in what may be termed the "political culture" of Ecuador.[6] Throughout the late nineteenth and early twentieth centuries, neither clearly articulated ideologies nor strong and well-disciplined parties informed Ecuadorian politics. The principal political parties, the Liberal and the Conservative, seldom produced leaders from within their own ranks. Instead, bold and aggressive men used these organizations as vehicles to advance their personal political ambitions. Personalistic and authoritarian military rulers dominated Ecuadorian politics.

These assertive, charismatic men and their followers battled recurrently over control of the national government. This meant that most administrations found themselves totally preoccupied with the foremost task of any government—staying in power. Beleaguered by violent enemies, leaders felt compelled to throttle free political expression and rig elections. Seeing the futility of electoral change, adversaries saw no recourse but military action. As a result, Ecuador was vexed by a nearly ceaseless and surely pointless cycle of "revolutions."

Part of the problem was that Ecuador's economy could not create enough positions considered suitable by the sons of the well-to-do (and the nation's thin middle class). Given the dearth of commercial opportunities in the economically somnolent sierra, many frustrated young men too often saw revolution as a sort of job application. Warring cliques emerged, fighting mostly over patronage, seldom over ideals.

### Government Revenue

Another serious problem facing government at any level in Ecuador was the sheer lack of revenue. Ecuador's frequent civil wars halted commerce, destroyed assets, and hindered efficient tax collection. Moreover, Ecuador was a relatively small, unindustrialized, and poor country. It is unremarkable that such a nation was perennially strapped for funds.

In addition, Ecuador did a poor job of collecting taxes. As in most countries, the rich successfully avoided paying; they were especially adept at blocking the imposition of any direct impost. The nation relied instead on tariffs collected at the Guayaquil customhouse. The tax system there was one of bewildering complexity. The code listed separate duties of widely varying amounts on every manner of import good. Many items carried two, three, or more special duties, each of which was collected individually. Some goods were taxed by weight, some by size, others by count, some by value, and others by a combination of those and other methods. Not unaware of the problems, Congress periodically adjusted and altered the tax code yet only managed to add to the confusion. Goods piled up on docks and rotted in warehouses as importers and customs officials gamely tried to balance their ledgers. Incessant bickering resulted as each tried to make sense of a tax code so confusing probably no one truly understood it. Countless merchants avoided the whole issue by smuggling their goods around the customhouse.

The government employed but a handful of bureaucrats and officials to collect and keep track of the imposts. Woefully short on training, they did not stand a chance against Ecuador's redoubtable tax code. Worse, each new government fired most of the employees from the previous administration and hired its own, losing in the process the few veteran officials who had pieced together some understanding of the tax code. The patronage system further hindered collections, for frequently the bureaucrats saw their tenure in office as a potentially lucrative, if brief, opportunity for self-enrichment. Short of funds, the government often found that it could not even meet its payroll, and salaries sometimes fell years behind. On occasion, the government paid employees in bonds or certificates for land. Such bills seldom traded at face value, and at times even the government refused to accept them. Employees had little choice but to dispose of this paper at a great discount in order to obtain cash. The poverty of officials did little to encourage honesty.

Given its lack of adequately prepared bureaucrats, the government had to rely on "tax farmers" to collect revenues. Those who collected taxes on aguardiente, for example, negotiated a price with the government for the right to collect the levy and kept anything in excess of that amount. The government had little idea of how much the tax farmer actually collected.

Ecuador spent much of its revenue unwisely. The near-constant threat of an internal military challenge forced successive administrations to divert scarce resources to the military. Sometimes that meant simply strengthening one's position with the military by raising the pay of high ranking officers. When internal civil war erupted anyway, resources had to be spent on warfare, further draining scarce funds.

Yet national revenues rose because of the success of the coastal cacao export economy. Eager to put the money to good use, government planners launched an assortment of ambitious public works projects. Frequently, though, the programs to build railroads, highways, bridges, or water works were not effectively coordinated. Congress mandated myriad programs and entrusted their oversight to specially created autonomous agencies. Each agency had specially earmarked sources of revenue, such as a surtax on a particular import item or an added tax on cacao exports. With each autonomous agency jealously guarding its domain, the president and his advisors found they could not even demand a review of their budgets. Half or more of Ecuador's national tax revenues went directly to the autonomous agencies.

The lack of central control might not have been a serious problem had the autonomous agencies, or *juntas,* successfully carried out their duties. But they completed few of their assigned projects. In 1905, for instance, fewer than 16 percent of the 346 public work projects were actually being carried out.[7] Sometimes the assigned revenues only covered the junta's administrative costs and left nothing for actual construction. The special juntas emerged as an answer to Ecuador's problem with regionalism and the strong urge toward local control. However, as a system of government, the autonomous agencies proved wasteful and ineffective.

The difficulties in revenue collection and expenditure led to other problems. More and more the government fell into debt, the servicing of which assumed an ever-larger share of the state's few resources. Because Ecuador had long since defaulted on its foreign debt, it could not attract foreign lenders. The national government had to turn to Guayaquil banks, the Banco de Ecuador and the Banco Comercial y Agrícola, for in Ecuador only the coastal cacao export economy generated ready cash. Quito regulated banking, approving or turning down charters and monitoring currency emissions. Coastal banks, then, were in a very poor position to deny the national government's repeated requests for loans. And if the bank's monetary policies were unsound, the Guayaquil bankers were not alone responsible.[8]

### Regionalism

The final piece of the national context, and central to understanding Guayaquil's political dilemmas, was the intense regionalism of Ecuador, "the political expression of the division and isolation imposed by geography."[9] Ecuador has historically lacked a strong sense of national consciousness. This is a country cut in half by some of the world's tallest mountains, and profound local differences—in ethnicity, language, religiosity, and culture—have developed naturally. The people of the coast and the sierra too often have regarded one another with a mutual sense of heart-felt contempt and dark suspicion. Most Ecuadorians never traveled outside of their native provinces and so tended to define their interests by household, extended family, village, or region. To these people, "nationalism" had little meaning.

During the colonial era, the sierra became home to an elite that fixed its efforts on exploiting the large population of Indians. Religion, education, and the arts soon came to be centered in Quito, "reinforc[ing] . . . [an] attitude . . . of cultural superiority [there, and a certain] . . . cultural defensiveness in Guayaquil." Meanwhile, the port harbored a special sense of separateness and a spirit of independence, born of its unique history. In 1804 the crown detached Guayaquil, but not the rest of the region of Ecuador, from the Viceroyalty of New Granada and attached it instead to the Viceroyalty of Peru. From 1820 to 1822, Guayaquil broke off and became an independent city-state, achieving its separation from Spain in advance of the provinces of the sierra. The municipal government of Guayaquil asserted a sentiment of autonomy repeatedly.[10]

Cultural differences divided Ecuador. People of the coast and the sierra spoke differently: the *d* in Quito was more clearly pronounced as a *th*, the *ll* as a *z*, and the *r* spoken with a hissing quality; on the coast, the *s* at the end of words became an *h*. Each held negative stereotypes of the other. To racist whites of the sierra, the swarthy montuvios of the coast were a bastard race—part European, Indian, and Negro—and living proof of the evils of miscegenation. Serranos referred to *costeños*, coastal residents, as "*monos;*" they belittled what they considered to be the port city's crass propensity for making money; and they sternly objected to Guayaquil's relatively lax religious attitudes. Costeños replied that serranos were "*longos,*" a term otherwise reserved for obsequious Indian houseboys. They saw *quiteños* as prideful and sanctimonious and claimed that the ostentatious piety of the sierra was wrought with hypocrisy.[11]

This national fragmentation came to be reinforced in several ways. Relations of production and market orientation developed along distinctly different paths in the sierra and the coast. Whereas the sierra counted on a largely unfree labor force that produced necessities for local consumption, the coast prospered under a system of mostly free wage labor that produced for the agro-export trade.

The lack of roads connecting the coast to the sierra further assured regional segregation—travel could take weeks during the dry season, and during the rainy season it was impossible. Even the 1909 completion of a national railway failed utterly in providing inexpensive transport. The railway, plagued by landslides and breakdowns, seldom showed a profit despite its high fares. As a consequence, leading businesses and families in the northern and southern sierra forged commercial ties to adjoining regions in Colombia and Peru, not to the Ecuadorian littoral.

"Less a nation than a series of loosely articulated regions," to the extent that any Ecuadorians showed an interest in national politics, they focused their energies on the spoils of office or on obtaining pork-barrel legislation to benefit their home districts.[12] Ecuadorians generally behaved as motivated by local needs and interests; as a result, the national interest suffered.

Such was the national context for coastal politics. For Guayaquil the principal political difficulty was that its cacao exports were the only important cash-producing activity in Ecuador; the import and export taxes on this trade provided almost all government revenue.[13] Ecuador had abolished the Indian tribute and the tithe on farm production by 1889. There remained no significant sierra tax.[14] Customs duties generated from 53 percent to 81 percent of ordinary national tax revenues from 1895 to 1925. Most of the money came from Guayas province (from 84 percent to 97 percent) and the rest from the other coastal provinces.[15] Still, the money had to be used first to pay the mounting bills of the national government in distant Quito and the sierra, not Guayaquil's expenses.

For example, the high school for boys in Guayaquil, the Colegio Nacional de San Vicente, had for its financial support in 1887 the proceeds of a 3.5 percent customs tax; the school in the highland city of Cuenca received the revenues from a 4.5 percent customs tax. In 1903, money from Guayas went to build a school workshop, a high school for girls, an arts school, and a new governor's office, all in Azogues, Cañar, in highland Ecuador. While these projects and countless others like them were no doubt worthy enough, Guayas politicians held that the sierra, not the coast, should pay for them. In some years Guayaquil received nothing from the national government for public works. For that which it did receive, Guayaquil hardly felt grateful. After all, most of the revenues came from the Guayaquil customhouse in the first place.[16]

Interregional battles resulted. Political elites in each zone—the traditional, autarkic, landed oligarchy of various districts in the sierra, and the non-immigrant merchants and great estate owners of the coast—worked assiduously to defend their own interests and, if possible, to seize control over the national government and use its power and resources to further advance their interests.

Unity might have come to the country if a strong single power block from any region had been sufficiently ascendant to impose its vision of national policy. But such was not the case in Ecuador; the regions remained fairly evenly balanced.[17] Despite the economic growth of the coast, Quito and the sierra always proved powerful enough to insist upon a large share of the revenues collected in Guayaquil. Quito, the seat of government since the beginning of colonial times, had the advantage of history on its side. Moreover, for all the demographic expansion of the coast, the sierra continued to have a much larger population. Led by a sturdy old elite with considerable social and economic resources, the sierra when challenged could quickly conscript Indians and field sizable and menacing armies. At the same time, many of the elite in Guayaquil were foreign merchants and frequently absent from Ecuador. For Guayaquil, this meant that the efforts of the resident local elite to oversee the city's progress were significantly restricted by the fiscal and political realities imposed by Ecuador's regionalism.

### City Government

Ecuador divided its government among a variety of branches and levels of authority. The presidents and their ministers had to contend with the power of Congress and with the autonomy of numerous special agencies. Each province had an elected governor who reported to the president's ministers. The governors, in turn, appointed numerous local officials. In Guayas province in 1910, they included five canton officials (*jefes políticos*) and thirty-seven parish officials (*tenientes políticos*).[18]

Like the national government, the municipal government of Guayaquil lacked adequate revenue. The largest share of funds for the municipality came from taxes on imports and exports, although the city government further realized proceeds from fees charged for potable water, street lighting, street cleaning, and spaces at the city market, from taxes on liquor, and from payments from the sale of city land. Smaller sums came from charges for surveying, the slaughterhouse, pier use, the rental of space in government buildings, and from taxes on peripatetic vendors, wheeled vehicles, meat, and tobacco.[19]

Guayaquil city revenues grew at a faster rate than did national revenues. In 1871, the national budget of 2.5 million sucres was thirty-seven times larger than the Guayaquil city budget of 68,000 sucres; by 1925 the national budget of 36.8 million sucres was only ten times larger than the Guayaquil city budget of 3.9 million sucres. Put another way, from 1871 to 1919 the Guayaquil city budget grew from 3 percent to 16 percent of the size of the national budget, while the population of the city only grew from 3 percent to about 5 percent of the national total. Per capita, the revenue of Guayaquil government rose from about 4.5 sucres in the 1870s to roughly 14.7 sucres by the 1900s, an increase of 320 percent; meanwhile, per capita revenue for the national government rose from about 3.4 sucres in the 1870s to 9.7 sucres by the 1900s, an increase of about 290 percent.[20]

In Guayaquil, city revenues generally grew faster than did population. Total city revenues rose from 68,000 sucres in 1871, when the city had a population of roughly 20,000, to 2.5 million in 1919, when the city's inhabitants numbered about 100,000. The population increased five times over and city revenues thirty-five times over (with negligible inflation in those years). In the 1880s, the population grew at a rate of 5.5 percent a year, while city revenues rose at a rate of 12 percent annually, or more than twice as fast. In the 1890s, the population of Guayaquil increased at a rate of 3.3 percent each year, while city revenues rose 11 percent annually, or more than three times faster. From 1900 to 1910, the population of the city rose about 3.1 percent per year, while city revenues actually declined at a rate of about 2.5 percent per year. And in the decade from 1910 to 1920, the city population rose at a rate of about 1.9 percent per year, while revenues grew about 8.6 percent annually, or about four times faster than the population.[21]

Schools, supported with both national and local tax money, usually took up 3 to 4 percent of the city budget.[22] City police, also funded with both city and national money, used from 3 to 12 percent of city revenues. The city provided financial aid to the Junta de Beneficencia for health services and hospitals in Guayaquil, in outlays ranging from 7 to 17 percent of the city budgets. City funds also went to run government offices, hold elections and festivals, provide for the jail, buy books for the library, pick up trash, print government documents, transport meat to the city, and support outlying rural districts.[23]

Public works, which could be supported with either national and local money (or both), used from 5 to 15 percent of city budgets. The city jail, for example, was built entirely with city funds. Other city-supported projects included a slaughterhouse, government office buildings, street paving, a new market, road construction, piers, laying pipe for potable water, sewers, street lights, parks, and many, many statues. However, most city public works projects were handled with national revenues, augmented by local funds. Still, by 1919 the city devoted more than 200,000 sucres, about 9 percent of the budget, to such ventures.[24]

In Guayaquil expenditures exceeded revenues, and the city's debt grew even more rapidly than that of the national government. The city debt ranged from 155,000 sucres in 1875 to 1,296,800 in 1889; 2,060,042 in 1892; 2,589,000 in 1904; fell to 2,479,600 sucres in 1905; rose again to 2,776,000 in 1908; and dropped again slightly to 2,390,000 in 1912. Over this forty-year span, the city debt grew some twenty times over. In the same period, the national debt of Ecuador grew not quite threefold, from 4.4 million sucres in 1877 to 12.6 million sucres in 1912.[25]

What these figures show is that the great leaps in city government revenues in the 1880s came from borrowing. Most of the money went to start the public works projects associated with rapid urbanization. Urbanization is expensive. As the city grew, it had to launch projects to provide water, dispose of sewage, and pave major streets. Start-up costs for these projects were

**Table 4.1.** Guayaquil city budgets, major expenditures, selected years, 1869–1925 (in percentages and in 1,000s of sucres)

| Year | Public works | Education | Charity and health | Police | Debt payment | Total |
|------|------|------|------|------|------|------|
| 1868 | n/a | n/a | n/a | n/a | n/a | 100 |
| 1870 | n/a | n/a | n/a | n/a | n/a | 94 |
| 1871 | n/a | n/a | n/a | n/a | n/a | 84 |
| 1887 | 14% | 4% | 17% | 8% | 10% | 100% |
| | 41 | 13 | 52 | 27 | 30 | 301 |
| 1889 | n/a | 4% | 15% | 12% | 31% | 100% |
| | | 14 | 54 | 43 | 115 | 372 |
| 1890[a] | 54 | 13 | 54 | 28 | 207 | n/a |
| 1891 | n/a | n/a | n/a | n/a | 39% | 100% |
| | | | | | 211 | 544 |
| 1892 | 5% | 3% | 12% | 3% | 50% | 100% |
| | 22 | 14 | 54 | 13 | 232 | 465 |
| 1893 | 3% | 3% | n/a | 6% | 59% | 100% |
| | 19 | 15 | | 31 | 332 | 560 |
| 1895 | 12% | 4% | 7% | 4% | 51% | 100% |
| | 69 | 22 | 43 | 25 | 304 | 593 |
| 1904 | n/a | n/a | n/a | n/a | 33% | 100% |
| | | 388 | 1,183 | | | |
| 1905 | n/a | n/a | n/a | n/a | 29% | 100% |
| | — | — | — | — | 255 | 896 |
| 1906 | n/a | n/a | n/a | n/a | 27% | 100% |
| | — | — | — | — | 255 | 933 |
| 1907 | 17% | 4% | 6% | 5% | 29% | 100% |
| | 211 | 51 | 72 | 58 | 363 | 1,237 |
| 1908[a] | 15% | 4% | n/a | n/a | 20% | 100% |
| | 180 | 52 | | | 229 | 1,175 |
| 1909 | n/a | n/a | 9% | n/a | 14% | 100% |
| | | | 96 | | 147 | 1,043 |
| 1913 | n/a | n/a | n/a | n/a | 245 | n/a |
| 1916 | 146 | n/a | n/a | n/a | n/a | n/a |
| 1918 | 10% | 3% | 5% | 4% | n/a | 100% |
| | 282 | 82 | 142 | 105 | | 2,857 |
| 1919[a] | 9% | 3% | 7% | n/a | 21% | 100% |
| | 213 | 84 | 167 | | 521 | 2,456 |
| 1925 | n/a | 3% | 7% | 2% | 20% | 100% |
| | | 117 | 283 | 94 | 785 | 3,868 |

**Table 4.1.** continued

| Year | Sale of city land | Food sale fees | Liquor tax | Customs revenue for sewers | Total |
|---|---|---|---|---|---|
| 1889 | 10% | 16% | 17% | 8% | 100% |
| | 37 | 61 | 63 | 31 | 372 |

| | Sale of city land | Marketplace fees | Imported liquor tax | Street lighting fees | Total |
|---|---|---|---|---|---|
| 1890[a] | 9% | 17% | 17% | 17% | 100% |
| | 30 | 60 | 60 | 60 | 346 |

| | Customs rev. for pub. wks. | Marketplace fees | Imported liquor tax | Lighting and street cleaning | Total |
|---|---|---|---|---|---|
| 1892 | 16% | 16% | 13% | 16% | 100% |
| | 75 | 75 | 61 | 74 | 465 |
| 1893 | 14% | 15% | 11% | 11% | 100% |
| | 76 | 77 | 60 | 58 | 526 |

| | Potable water fees | Marketplace fees | Imported liquor tax | Lighting and street cleaning | Total |
|---|---|---|---|---|---|
| 1895 | 14% | 13% | 11% | 10% | 100% |
| | 84 | 75 | 64 | 60 | 593 |

| | Potable water fees | Marketplace fees | Liquor taxes | Cacao export tax | Total income |
|---|---|---|---|---|---|
| 1907 | 8% | 8% | 15% | 29% | 100% |
| | 104 | 102 | 184 | 360 | 1,237 |

| | Potable water fees | Marketplace fees | Liquor taxes | Cacao export tax | Total income |
|---|---|---|---|---|---|
| 1908[a] | 13% | 7% | 8% | 38% | 100% |
| | 147 | 83 | 94 | 450 | 1,175 |
| 1913 | 8% | 4% | 4% | 27% | 100% |
| | 157 | 84 | 73 | 537 | 1,997 |
| 1918 | 6% | 4% | 26% | 19% | 100% |
| | 175 | 113 | 729 | 550 | 2,857 |
| 1919[a] | 7% | 5% | 7% | 27% | 100% |
| | 175 | 115 | 160 | 650 | 2,456 |
| 1925 | 11% | 5% | 5% | 13% | 100% |
| | 426 | 210 | 210 | 500 | 3,868 |

Sources: Los andes (Guayaquil), 14 March 1868, 20 January 1869, 6 April 1870 (cited in unpublished research notes of Julio Estrada Ycaza); MI, Informe, 1871, 1887; PCC, Informe, 1887, 1889, 43–53; 1892, 31–37, tables P–U; 1916, 8; 1919, 10, xxiii; CC, Gaceta municipal no. 479, 5 January 1895, 529–43; 1908, 207–8, 347; CC, Informe, 1907, 71–85; 1918, 51–76; 1925, 255–73; PCC, Balance de la contabilidad municipal, 1909; El Ecuador: guía, 228–29; TM, Informe, 1915; América libre, 131.
[a]Estimate.

high, and the city had to borrow from the Banco de Crédito Hipotecario (at 15 percent interest) and the Banco del Ecuador (at 9 percent interest). Later the city shifted its debt to the Banco Territorial and the Banco Comercial y Agrícola.[26]

After the heavy borrowing of the 1880s, debt interest became by far the largest item in the city's budgets. Such payments rose from 115,000 sucres, or 31 percent of the budget in 1889, to 332,000 sucres, or 59 percent of city outlays, in 1893. After this time the proportion of the city budget devoted to interest decreased as the city temporarily halted further borrowing; by 1909, debt payment took but 14 percent of city funds. But by 1919, the city's debt payment had risen to a new high of a half million sucres (21 percent of the city budget).[27]

Distressed by revenue shortfalls and cost overruns, City Treasurer E. Aguirre Overweg in 1919 prepared an accounting, making all too plain the extent of the city's problem.[28] As Overweg documented, the local tax on aguardiente fell short by 97,000 sucres, the cacao export tax 80,000 sucres short, and city debt collection 39,000 less than expected, for an overall short-fall of 216,000 sucres. At the same time, public works cost 46,000 sucres more than planned, and street cleaning 16,000 sucres more, for a total overrun of 84,000 sucres.

In sum, the city revenues and expenditures both rose as a crush of mi-grants to Guayaquil generated new urban needs. Unable to raise enough rev-enues through taxes to pay the heavy start-up costs for necessary new pub-lic works projects, the city turned to loans, especially in the 1880s. As the debt ballooned, the city slowed further borrowing and struggled just to keep up interest payments on its previously incurred obligations. But the city's pop-ulation continued to grow, and Guayaquil could not afford to borrow more, so existing city services quickly became swamped.

Quito had a city budget in 1871 of 35,494 sucres in revenue but 48,560 in expenditures.[29] In 1909, the province of Pichincha, in highland Ecuador, brought in 525,035 sucres in tax revenues but spent 3,264,534 sucres.[30] Quito made up its shortfall with money taken from Guayaquil. The sierra con-sumed, but did not produce, government revenues. The cacao economy of the coast had to pay all the heavy national expenses as well as provide tax revenue for the urgent social needs of the city of Guayaquil. This double bur-den it could not bear.

A final indignity to officials in Guayas was Quito officials' intrusion into local matters. To some, that might have seemed a baseless local complaint, given the problems of decentralization that faced the national government. After all, the executive branch of government had long decried the power of both the ubiquitous autonomous agencies and the regionalist-dominated Congress. But while fiscal decentralization certainly eroded the president's power, he could still exercise significant control in non-fiscal matters. City authorities also decried the power of the special agencies charged with carrying out programs created by Congress; they resented any effort by any part of the national government to usurp local control.[31]

**Table 4.2.** Guayaquil city government income versus Ecuadorian national government income, selected years, 1857–1925 (in sucres—pesos before 1884)

| Year | Guayaquil revenues | National revenues |
|------|--------------------|-------------------|
| 1857 | 41,437 | 1,276,000 |
| 1868 | 75,468 | 1,442,000 |
| 1869 | 76,418 | 1,664,000 |
| 1871 | 84,228 | 2,483,000 |
| 1875 | 105,400 | 2,849,000 |
| 1876 | 118,000 | 2,387,000 |
| 1881 | 113,003 | — |
| 1882 | 173,570 | 2,212,000 |
| 1883 | 272,000 | 2,683,000 |
| 1884 | 285,000 | 3,164,000 |
| 1885 | 297,000 | 2,524,000 |
| 1886 | 273,498 | 3,176,000 |
| 1887 | 300,871 | 4,479,000 |
| 1888 | 438,000 | 4,047,000 |
| 1889 | 372,000 | 3,111,000 |
| 1890[a] | 346,000 | 4,183,000 |
| 1891 | 465,108 | 3,584,000 |
| 1892 | 465,018 | 3,799,000 |
| 1893 | 526,302 | 4,326,000 |
| 1895 | 593,439 | 5,128,000 |
| 1904 | 1,183,000 | 8,559,000 |
| 1905 | 896,000 | 11,538,000 |
| 1906 | 933,000 | 12,922,000 |
| 1907 | 1,237,000 | 12,571,000 |
| 1908[a] | 1,175,000 | 12,807,000 |
| 1909 | 1,043,000 | 15,895,000 |
| 1913 | 1,997,000 | 19,845,000 |
| 1918 | 2,857,000 | 13,826,000 |
| 1919 | 2,456,341[a] | 15,178,000 |
| 1925 | 3,868,000 | 36,816,000 |

*Sources: Los andes* (Guayaquil), 20 January 1869, cited in unpublished notes of Estrada Ycaza; MI, *Informe, 1871;* GG, *Informe, 1877,* 24; PCC, *Informe, 1887, 1889,* 17, 43–62, *1892,* 31, tables S-U, *1919,* 10, xxiii; CC, *Gaceta municipal* no. 479, 5 January 1895, 529–43; PCC, *Balance de la contabilidad 1909;* TM, *Informe, 1915;* L. A. Rodríguez, *Search for Public Policy,* appendix K.
[a]Estimate.

Municipal officials had cause to complain, for at times the presidents sought to take control over even rather minor local decisions. A few examples suffice. In 1900 President Eloy Alfaro issued a decree regulating fruit juice sales in Guayaquil. The order affected only such sales and only Guayaquil. In 1902, President Leonidas Plaza sent forth a decree regarding the details of church construction in the city of Guayaquil. In 1909, President Alfaro ordered the establishment of the position of porter at the governor's office in Guayaquil. Later, a separate presidential directive set the porter's salary (60 sucres a month). In 1910, Alfaro issued a decree that picked up the costs for the funeral of Dr. César Borja.[32]

To be sure, Ecuador is a small nation, but certainly some of these matters would have been more appropriately dealt with at the local level. Had these decrees involved all of Ecuador, it is possible that one might construe the actions as necessary measures to arrange a coherent national policy. But the directives cited, and numerous others like them, applied solely to a particular city, town, village, or person. Little wonder then that municipal officials felt that the national government meddled needlessly in their affairs.

Guayaquil officials felt that the national government got in the way, told Guayaquil what it needed and where, and generally tried to usurp local authority. Moreover, serranos tended to monopolize the coveted positions in the national bureaucracy in Quito. That quiteños largely controlled this critical source of white-collar employment deeply angered guayaquileños with middle-class aspirations. That politics were the biggest business in Quito was all the more galling since Guayaquil's busy commerce filled the national treasury.[33]

Rapid urbanization in the late nineteenth century was a common Western phenomenon, and most cities had trouble providing social services for their growing numbers. However, Guayaquil's political situation gave it additional problems. The city had an ongoing struggle for local political control against the interests of the national government in Quito. The busy commerce of the cacao region generated the main part of the nation's wealth, but the tax revenues from this economic activity had to be shared with all of Ecuador. There was but a limited amount of revenue available to Guayaquil.

# Chapter Five

# The People of Guayaquil
## Daily Lives of the Poor and Rich

The success of the cacao trade changed the face of Guayaquil. The population of the city and indeed the entire coast began to grow rapidly. Guayaquil flourished; the city became a much larger, a much more exciting place to live. From economic change emerged new social patterns as people adapted to make a living and make a life in Guayaquil.

### Population

The population of the coastal provinces of Ecuador increased seven times over from 1873 to 1926, from 165,280 to 1,115,264; that of Guayas Province rose not quite as fast, increasing fivefold, from 94,411 in 1877 to 483,508 in 1926. And the growth of Guayaquil was similarly unprecedented: in 1870 the city numbered about 20,000 to 25,000 people; by 1890, about 45,000; by 1900, 60,000; by 1910, 80,000; and more than 120,000 in 1925 (see tables 1.1 and 5.1). Of all Guayas residents, about one-quarter to one-half lived in urban Guayaquil during this period.[1]

Guayaquil's growth was rather remarkable given that deaths in the city usually exceeded births. Of course, during the late nineteenth and early twentieth centuries most cities, especially port and tropical ones, exhibited the same grim pattern.[2] Close human proximity and poor sanitary conditions combined to spawn lethal diseases in most urban settings. Cities maintained or increased their numbers only by drawing a steady stream of fresh recruits from the healthier countryside.[3] Still, Guayaquil's record was particularly bad: in 1889, 1897, and 1912, the city had over one thousand more deaths than births (see table 5.2).

**Table 5.1.** Population of Ecuador, coastal Ecuador, and Guayas province as a percentage of Ecuador's total population, selected years, 1857–1926

| Year[s] | Guayas | Coastal provinces | Ecuador |
|---|---|---|---|
| 1839 | — | — | 612,789 |
| 1841 | 41,723 | 65,364 | 642,967 |
| | (7%) | (10%) | |
| 1848 | 80,000 | 132,000 | 768,000 |
| | (10%) | (17%) | |
| 1853 | 75,365 | 107,162 | 695,115 |
| | (11%) | (15%) | |
| 1857–58 | 91,620 | 128,257 | 748,297 |
| | (12%) | (17%) | |
| 1864–65 | 81,580 | 178,166 | 873,606 |
| | (9%) | (20%) | |
| 1871 | 90,000 | — | — |
| 1873 | 87,427 | 165,280? | 843,505 |
| | | (20%) | |
| 1874 | | 174,429? | |
| | | (21%) | |
| 1875 | 83,397 | — | — |
| 1877 | 94,411 | | |
| 1886 | 95,640 | 224,717 | 1,004,651 |
| | (10%) | (22%) | |
| 1889 | 98,042 | 242,118 | 1,271,761 |
| | (8%) | (19%) | |
| 1894 | 150,000 | — | 1,500,000 |
| | (10%) | | |
| 1905 | 194,150 | | |
| 1909 | 231,200 | 481,200 | 1,642,856 |
| | (14%) | (29%) | |
| 1915 | 192,000 | — | 1,743,360 |
| | (11%) | | |
| 1926 | 483,508 | 1,115,264 | 2,929,314 |
| | (17%) | (38%) | |

*Sources: Los andes* (Guayaquil), 29 August 1863, 13 September 1865, cited in unpublished notes of Estrada Ycaza; MI, *Informe, 1871, 1886,* 22, *Anexos al informe, 1910,* 16; *El comercio* (Guayaquil), 21 May 1875, cited in unpublished notes of Estrada Ycaza; GG, *Informe, 1877,* 2–7; L. F. Carbo, *El Ecuador en Chicago,* 42, 367; MIP, *Informe, 1910, 1916,* viii; Estrada Ycaza, *Regionalismo y migración,* 262; Chiriboga, *Jornaleros,* 23; L. A. Rodríguez, *Search for Public Policy,* 203–5.

Guayaquil was considerably less healthful than neighboring districts. In 1902, deaths outnumbered births in Guayaquil canton by 17 percent, while in all other cantons of Guayas province the reverse was the case: Yaguachi canton had 44 percent more births than deaths, Santa Elena canton had 46 percent more, and Daule Canton had 73 percent more.[4]

**Table 5.2.** Births and deaths in Guayaquil and Ecuador, selected years, 1843–1929

| Year | Guayaquil births | Guayaquil deaths | Guayaquil differences | Ecuador |
|------|------|------|------|------|
| 1843 | 1,303 | 1,044 | +259 (+20%) | — |
| 1848 | — | — | — | (+40%) |
| 1857 | 3,422 | 1,122 | +2,300 (+67%) | — |
| 1889 | 2,461 | 3,568 | −1,107 (−31%) | — |
| 1890 | 2,683 | 3,130 | −447 (−14%) | — |
| 1891 | 2,749 | 2,882 | −133 (−5%) | — |
| 1892 | 2,597 | 2,355 | +242 (+9%) | — |
| 1897 | 1,965 | 3,806 | −1,841 (−48%) | — |
| 1898 | 3,102 | 2,576 | +526 (+17%) | — |
| 1901 | 3,640 | 3,402 | +238 (+7%) | (+21%) |
| 1902 | — | — | — | (+35%) |
| 1903 | 3,397 | 3,174 | +223 (+7%) | (+35%) |
| 1904 | 3,562 | 2,860 | +702 (+20%) | (+42%) |
| 1905[a] | 3,324 | 3,103 | +221 (+7%) | — |
| 1907 | 3,161 | 3,702 | −571 (−15%) | (+34%) |
| 1908 | 3,546 | 3,510 | +36 (+1%) | — |
| 1909 | 3,586 | 3,631 | −45 (−1%) | — |
| 1910 | 3,771 | 3,177 | +594 (+16%) | |
| 1911 | 3,704 | 3,368 | +336 (+9%) | |
| 1912 | 4,071 | 5,300 | −1,229 (−23%) | — |
| 1913 | 6,126 | 3,981 | +2,145 (+35%) | — |
| 1914 | 5,720 | 3,573 | +2,147 (+38%) | (+44%) |
| 1915 | — | — | — | (+37%) |
| 1917 | — | — | — | (+44%) |
| 1918 | — | — | — | (+43%) |
| 1919 | — | — | — | (18%) |
| 1920 | — | — | — | (+36%) |
| 1928 | — | — | — | (+47%) |
| 1929 | 9,073 | 5,551 | +3,522 (+39%) | (+46%) |

*Sources:* PCC, *Informe, 1887, 1889, 1892;* IP, *Informe, 1890, 1891, 1897, 1898, 1903, 1904, 1905, 1910;* Gallegos Naranjo, *1900 almanaque;* Paz, *Guía;* MI, *Informe, 1903;* MIP, *Anexos a la memoria, 1903,* lxii, *Memoria, 1905, 1908, 309, 1910, 1916,* lxxxvi-cxlii, *1919,* cviii-cxvi, *1921,* 137–38; GG, *Informe, 1907;* SS, *Informe, 1911, 1913, 1914;* RC, *Informe, 1929–30;* and adapted from table 7.3.
*Note:* +% = more births than deaths; −% = more deaths than births.
[a]Estimate.

Guayaquil was considerably less healthful than the sierra. The year 1920 was typical: highland Pichincha province had 26 percent more births than deaths; Guayas had 13 percent more. In 1912, an extreme example, deaths surpassed births in Guayaquil by 23 percent, whereas in Quito in 1911–12, births outnumbered deaths by 16 percent. If on occasion Guayaquil and Guayas could post a better birth/death record than Quito and Pichincha province, usually they did not.[5]

Guayaquil was considerably less healthful than the rest of Ecuador. In 1902 for example, while births outnumbered deaths in Guayas province, in Quito, and in Ecuador as a whole, only in the city of Guayaquil did deaths exceeded births. For Ecuador throughout the late nineteenth and early twentieth centuries, births consistently outnumbered deaths. Between 1901 and 1920, there were typically at least one-third more births than deaths. In Guayaquil this situation obtained only part of the time. While population in Ecuador continually rose from natural increase, in Guayaquil it often did not (see table 5.2).[6]

Immigration from Europe represented the leading source of population growth for several important South American cities of the era, notably Buenos Aires, Sao Paulo, Rio de Janeiro, and Montevideo. In Guayaquil, though, it played far less of a role. In Rio de Janeiro, immigrants made up from one-third to one-fifth of all residents from the 1870s to the 1920s; in Sao Paulo the immigrant population grew from 8 percent of the city total in 1872 to 55 percent in 1893; and in Buenos Aires, by 1914 immigrants totaled 49 percent of the population.[7]

During its colonial past, when Guayaquil was the leading shipbuilding and ship repair center on the Spanish Pacific, the city teemed with foreigners.[8] But in the national era Guayaquil no longer drew a great inflow of immigrants. However, the city did manage to attract some wealthy foreign merchants whose economic importance exceeded their numbers.

Available evidence—rare Guayaquil censuses, by necessity supplemented by cemetery lists and police arrest records—provide some idea, if not an exact count, of the number of immigrants to Guayaquil.[9] The census in 1890 reported a 10 percent foreign population in the city; that of 1899 showed a 15 percent total. Foreigners made up between 4 and 8 percent of those who died in Guayaquil in the years 1890 through 1914. Of course, city death totals underrepresent the actual foreign presence; long-distance immigration is selective of young men, a relatively healthier cohort. Police records showed a higher percentage of foreigners, although in this case immigrants would have been overrepresented given both selective, anti-foreign, law enforcement practices and young men's greater proclivity for rowdy lawbreaking. Between 1897 and 1909, foreigners made up about 15 to 20 percent of those arrested in Guayaquil. Overall, probably a tenth of Guayaquil's population was foreign-born during this era, although their presence was declining after 1914. By 1924 only 1 percent of those who died in the city had been of foreign birth.

Still, because Guayaquil was the nation's major port, it drew more immigrants than did other places in Ecuador. In 1877, only fifty-four of the 23,265 residents of nearby Daule canton were foreign-born. In the same year, twenty-six of the 15,572 people of the coastal city of Santa Elena were for-eigners. In Machala canton of the south coast, about 7 percent of the residents in 1877 came from other nations. Overall, Guayaquil was home to about one-quarter of Ecuador's immigrants.[10]

Not surprisingly, well over half the immigrants to Guayaquil came from neighboring Peru and Colombia, with far smaller numbers coming from China and Italy. This was an age of overt racism, so like other South Ameri-can nations, Ecuador sought white European settlers. Congress passed an immigration law in 1889 to encourage such people. Few came. One scheme called for European settlement of the Galapagos Islands, with each immi-grant entitled to a cow and a plot of land. The plan failed, due no doubt to the islands' virtual absence of fresh water.[11] Despite this plan and others like it, Europeans mostly avoided Ecuador.

Ecuador was just too far away. European immigrants typically selected nations with an Atlantic orientation. To most, proximity to Europe was a crit-ical consideration, for many planned to live only temporarily in South Amer-ica. Indeed some workers, the "swallow migrants," came only to help at har-vest time, afterward returning to the northern hemisphere in time to help bring in crops there.[12]

Worse, Guayaquil carried a reputation as one of the most disease-in-fested cities of the world. Sadly, this was a reputation that the city all too richly deserved. Guayaquil's well-known and continuing problems with yellow fever, bubonic plague, and other dreaded diseases obviously damp-ened enthusiasm for immigration.[13] Finally, Ecuador's frequent internal wars also provided additional discouragement, if such were needed. De-spite an abundance of coastal farm land that was inexpensive and fertile (if admittedly generally remote and inaccessible), the coast and Guayaquil did not attract vast numbers of working-class white immigrants. And for rich visitors from the United States and Great Britain, Guayaquil seemed a cul-tural backwater, oppressively hot, dull, and dirty. Still, when authentic money-making opportunities tempted, some wealthy foreign entrepre-neurs came anyway.[14]

Only a few foreign small businessmen came to Guayaquil. Frequently Chi-nese or Syrian, the success of these immigrant shopkeepers earned them the bitter enmity of the locals. Syrian and Chinese merchants could not join the Chamber of Commerce nor expect entry into the prestigious Club de la Union. Chinese suffered special contempt; they endured racist attacks in many parts of the South American continent, and it was no different in Ecuador. Viciously racist anti-Chinese articles commonly appeared in

Guayaquil city papers. The national government added to the pressure, passing a law in September 1889 banning Chinese immigration. The lawmakers disingenuously claimed this as an effort to halt the arrival of undesirable Chinese "coolies," but they clearly had others in mind; there were few coolies in Ecuador. Seventy-three Chinese lived in Guayaquil in 1903, of which sixty-four worked as small shopkeepers. The government was after Chinese businesses. Up the coast in Manta, the Chinese were particularly noted for their active role in facilitating the coasting trade with Guayaquil. At times the government seized these and other Chinese homes and commercial assets.

When political upheavals set looters loose in Guayaquil, these individuals often singled out the stores of Chinese for special attention, as Ramon Noriega, a Chinese immigrant, learned during the civil war of 1912. A mob attacked and plundered his hotel while witnesses stood by and looked on. Anti-Chinese attitudes persisted. A handsome 1920 volume promoting commerce in Guayaquil stated that "all the territory of Ecuador offers a broad field [for investment] to all the races (with the exception of the Mongolic)."[15] Rich white businessmen from other Latin American nations, the United States, or Europe, however, found easy acceptance in elite circles in Guayaquil. Intermarriage with the local rich, especially by German immigrants, was not at all uncommon.[16]

So it was not natural increase, and not immigration, but internal migration from the sierra that fed the growth of Guayaquil and its hinterland. In 1824 the littoral accounted for but 15 percent of the national population; by 1926 the coast had 38 percent of Ecuador's total. At least a third of the people who lived in Guayaquil in 1899 had moved from elsewhere in Ecuador; slightly more than half of these migrants had traveled down from the sierra.[17] Internal migration was a broad South American phenomenon. In Rio de Janeiro, for example, internal migrants equaled 9.2 percent of the city population in 1872, 26.1 percent in 1890, and 26.6 percent in 1920.[18] In Buenos Aires internal migrants totaled 11 percent of the city's population in 1914.[19]

In Ecuador's coastal lowlands, cacao workers shifted easily from estate to estate and traveled about in all directions, especially when demand for labor went slack after the harvest. They drifted with the fluvial currents, floating downstream to where all the rivers met: in Guayaquil. Arriving on makeshift rafts, their balsas, bringing loads of charcoal, fruit, or straw hats to sell, migrants might spend a few days peddling their wares and taking in the city. Many decided that they liked Guayaquil well enough to stay, or perhaps they simply lacked the money for the trip back upriver on steam-powered lanchas. Some never really settled; they wandered back and forth from hacienda to city, scouting about for the best work opportunities. In 1908, for example, 1,903 people entered Guayaquil and 1,855 left; in 1909, 1,744 migrants entered and 1,240 left. Those who remained in Guayaquil changed residences frequently.[20] As Police Chief R. T. Caamaño put it, Guayaquil had an immense "floating population."[21] The phrase may be taken literally, for many newcomers crowded along the river bank and estuary, living in balsas, for want of more firmly planted dwellings.

Considering the limited employment opportunities available in Guayaquil for working people, as well as the disease and urban problems of the city, one might well wonder why so many came. But if one could secure steady employment, there was the chance to build a better life for oneself and one's family. In addition, education, the first step in upward mobility, was relatively more available in Guayaquil. In contrast to the sierra, Guayaquil could at least offer hope.[22]

### Gender, Marriage, and Children

Guayaquil was a city of females. There were only eighty-three males for every one hundred females in 1890 and still in 1919 only eighty-nine males for every one hundred females.[23] Young women from the surrounding countryside found it more appealing to settle in the city; men had greater commercial value as agricultural field hands.[24] Moreover, young men in Guayaquil ran the added risk of impressment into military service; Ecuador's frequent state of civil war

Balsas along the riverfront, ca. 1900.

provided many opportunities for military service, and perhaps, an early grave.[25] It is also likely that census data on gender represented something of an undercount of males; men had good reason to hide when government authorities showed up in the neighborhood.

Guayaquileños were not the marrying kind. Other Ecuadorians were. Marriages were typically twice as common in Quito as in Guayaquil, though the cities were roughly the same size. In Ecuador as a whole in 1929, Guayaquil men were only half as likely to marry by age 20 as other Ecuadorian men. In Guayaquil the institution of marriage was chiefly for the well-off; men especially tended to marry only if they had established themselves financially. In the sierra, marriage was for rich and for the impoverished but pious Indian underclass. Serranos also tended to marry earlier in life than did guayaquileños who married.[26]

The regional differences may in part be explained by the fact that in the tradition-bound sierra, the Church had a larger presence. Of the 490 secular clergy in Ecuador in 1871, only fifty-one lived in Guayaquil and, in fact, on the entire coast. That same year, Guayaquil and the coast had only five monasteries and convents tended by twenty clerics, while Quito had fifteen such institutions and 185 clerics.[27]

Guayaquileño couples produced many children, but mostly not "legitimate" ones—usually much less than half were so regarded (see table 5.3). Such was the case throughout the coast, but not in the sierra. Over half the children born in 1902 in the coastal cantons of Daule and Yaguachi were "illegitimate," while in Quito that year, only one in five infants were conceived outside of marriage. Sixty-two percent of the children born in Guayas province in 1919 were deemed illegitimate, while in Pichincha 16 percent were. That same year, about one-third of all children born in Ecuador were considered illegitimate, but a wide majority of those born in the coastal provinces were so regarded. Six in ten born in Guayas in 1920 were of unmarried parents; one in three in all Ecuador were. Sixty-five percent of all births in Ecuador in 1929 were regarded as legitimate, whereas only 45 percent of those in Guayaquil were.[28]

Clearly, guayaquileños held attitudes similar to other residents of the coast: most did not favor formal marriage. While many guayaquileños had come from the sierra, these migrants had broken the bonds of tradition by their act of separation from their highland homes. Through their actions, they demonstrated that they felt some distance from Church guidance and regulations. However, the practice of entering into informal unions did not only reflect rejection of Church strictures—sheer lack of funds and the cost of a church wedding led many to forego the ceremony.[29]

**Table 5.3.** Marriages, births, and "illegitimacy": in Guayaquil, selected years, 1890–1929

| Year | Marriages | Births | No. illegitimate | % illegitimate |
|------|-----------|--------|------------------|----------------|
| 1890 | 300 | 2,683 | — | — |
| 1891 | 231 | 2,749 | — | — |
| 1892 | 251 | 2,597 | — | — |
| 1897 | 165 | 1,965 | 1,144 | 58 |
| 1898 | 241 | 3,102 | 1,604 | 52 |
| 1901 | 442 | 3,640 | — | — |
| 1903 | 198 | 3,397 | 1,933 | 57 |
| 1904 | 252 | 3,562 | 1,965 | 55 |
| 1905[a] | 350 | 3,324 | 1,892 | 57 |
| 1907 | 378 | 3,161 | 1,915 | 61 |
| 1908 | 386 | 3,546 | — | — |
| 1909 | 407 | 3,586 | 2,075 | 58 |
| 1910 | 384 | 3,771 | — | — |
| 1911 | 396 | 3,704 | 2,142 | 58 |
| 1912 | 471 | 4,071 | — | — |
| 1913 | 660 | 6,126 | — | — |
| 1914 | 1,013 | 5,720 | — | — |
| 1929 | 980 | 9,073 | 4,993 | 55 |

*Sources:* IP, *Informes, 1890–1910;* PCC, *Informe, 1892;* Gallegos, *1900 almanaque,* 145; Paz, *Guía, 1901;* GG, *Informe, 1907;* SS, *Informe, 1911, 1913, 1914;* RC, *Informe, 1929–1930.*
[a]Estimate.

## Jobs

For the crush of newcomers, Guayaquil could offer steady work for few. Only a handful of positions were to be found in the limited manufacturing sector, for Guayaquil developed almost no industry. Entrepreneurs avoided such investments—wisely too, given the city's relatively modest size, its most unpromising consumer base of impoverished, underemployed workers, a still rather thinly populated hinterland, awesome geographic barriers to potential highland markets, and long distances separating them from foreign consumers. Instead, the Ecuadorian and foreign entrepreneurs who profited from the cacao trade—especially importers, exporters, and the owners of great cacao estates—found in real estate speculation, retail sales, opulent living, and extended foreign travel sufficient outlets for their money.

A few workers took employment at the rice-processing plant north of town or as hands in some of the small manufacturing shops scattered through the city. But such job opportunities were rare. There were but sixteen small "factories" in 1883, when the city population was 36,000; in 1909, when the city's inhabitants numbered 80,000 people, there were still only forty small firms, producing such items as beer, ice, cigarettes, cigars, biscuits, candy, noodles, brooms, bags, and power. As a rule, local industry did not challenge imports: if an item could be imported, it was.[30]

Some of the more fortunate might secure steady employment as skilled service workers, such as teachers, reporters, or cashiers, or as steadily employed unskilled service workers, such as restaurant help, trolley conductors, or bellhops. But most people found only sporadic employment as unskilled service-sector workers. Indeed, the proportion of people taking such jobs steadily increased. Most men settled for employment as day laborers, especially as cacao handlers (*cacahueros*)—sorting, drying, and bagging cacao—or as dock workers, hauling the bags aboard and unloading the vessels returning with consumer items from Europe and the United States. Women typically took jobs as seamstresses, cooks, laundresses, maids, or prostitutes. Many people worked in itinerant retail sales, roaming the streets shouting the names of their products. Some turned to begging, and others to crime.[31]

The service sector was an important source of jobs in other Latin American cities of the times. Such was the case even in cities like Santiago, Chile, that developed much more industry than did Guayaquil. In urban Brazil, June Hahner found that "many [people] lacked steady employment and, . . . often just waited on street corners for jobs." In Rio de Janeiro in 1872, she

Drying cacao, ca. 1910

notes, "domestic service . . . employed sixty-three percent of the city's total female labor force," and by 1920, 50 percent were still so employed.[32]

Guayaquil's active commerce had a mixed effect on artisan and middle-class jobs, at the same time creating and eliminating some of the scarce, better-paying positions. Guayaquil supported a variety of artisans: masons, carpenters, butchers, leather workers, teamsters, blacksmiths, coopers, mechanics, painters, bakers, barbers, typesetters, shoemakers, printers, hat makers, glass makers, tailors, plumbers, silversmiths, marble workers, and others.

But if the number of people working in these trades probably increased as Guayaquil grew, their percentage of the total workforce steadily dropped. There were 353 artisan shops in the city in 1890; by 1912, after twenty-two years of rapid population growth, there were eight fewer.[33] Police arrest totals (the available evidence used because complete manuscript census returns or labor department reports do not exist for this period) show a declining percentage of artisans among those arrested, although the tallies may of course merely reflect shifting law enforcement practices. Police arrest records from 1897 to 1909 show a steady drop in the percentage of artisans among those arrested: they represented 41 percent of those arrested in 1897 but only 18 percent in 1909.[34]

Guayaquil's steady stream of cheap, modern consumer imports gradually diminished the need for old-style artisans. The many small retail shops in Guayaquil offered imports of every variety: shoes, hats, ready-made and pre-dyed clothing, hardware, as well as patented cures for yellow fever, fine European liquors, and expensive Japanese cloth. Guayaquil had nearly 200 retail stores in 1883; by 1909, it had almost 400.[35]

The ranks of white-collar professionals who counted, sorted, and kept track of the profits grew modestly (see table 5.4). The economy generated a greater need for people of some education who could staff the private offices of banks and commission houses or run the government bureaucracy. The number of physicians and lawyers also grew as more people wanted and could afford their services. Still, there were relatively few white-collar jobs in Guayaquil.

For the unskilled service workers who made up the bulk of the city's adult population, wages were low (see table 5.5). The men who worked irregularly as day laborers earned about seventy-five cents per day in the 1880s; after the turn of the century, they took in one or sometimes two sucres per day. Women earned less. Seamstresses or cooks received from four to twelve sucres a month. This money did not go far (see table 5.6). A pound of lard and a pound of corn together cost more than a seamstress could earn in a day. A pair of shoes cost a male day worker a quarter of his monthly earnings. Even

**Table 5.4.** Professionals in Guayaquil, selected years, 1883–1912

| Year | Professionals[a] |
| --- | --- |
| 1883 | 90 |
| 1890 | 143 |
| 1898 | 132 |
| 1899 | 143 |
| 1903 | 157 |
| 1904 | 171 |
| 1905 | 173 |
| 1906 | 173 |
| 1909 | 194 |
| 1912 | 239 |

*Sources:* Gallegos Naranjo, *1883 almanaque;* IP, *Informe, 1890, 1891, 1898, 1903, 1904, 1905;* Gallegos Naranjo, *1900 fin de siglo almanaque;* Barbosa, *Almanaque ilustrado; El Ecuador: guía; Guayaquil en la mano 1912.*
[a]Attorneys, doctors, dentists, notary publics, midwives, accountants.

death was expensive. At twenty-seven sucres, even a simple burial cost half a month's wages. The forty to fifty sucres a month that steadily employed laboring men earned must have seemed quite small when compared to the 150 sucres per month a university teacher earned or a judge's salary of 350 sucres per month.[36] For most residents of the city, Guayaquil offered just a chance at a better life, not the reality of it.

### Elites

The number of wealthy people in Guayaquil grew rapidly from 1870 to 1925, as too did the size of their fortunes. Economic growth in Guayaquil paid handsome profits to some. But if cacao was important to Ecuador's economy, it was not the only way men enriched themselves in Guayaquil during this period. Indeed, a minority of Guayaquil's elites owned cacao-producing estates. Some made money in exporting cacao, but the greatest wealth came from the importing business.

For purposes of analysis, the fifty-five years from 1870 to 1925 may be divided into four parts: 1870–96, 1897–1908, 1909–19, and 1920–25. For the first period (1870–96), we may use the declared business losses after the fire of October 5 and 6, 1896 (a blaze that destroyed at least half the city and claimed the entire commercial district), to provide information on elite wealth.[37] Obviously this is hardly a perfect source; we will use it because it is the only source. The listing does at least provide a rough picture of the wealth of Guayaquil's elite; those who had something to lose, lost it in the 1896 fire.

Twenty-four men possessed fortunes of 100,000 sucres or more by 1896

**Table 5.5.** Wages and salaries in Guayaquil, selected years, 1881–1925 (per month in sucres—pesos before 1884)

| Type of employment | 1881–1900 | 1904–1912 | 1918–1925 |
|---|---|---|---|
| Waiter | — | 6–20 | — |
| Soldier (one-year recruit) | — | 8 | — |
| Laundry worker | 8 | — | — |
| Porter's helper | — | — | 50 |
| Porter | 8 | 50 | 60 |
| Seamstress | — | 9–12 | — |
| Cook (female) | 10 | 4–12 | — |
| Day laborer | 12–23 | 30–60 | — |
| Jail helper | — | — | 36–50 |
| Janitor | 16 | 30 | — |
| Water carrier | 24 | — | — |
| Police officer | — | 40 | 60 |
| Assistant guard (jail) | — | — | 60 |
| Schoolteacher's helper | 40 | — | — |
| Elementary school teacher | 24–60 | 60 | — |
| Guard | 40 | — | — |
| Customhouse helper | — | 60 | — |
| Clerk | 50 | 90 | — |
| Railway worker | — | — | 62–77 |
| Army lieutenant | — | 80 | — |
| Doorman | — | — | 80 |
| Carpenter | 108 | — | — |
| Customhouse inspector | — | 120 | — |
| High school teacher | — | 122 | — |
| Gas co. engineer | 140 | — | — |
| University professor | — | 150 | — |
| Jefe político | — | 300 | — |
| General (army) | — | 300 | — |
| Superior Court judge | — | 350 | — |
| Customhouse director | — | 500 | — |
| City treasurer | — | 500 | 500 |
| Governor | — | — | 600 |

*Sources:* PCC, *Informe, 1881, 1892, 1907, 1918, 1925;* USCD, "Report," 31 May 1890; IP, *Informe, 1898, 1904;* MIP, *Informe, 1899,* 231; PCC, *Actas de las sesions efectuadas por el ilustre concejo municipal de Guayaquil, primer trimestre, 1899,* 138, *Estado de la municipalidad, 1905; El Ecuador: guía; El Grito del pueblo,* 3 and 14 January 1912; CC, *Gaceta municipal: actas de las sesiones efectuadas por el ilustre consejo municipal de Guayaquil, 1912,* 19; GBFO, "Report," 1924, reprint of, A. J. Andrade, *Informe del interventor fiscal de "The Guayaquil and Quito Railway Company" por el año de 1923* (Quito, 1924), 36, and reprint of *Registro oficial,* 8 November 1924, 474; Guerrero, *Los oligarcas,* 30.

**Table 5.6.** Prices of selected commodities and services,
Guayaquil, 1904

| Item | Cost in sucres |
| --- | --- |
| haircut | .20 to .60 |
| shoes | 6.00 to 12.00 |
| hat | .20 to .30 |
| felt hat | 6.00 to 12.00 |
| dress coat | 45.00 to 60.00 |
| cotton underwear | 1.00 to 1.60 |
| wool socks | .40 |
| coarse cloth | .40 (per yard) |
| tallow candles | 1.25 (each) |
| cane (housing material) | .50 (per piece) |
| coarse sugar | .78 (per pound) |
| onions | .10 (each) |
| beans | .07 (per pound) |
| wheat flour | .07 (per pound) |
| eggs | .48 (per dozen) |
| lard | .29 (per pound) |
| corn | .07 (per pound) |
| potatoes | .05 (per pound) |
| plantanos | .01 (each) |
| oranges | .04 (each) |
| corvina (fish) | .20 to 1.00 (each) |
| chickens | .40 to .80 (each) |
| beef | .25 (per pound) |
| milk | .10 (per liter) |
| soda pop | .40 (per dozen bottles) |
| coarse tobacco | .28 (per pound) |
| aguardiente | 1.75 (per gallon) |
| beer | 10.00 (20 liter barrel) |
| mule | 30.00 |

*Source:* IP, *Boletín de información, 1904.*

(see table 5.7 and the appendix). That was a considerable sum; by comparison, a rural schoolteacher earned 240 sucres a year in 1893, and an ordinary police officer made 360 sucres a year in 1895.[38] Eighteen of the twenty-four businessmen (75 percent) were involved in the import trade—easily the single most important business activity of the group of leading Guayaquil businessmen. Of the importers, six also earned money by exporting. Of the total twenty-four men, ten were exporters (42 percent). Twenty-two of all elites (92 percent) were merchants, either importers, exporters, or both. Eight men were involved in banking (33 percent), either as major shareholders or by serving on the board of directors of one of Guayaquil's financial institutions.

Only seven of the total owned cacao plantations (29 percent). Three of the twenty-four operated retail outlets.

Most of the men managed over the years to maintain or even enlarge their fortunes. While some died and some foreign-born returned home to Europe, still over half—fourteen of the twenty-four—claimed fortunes of 100,000 sucres or more in 1909.

The Aspiazu brothers had the most lucrative business in Guayaquil in 1896, worth 800,000 sucres, money they made mostly by growing cacao. Indeed, the Aspiazus were among the most famous cacao-growing families in Ecuador, although they also integrated their financial holdings vertically into exporting and banking. The first Aspiazu to come to Ecuador was Julian Antonio de Aspiazu, born in the Basque province of Guipuscoa, Spain.[39] Julian arrived some time in the late eighteenth or early nineteenth century and made his way to Palenque parish, Vinces canton, in the district that later became Los Ríos province. He served as a minor government official: as *colector de rentas reales* (rural tax collector) in the *partido de* San Nicolas; in Palenque, from 1804 to 1817, as *teniente de governador* (assistant to the governor); and later as a *justicia mayor* (judge) in Palenque.

Julian Aspiazu's son, José María de Aspiazu y Aviles, became a richer man than had been his father. Like his father, José got involved in politics: in 1835, the town of Baba elected him mayor. José married María Rosa Coto y Chavauniz of a wealthy colonial land-owning family. Sensing the bright fu-

**Table 5.7.** People and companies worth 100,000 sucres or more, Guayaquil, 1870–1925

| Occupation or economic tie | 1870–1896 No. | % | 1897–1908 No. | % | 1909–1919 No. | % | 1920–1925 No. | % |
|---|---|---|---|---|---|---|---|---|
| Merchants | 22 | 92 | 30 | 81 | 39 | 65 | 29 | 71 |
| Importers | 18 | 75 | 28 | 76 | 30 | 50 | 25 | 61 |
| Exporters | 10 | 42 | 14 | 38 | 23 | 38 | 12 | 29 |
| Banking | 8 | 33 | 17 | 46 | 18 | 30 | 8 | 20 |
| Factory owners | 0 | — | 6 | 16 | 11 | 18 | 6 | 15 |
| Foreign insurance company representatives | 3 | 13 | 12 | 32 | 2 | 3 | 1 | 2 |
| Consular officers | 4 | 17 | 10 | 27 | 4 | 7 | 1 | 2 |
| Foreign ship line representatives | 3 | 13 | 6 | 16 | 4 | 7 | 1 | 2 |
| Retail sales | 3 | 13 | 2 | 5 | 38 | 63 | 19 | 46 |
| Cacao growers | 7 | 29 | 12 | 32 | 11 | 18 | 6 | 15 |
| Total | 24 | | 37 | | 60 | | 41 | |

*Sources:* Adapted from appendix.

ture for cacao, José invested the profits of his wife's cattle ranches in buying up vacant hacienda land.

The offspring of José and María benefited handsomely from their father's acquisition of prime cacao-growing properties. By 1900, the Aspiazus owned thirty large estates and perhaps held more land than any other family in the province of Los Ríos. Their son, Pedro José Aspiazu, controlled twelve separate properties in Los Rios by 1883, some as large as 10,000 hectares, or 24,741 acres. Their daughter, Mercedes, married Lisimaco Guzmán, the single largest cacao exporter in Ecuador.

More representative of the group of elites for this first period of years (1870–96) was Juan Kruger. Kruger, a German, founded a small hardware importing business in Guayaquil in 1883. Kruger expanded his holdings, representing steamship lines and selling German fire insurance. Kruger also became the owner of a cacao hacienda, the "San Remo." By 1896, he was worth 100,000 sucres.

Half of the twenty-four elites diversified, spreading their money into several economic activities. Of the other twelve, nine worked solely as importers. For this early period, the pattern that emerges is one of a merchant—especially import—elite that possessed significantly diversified holdings.

A 1901 listing of capital assets in Guayaquil (see table 5.8) provides further information on elite economic activities. Banks, importers, and exporters had the greatest amounts of capital in Guayaquil. While it is not surprising that banks had a great deal of money, what is interesting is the vastness of the combined personal fortunes of the commercial elite. Merchants, both importers and exporters, had almost as much in capital assets (13,260,000 sucres) as did all the banks in Guayaquil combined (13,618,000 sucres). Agricultural estates were an important component of elite holdings, but these provided little liquid capital. It is one thing to own a hacienda, quite another to have ready cash at one's immediate disposal. In terms of the overall net worth of the city, the breakdown for 1901 underscores the pattern noted earlier: for the businessman interested in amassing liquid capital assets, the money was in importing.

The years 1897 to 1908 brought continued expansion and diversification in the holdings of elites. By 1903 the list of men worth 100,000 sucres or more had grown from twenty-four to thirty-seven (see table 5.7 and the appendix).[40] Thirty of the thirty-seven (81 percent) were merchants—importers, exporters, or both—about the same proportion as in the first period. Again most of the merchants were importers; less than half were involved in the export trade. In a modest increase from 1896, almost half the elites had interests in banking. And as in the first period, agriculture was not the most

Banco del Ecuador, ca. 1900.

important source of wealth. Only eleven of the thirty-seven had noteworthy cacao holdings. Oddly, in the port city of cacao country, a decided minority of the elites—less than a quarter—grew cacao. Significantly, one new source of wealth appeared in the second period (1897–1908). Six of the thirty-seven men (16 percent) owned small factories.

The wealthiest name in the years 1897–1908 was again Aspiazu. The Aspiazu brothers had 800,000 sucres in capital. By this period they had added the sale of German fire insurance to their economic activities, but they continued to focus on producing and exporting cacao.

More typical of this group of rich men in Guayaquil for the years 1897 through 1908 was Enrique Rohde. Rohde founded an import and export firm in Guayaquil in 1880. In 1901 he had accumulated 400,000 in capital assets and by 1903 had 500,000 sucres. Rohde also owned a line of steam-powered river boats, a small factory that made soap and candles, and a cotton-combing factory; he sold fire insurance (the Phoenix Insurance Company), represented German steamship lines in Ecuador, served as a top official of two banks (the Banco del Ecuador and the Banco Territorial), and held the post of executive officer for the Chamber of Commerce. Rohde diversified.

Of all elites in the second period, about one-third had strong overseas connections, mainly to Europe. These foreign-born traders benefited from their detailed knowledge of European markets, and they enjoyed easier access to European insurance, shipping lines, and lines of credit. Guayaquil importers frequently represented foreign insurance firms, for the 1896 fire had easily bankrupted most Ecuadorian insurance companies. They served as consul officers for one or more foreign nations, a position of no small advantage given consuls' privileged access to trade information. Some also sold space on foreign vessels.[41]

The leading role that foreigners played in Guayaquil's retail trade had a direct Latin American parallel only in Rio de Janeiro. Foreigners there, especially the Portuguese, dominated retail commerce. But Ecuador and Brazil were unique in this regard; foreigners did not commonly play a leading role

**Table 5.8.** Number of businesses and their net worth, Guayaquil, 1901 (value in 1,000s of sucres)

| Type of business | No. | Worth | % of Guayaquil's capital assets |
|---|---|---|---|
| Banks, S&L's | 7 | 13,618 | 39 |
| Importers | 391 | 8,831 | 25 |
| Exporters | 30 | 4,429 | 13 |
| Financiers | 141 | 2,313 | 7 |
| Fire insurance companies | 14 | 2,230 | 6 |
| Companies | 13 | 1,145 | 3 |
| Factories | 34 | 852 | 2 |
| Steamboat companies | 19 | 376 | 1 |
| Retail lumber | 11 | 357 | 1 |
| Drugstores | 19 | 238 | 1 |
| Hotels, bars | 36 | 144 | — |
| Barbers | 8 | 85 | — |
| Candy, bakery stores | 18 | 52 | — |
| Tailors | 11 | 48 | — |
| Small boat companies | 13 | 45 | — |
| Tobacco stores | 12 | 24 | — |
| Plumbers (water & gas) | 6 | 20 | — |
| Total | | 34,801 | |

*Source:* GG, *Informe, 1901.*

in the retail trade of other Latin American countries, where foreign domination of overseas commerce forced "native businessmen [to take] . . . refuge in internal trade."[42]

Foreign predominance among overseas traders in Guayaquil was, however, a pattern often noted throughout Latin America for nearly all of nineteenth and early twentieth centuries. In Rio de Janeiro 1871–98, Salvador 1873–74, and Belém and Sao Luís 1855–74, three-fifths to four-fifths of overseas merchants were foreigners. In Montevideo in the mid-nineteenth century, "foreign importers outnumbered natives by a ratio to seven to one."[43] Even when a European merchant family maintained operations in Latin America for several generations, the business typically stayed in the hands of the foreign-born. When selecting someone to take over the family business, foreign merchants showed a marked preference for young, bright, and willing, if poorer, nephews or other male family members from their European homeland. By contrast, the well-born children of elite merchants apparently found little to recommend a long apprenticeship clerking for their fathers' firms. These boys' lack of fluency in European languages and other deficiencies in their educations may also have steered them away from following in the family trade. So in Guayaquil, as in most Latin American cities of this time, the foreign-born dominated international trade.

The third period, 1909–19, brought some changes in the size and make up of the elite (see table 5.7 and the appendix). While merchants still predominated in this group of sixty men worth 100,000 sucres or more in 1909, a number of moderately wealthy retailers had crept onto the lower half of the list. Merchants, especially importers, were the single largest occupational group among the elites in this period, but retailers had become almost as important. The number of retailers had grown from two in the previous period to thirty-eight (63 percent) of the elites in the third period. Ownership of "factories" (usually little more than overgrown hand-manufacturing shops) had also become a possible path for getting rich. About one-sixth of elites owned such manufacturing shops.

The business of Lisimaco Guzmán and Sons, with total assets of 1,000,000 sucres, topped the list of elites for the period 1909–19. The leading cacao exporter of this era, Guzmán widely diversified his holdings after he joined in founding López and Guzmán Exports in 1880. Guzmán bought and sold letters of credit, represented foreign shipping lines and insurance companies, sold imports to the interior, held a post on the board of directors of the Banco del Ecuador, and speculated in urban real estate.

A representative example of the new group of retailers was Adolfo Poppe, a German immigrant. Poppe came to Guayaquil and set up an importing firm and retail outlet for hats, ready-made clothing, and perfume. He had amassed 250,000 sucres by 1909. By 1920, Poppe had returned to Europe.

Finally, the fourth period, 1920–25, shows a continuation of prior trends, although the building cacao export crisis of the 1920s already could be discerned. Most of the leading men (71 percent) were still merchants, although only twelve of the twenty-nine, fewer than ever before, were cacao exporters. Bankers too were less represented among the well-off: their proportion fell to its lowest level, 20 percent, down from 46 percent of the elite in the years 1897–1908. Factory ownership (15 percent of the elite) continued at around earlier levels. Ties to retail sales (46 percent of the elite) and ownership of cacao estates (15 percent) fell off some also.

Lisimaco Guzmán again topped the list of the wealthy, with the impressive sum of 1,300,000 sucres. More typical of the group were the Levy brothers, Felipe, Theodore, Alberto, and E. Levy Gildred. The Levys had set up an import-export house in 1913 and by 1920 operated several branch outlets throughout Ecuador. The Levys specialized in the sale of imported cars and farm equipment but also made money exporting cacao and coffee.

Overall then, through the era 1870 to 1925, the elite of Guayaquil were not predominantly cacao growers or even large rural landowners. In fact, many of the owners of cacao estates had surprisingly limited liquid capital assets. Not one person in the provinces of El Oro, Esmeraldas, or Los Ríos had even 100,000 sucres in liquid capital in 1909.[44] Moreover, many estate owners actually ran deeply in debt. Only the wealthiest landowners could afford to move to the city.

Guayaquil did not produce elite-class factions grounded in different forms of wealth.[45] This city was too small and the range of economic opportunities too narrow for such factions to emerge within the commercial community. The one possible rivalry that might have developed, that of nascent industrialists versus importers of foreign manufactures, never got started. Like many Latin American cities of this era, Guayaquil made few moves toward industrialization, and such industry that developed was very unsophisticated. Guayaquil's "factories" carried out no complicated tasks and most of the labor was performed by hand. Most of the region's industry either involved native handicrafts, such as the weaving of straw hats, or produced items that could not be easily imported, such as electricity, paving stones, or ice. Guayaquil's industry operated in the territory left over by the import trade. Moreover, the few manufacturers did not have interests that opposed those of the merchants. Indeed, as we have seen, they were often the same people.

From 1870 to 1925, then, as the city expanded, merchants became wealthier and wisely protected their fortunes by investing in other economic activities. Likewise, some landowners became involved in banking, cacao export, and the city's commerce. Toward the end of the era, from 1909 to 1925, retail sales had become the chief economic sideline activity of the elites. The merchants arranged the overseas sales of growers' cacao and then imported European and U.S. consumer items to be peddled in the shops and streets of Guayaquil. Factories appeared, but most of them were small and primitive. Guayaquil was a commercial entrepot, and its elites were merchants who had diversified their holdings. The fortunes of these men and their families rose with cacao shipments aboard.

### Lives of the Poor and the Rich

Guayaquil, like most cities, could be at once beautiful and ugly, exciting and exasperating: the movement and commotion of the crowd, the arrival of a ship, a fight, an accident, a thief, the quiet of the morning, the sounds of the birds, the colors of the sunset, the cool breezes and the beauty of the river and Santay Island in the evening. It was elegant, with its immaculately groomed parks, somber bronze statues peering out over the gently flowing Guayas River, and lovely colonial-style homes with their characteristic second-story overhangs and wooden slat windows that opened from the bottom to catch cool updrafts. It was squalid, with its hideous slums, legions of roaches, swarms of mosquitoes, and the intense heat and humidity of the equator. The city smelled wonderful: of cacao drying in the streets, of plantains frying, or of bread baking. The city reeked: from the slaughterhouse, men urinating by the riverbank, from the garbage, manure, chickens, pigs, and raw sewerage. But mostly Guayaquil teemed with life. Iguanas ate leaves and small birds in the trees in the parks, the river swam with fish, and bats sped about among the buildings at dusk. People walked, ate, sat, and filled the city with the sounds of their talking, laughing, and music.

The diet of ordinary guayaquileños included a blend of domestic staples and imports. At the market one could find numerous local products: peeled rice, lentils, potatoes, corn, noodles, beef, chicken, various seafoods, onions, beans, oranges, bananas, lemons, melons, pineapples, garlic, cilantro, anise, cloves, peppers, peanuts, sugar, cacao, coffee, butter, cheese, eggs, crackers, cookies, and a great deal more. However, people also looked to imports to provide other basic necessities, such as olive oil, cooking oil, lard (guayaquileños preferred fried foods), and wheat flour. Imported rice and coast-grown plantains served as the dietary mainstays.

Many people found room around their homes or in adjacent streets for a few chickens. Some families also kept goats, good for milk or for making the coastal specialty, seco de chivo, roasted goat ribs. Other favorites included tripe in peanut butter sauce, or *colada*, a heavy, meat-bone soup thickened with barley flour and sweetened. The typical meal included rice or lentils, fried plantains, and perhaps some fried fish or fried chicken. Given the bounty of the coast, in Guayaquil it was not hard for everyone to get enough to eat.

The poor generally lived in simple dwellings of their own fabrication. Typically the homes followed the style of the rural coastal montuvios' dwellings. Those living out by the estuary placed their shacks on stilts standing about one to three feet above the ground to avoid the floods of the rainy season. They built the walls and floors of flattened bamboo and the roofs of thatch or, if they could afford it, of metal. In the city center the poor built their homes of the same materials, although most had no need to elevate the structures.[46]

Ordinary people found many ways to amuse themselves after work and on Sundays. Those able to read—about two of three guayaquileños—might buy a newspaper. By 1902, one could pick from thirteen, including four dailies. By 1880, the papers offered news of the world delivered by mail— the telegraph cable did not yet reach from Panamá. By 1925, the papers carried direct wire-service stories from United Press International and Agencia Havas. The papers also presented poetry, featuring the efforts of local authors. If the paper offered nothing very interesting, one could try the public library. The city finished the building in 1862, and by 1892 it held 7,000 volumes. The city council spent 1,000 sucres in 1907 on new books and magazines, and in 1920 the city opened an improved new facility.[47]

The city library and museum, ca. 1920.

Given the density of its settlement pattern, Guayaquil had little greenery. Already by 1880 the once-wide streets had become narrow and crowded. As one R. Quevedo complained in a petition to the city council in 1893, Guayaquil severely lacked clean and safe places for one to go and relax.[48] Zoning laws were unknown, and factories operated full-blast next to residential neighborhoods. As the city paper, *El grito del pueblo*, editorialized in 1912, Guayaquil had an "ugly appearance."[49]

Hence, the few city parks and the riverfront, adorned with flowers, trees, and statues, served as critical refuges. The Malecón (waterfront), a favorite spot for a pleasant evening stroll, overlooked the Guayas River and was graced with a statue of poet José Joaquin de Olmedo (1780–1874). A statue depicting the famous 1822 meeting of Simón Bolívar and José de San Martín, rose nearby at the rotunda. Downtown, by the cathedral, stood Seminario Park, which sported a French-made monument of Bolívar on horseback. Centenary Square, at the edge of the downtown district on Avenida 9 de Octubre, boasted a tall spire of bronze and marble entitled "The Column to the Heroes of the Independence of the City," representing history, justice, patriotism, and heroism. In these formal manicured parks, the grass, trees, and flowers were kept carefully behind short fences. Guayaquil's parks were for walking, sitting, and looking, not for running, jumping, and athletics.[50]

After the appearance of streetcars in 1882, people discovered that the vehicles did more than just make it easier to get around. Riding on the open upper decks was a good way to enjoy a breeze on hot nights, and in 1920 the ride was still a bargain at 5 cents.

Children enjoyed swimming, especially in the calm waters of the estuary. On especially hot days adults would join the fun, their lack of swimsuits raising the eyebrows of passersby. At night young women and men came down to the waterfront or to the parks to engage in the evening ritual of flirting and courtship. By the 1870s, the city hired a band to play in the parks for free. Some people danced, others just listened. Men smoked, gossiped, read, and gambled, and, judging by the countless small bars and by police records, many found diversion in drinking and visiting prostitutes.[51]

Nearly everyone enjoyed playing the lottery—both the legal and illegal ones—that kept up a swift business even during Ecuador's fierce civil wars. The jackpot reached 10,000 sucres by 1925. Bull fights at American Park, ubiquitous cockfights (with even a hired city inspector to assure the honesty of the proceedings), and the cinema provided other diversions. The Eden theater was in business by 1912, and by 1925 there were at least two more, the Colon and Ideal, from which to choose. And there were sports; by 1916, local soccer teams held matches at the stadium.[52]

Seminario Park, 1889.

Special days and events provided further entertainment. Although Guayaquil was not a city particularly noted for religious piety, frequent saints'
days always brought special festivities. Women put on home-sewn dresses
fashioned of fine Japanese cloth and modeled after styles in Europe or the
United States. Men wore their black Sunday-best suits, starched white shirts,
and black neckties, their hair slicked back and parted in the middle. Secular
holidays also provided occasion for revelry. The city erected a permanent
structure to house circuses and fairs. Even into the 1880s, people continued
the colonial custom of celebrating carnival. Kids ran around and played
pranks; adults drank heavily, especially *aguardiente*. And Guayaquil Independence Day meant a parade, speeches, and pigs roasted right out on the
street. (Each pig had small flags adorning each nostril, one for Guayaquil,

one for Ecuador.) When the city dedicated its statue to the heroes of independence in Centenary Square in 1917, all Guayaquil turned out. President
Alfredo Baquerizo Moreno gave a speech, as did most other city dignitaries.
Well-rehearsed schoolchildren sang the national anthem, read poetry, waved
flags, raced about in athletic events, and otherwise frolicked.[53]

For the elite, the city's small size afforded the opportunity to become well-
acquainted with one another. As their economic interests intertwined, so too
did their social connections; they attended the theater together, escaped
Guayaquil during the hot rainy season together, and they married one another. Of course, this coastal elite did not mix with the sierra aristocracy.
(Even today these regional elites are mutually exclusive.) In part, this segregation stemmed from the lack of economic ties between coast and sierra, although, as we have seen, cultural differences played a role as well.[54]

The affluent of Guayaquil partook of various diversions. Many enjoyed
betting on the horses at the track. By 1900, the card featured three races a day
of running thoroughbreds brought in from all over the world. After the turn
of the century, automobiles crowded in front of the Jockey Club, with Buicks,
Fords (at 2,950 sucres in 1925), and Alfa Romeos the most popular choices.
Given the primitive state of the roads, it was one of the few places a person
could go in an automobile. The cars, tires, most of the gasoline, and all the
parts had to be imported.[55]

The literary-minded could read short stories or poems (such as the wist-
ful "Impossible Love" by Miguel Rasch Isla) featured in local society magazines such as *Patria*. Women might spend a quiet afternoon sitting amidst the
cool ferns of an interior patio, catching up on the news of weddings, en-

Eating snow cones, ca. 1920.

The racetrack, ca. 1880.

gagements, and other social events. Women could purchase the latest foreign fashion magazines, such as *La Moda Elegante Ilustrada de Madrid*, although the price was a stiff twenty-one sucres a year in 1880 and twenty-six sucres in 1912. Guayaquil imported fifty-six magazines by 1925 whose prices ranged from three and a half to forty sucres a year, with titles in poetry, fashion, sports, short stories, needlework, and crime. One could also sample from newspapers and novels imported from around the world.[56]

For those who did not care to read, there was the theater, although even in 1880 tickets could be costly—top seats ran five sucres. Still, there might be

A view inside the home of a "gente bien," ca. 1920.

something worth seeing: in 1886 Sarah Bernhardt came to Guayaquil. By 1907 Guayaquil had three theaters from which to choose, although most regarded the Teatro Olmedo as the most elegant. And there were parties; in 1900 Antonio C. Cabezas advertised that he would play dance music at private affairs. Concerts or special fundraising dinners and awards ceremonies to toast leading citizens and philanthropists afforded further opportunities to meet and socialize. Mustachioed men donned tuxedos, while the women might show off new French fashions. The Belen del Huerfano, the Club de Damas Siglo XX, and the Sociedad Filantropica all held fundraisers for city hospitals or camps for poor children. Young men of the wealthier families joined soccer clubs; the winners got their pictures in the paper. When the young men got older, they might join other notable males at the Club de la Union to while away the late afternoons relaxing, drinking, and hatching business deals.[57]

The elite, the "gente bien" or "*gente decente,*" could afford to live graciously. Judging by photos in the papers, some owned rather significant yachts; the papers reported further on the sumptuous banquets held onboard. Many wealthy families owned vacation homes on Puna Island or at the beach at Playas or Salinas, and they fled Guayaquil during the hottest months. The wealthy adorned their homes with telephones, indoor plumbing, refrigerators, typewriters, various Westinghouse kitchen appliances, and even gas lights and stoves. Special imports including American whiskey such as Old Grand Dad, champagne (at four sucres a bottle in 1925), fine soaps, Scott tissue, or Ever-Sweet underarm deodorant, they could purchase at better stores. And if they could not find what they were looking for, they could always order by catalog from Wanamaker's of New York. If one bought an imported French piano, Eduardo Neumane advertised that he could teach aspiring pianists how to play.[58]

Higher status tended to accrue to those with lighter skin hues, a college degree (especially in law or medicine), fine clothes, a refined manner, a wife who belonged to the Charitable Society, a big house and, above all, money. Status conferred many privileges. Common people would stand to one side of the sidewalk as "gente bien" walked by. The elite might appropriately glide to the front of any line. More importantly, one might secure a good job for one's son in the government bureaucracy. High status and wealth might also exempt a person from prosecution for criminal wrongdoing.[59]

A further benefit was freedom from conscription. For most males impressment into the army was always a possibility. Ecuador's frequent internal wars generally brought forced recruitment into the army, although technically this was illegal. Military service was something to be avoided at any

price. Sons of the well-to-do could afford that price, and they either purchased their exemptions or used family influence to avoid military duty.[60]

The cacao economy flourished, and Guayaquil grew as the distribution
and commercial center for this trade. The city developed a vast service sector but only a very modest hand-manufacturing sector. The advance of commerce in Guayaquil sparked ever-higher levels of internal migration from
the sierra to the coast, although most of the newcomers to the city fell into an
expanding class of only partially employed workers in low-paid, service-related jobs. Of course, some people in Guayaquil became quite wealthy. The
richest were those most closely associated with overseas trade, although all
elites showed a marked tendency toward economic diversification. The elite
class that emerged in Guayaquil became one that was ever more numerous,
interconnected, and affluent.

*Chapter Six*

---

# Life in Guayaquil
## Servicing a Growing City

Guayaquil spread out geographically as its population increased. Set on the western bank of the broad, muddy Guayas River, thirty miles north from the Pacific Ocean, Guayaquil occupied mostly flat and rather featureless land. Only the steep Santa Ana and Carmen hills, at the northern boundary, provided relief. To the west, the city stopped at the Estero Salado salt marshes, and to the east, the riverbank marked the edge of town. No natural obstacles stood to the south, and the city grew accordingly.

But the urban growth of Guayaquil came chaotically. Careful planning and strict zoning laws were unknown, and the city became a maze of winding paths and makeshift hovels. The riverfront grew increasingly crowded with wooden docks served by a tangle of rail lines. As migrants overwhelmed the existing supply of housing, people built cane and thatch homes atop poles on the saltwater estuary to the west, began to work up the sides of the Carmen and Santa Ana hills to the north, and squeezed dwellings into vacant spaces in the city center, while others lived in balsas that crowded along the west bank of the Guayas. Some people lacked even these minimal forms of shelter. As Blair Niles, a tourist visiting Guayaquil in 1921, wrote: "in the shadows, on doorsteps, or stretched upon the sidewalks, the manual laborers of Guayaquil slumber."[1] Guayaquil was no longer the small town it had been in 1870, when it had three urban parishes and a modest number of houses clinging to the west bank of the Guayas. By 1925, the city center was bordered to the south and east by new suburban settlements built by the recent migrants to the city.[2]

But even as the city spread, it remained compact and crowded. In the center of town, along Avenida 9 de Octubre (about eight blocks south of the hills), the business district stretched south and north and extended westward away from the wharves and warehouses by the Malecón. The outside walls of most businesses were of bamboo stalks split in half and reaching up two stories. The central city had some buildings of concrete, although given the high cost of cement, some buildings used the material only as a veneer. Here stood the domed Gobernación or governor's offices, the heavy stone Secretaría Municipal of city government, the library, churches, banks, currency exchange shops, store after store featuring small imports, and innumerable bars and restaurants. All along the sidewalks, peddlers stacked their wares— fruit, jewelry, clothing, and much, much more—forcing pedestrians into the street. The building density made Guayaquil a walking city; people could get where they were going on foot.

As with other quickly growing cities, Guayaquil had difficulty providing social services to keep pace with its increasing population. There are high start-up costs for putting in place necessary urban facilities and services that are not always needed in less crowded towns or rural districts. The geographic expansion of Guayaquil required the building of new street lights, fire houses, schools, jails, and more. Yet city efforts constantly seemed one jump behind the bounding population growth. Slum districts developed that teemed with people, especially children, and were ridden with filth and disease.

In some services, Guayaquil made notable progress. Significantly, crime did not become one of the city's major problems. Despite the perception of some contemporaries that Guayaquil was in the midst of a crime wave, the incidence of violence and theft actually increased only slightly. In other aspects, though, Guayaquil broke down under the strain of its growing population burden. Earlier systems for urban provisioning that had worked well when the city was smaller swiftly became inadequate.

### Paving, Lights, and Power

Colonial Guayaquil exhibited "a relatively egalitarian social system" and cultivated "a humane case of urban development within a colonial system."[3] City leaders continued to show some concern for social services into the late nineteenth and early twentieth centuries. Certainly they cared about their city, but more to the point, a foul urban environment was bad for business. Nothing could scare away potential investors and foreign vessels more surely than a citywide epidemic. From both a sense of community pride and pecuniary self-interest, city leaders sought to improve their city.

Street paving was one service Guayaquil did not keep up. Only major thoroughfares were paved; seasonal heavy rains turned the many dirt roads

Guayaquil, 1909. Reproduced from Compañia Guía del Ecuador, *El Ecuador: Guía comercial, agrícola e industrial de la república* (Guayaquil: Talleres de Artes Graficas de E. Rodenas, 1909).

to thick mud that halted urban transport. Without funds to address the problem, the city council tried instead to ban wheeled vehicles from all city dirt roads during the rainy season. The measure failed. The Malecón, visitors' first glimpse of the city, offered an especially sordid, raw appearance. In working-class neighborhoods, trash often served as landfill. Wrote one visitor in 1914: "The upper or northern part [of Guayaquil] is inhabited by the poorer classes. The streets in this section are tortuous, badly paved and undrained, pestilential and dirty, and in large part responsible for the evil reputation of Guayaquil as a centre of fever and plague."[4]

The streetlights, poorly constructed by foreign firms, never shone brightly. Gas-burning streetlights first appeared in 1870; within three years, the city had dim gas lights on most of the major streets, and by 1890, the gas lanterns numbered more than one thousand. The city acquired somewhat brighter electric lights beginning in 1873. In 1909 it had 1,320 gas lanterns downtown and 1,042 electric ones in the surrounding districts. In 1920 there were 1,792 gas and 1,533 electric lights, an increase of only 963.[5]

Yet even where streetlights went up, the city was little better for it. Dismayed citizens presented to the city council in 1876 a petition, bearing four pages of signatures, complaining about the streetlights' inadequacy.[6] But little

Guayaquil from above, 1922. Looking to the west.

was done; indeed, when the city subsequently failed to pay its gas bill, the power company shut the lights off altogether. This would not be the only time.

Its high charges and poor service wrought nearly constant complaints about the light and power company. Gas supplies were so low in 1880 that street lamps cast about as much light as a candle. City Commissioner Alberto Reina said the lights were so dim that people were in danger of bumping into one another even when directly under one of the lanterns. Service for broken lamps was virtually nonexistent. Even the new electric lamps provided little improvement. J. A. Cortes García, acting president of the city council in 1919, summed up the grievances by noting that the worst problem was "the exorbitant charge demanded for [such] deficient service."[7]

A 1925 report by a U.S. commission studying the provisioning of light and power for Guayaquil pointed to some of the continuing concerns. Commissioners M. L. Stewart and C.A. McKenney noted that "public service was not satisfactory": the electrical power plant produced only 800 kilowatts for the entire city. "We have never seen or heard of a city with a similar situation in the world, illuminated in a manner as manifestly inadequate as this. . . . In fact, it isn't even necessary to leave Ecuador to find a surprising comparison. The city of Quito, with [in 1925] a smaller population than Guayaquil has at its disposal an adequate and steady supply of electricity of about three and a half times more than Guayaquil;" the company in Quito was soon to add more generating capacity that would give the capital five times more power than Guayaquil. Worse, the report went on, even Guayaquil's present insufficient output could not be assured. The existing plant was very unstable, and "a major accident had to be expected" at any time. The power plant depended on three diesel motors, each in questionable, unserviced condition. All three worked at full capacity around the clock without backup. Moreover, the power lines strung throughout Guayaquil were also, the commissioners said, of "inferior quality." They recommended a generating capacity for Guayaquil of 3,000 kilowatts, about four times more than the existing level, and called for a complete rewiring of the entire city. The existing generators had some limited utility as a backup system, the commissioners suggested. Finally, Guayaquil should turn to water power as an energy source—oil and coal were too expensive in Ecuador, and one readily available source was inappropriate: "reduced to its simplest terms, burning wood to generate power is an economic crime," the commissioners concluded.[8]

### Fire

Fires repeatedly ravaged Guayaquil, causing deaths and enormous financial losses. Beyond the damage to private property, blazes destroyed costly government buildings and forced the city to build new schools and other facilities. In the colonial era, city fathers made a studied effort to impede the spread of fires by leaving wide streets and by clearing vacant lots of debris. But in the rush of urban growth during the cacao boom years, such wise practices were forgotten. For this Guayaquil paid dearly, for a major fire occurred on average every three years.[9]

The fire department did not do a very good job of protecting Guayaquil. By all reports the force lacked adequate equipment and access to water.[10] Nevertheless, Police Chief R. T. Caamaño proclaimed in 1891 that the city had turned the corner on the problem. "We can say without doubt," he wrote, that "there is no danger" from fire any longer.[11]

On October 5, 1896 at 7:45 P.M. a fire started at the "La Joya" boutique near the waterfront in Guayaquil. The blaze quickly raged out of control in all directions. The fire burned all night, throughout the next day, and on into following evening. Panic-stricken people rushed about, vainly attempting to rescue their belongings. Gougers arrived to take advantage; they offered their services in saving furniture but charged rates in excess of the objects' actual value. Many residents managed to drag most of their possessions outside, only to have the fire claim them there. The blaze trapped people along the riverfront. In a scene of complete bedlam, people crowded onto boats and canoes while others tried to launch rafts crammed with furniture. The fire all but leveled the city: it gutted ninety-two city blocks, and reduced the down-

Firemen showing off their new equipment, 1891. A few years after this photo was taken, much of the city burned to the ground.

town commercial district to cinders. The U.S. minister to Ecuador visited the scene afterwards and concluded: "the whole city has been destroyed."[12]

The fire of 1896 killed thirty-six people and left perhaps 18,000 homeless. A third or more of Guayaquil's population fled the city. The surrounding villages soon had overflow populations of refugees from Guayaquil. Basic supplies became precious and costly. Charity was niggardly; the huge losses suffered by the wealthy discouraging philanthropy.[13]

On July 16, 1902, it happened again. This fire, named "Iglesia de San Agustin" for its starting location at the church, lasted fifteen hours and claimed twenty-six city blocks. With two major fires in six years, at last the city took effective action to forestall further disaster. City leaders L. García, José Luís Tamayo, and Urvina Jado founded the Junta Proveedora charitable society in the months that followed and arranged the purchase of new equipment from the United States. Meanwhile, city officials established a new building code, which they actually began to enforce at least in the downtown area. They widened streets, lowered the allowable building height, and forbade the use of easily flammable construction materials. More importantly, the city government got serious about furnishing adequate water supplies to the fire department. It completed a system in 1905 to pump river water to three large holding tanks on Santa Ana hill overlooking Guayaquil. Not all the problems had been fully addressed, though. Most of the city still lacked fire alarms in 1912.[14]

The fire of 1902 was the last citywide blaze that Guayaquil endured. The two blazes left the older established downtown section all but ruined; as a result of the fires, though, Guayaquil became a somewhat more pleasant place to live. The flames had claimed many ramshackle and rat-infested wooden structures. Modern concrete and steel edifices came in their place. The city widened downtown streets, and trees lined the newly spacious and rather more attractive avenues in central Guayaquil.[15]

### Policing and Crime

Law enforcement, like other municipal services, also suffered from a serious lack of funding. The city jail housed mostly petty criminals—more serious offenders went to the national penitentiary in Quito—yet the jail proved insufficient even for its limited designation, for many inmates found it quite easy to escape. As one might expect, Guayaquil's jail was crowded and unclean.[16] The experience of Samuel Wisdom, a Guayaquil workman, likely reflects the circumstances of many incarcerated in Guayaquil. Wisdom, a Jamaican, found a job in 1908 as coachman for Antonio Gomez, "a respectable and wealthy citizen of Guayaquil."[17] But Wisdom soon wrecked the coach, and Gomez had Wisdom thrown in jail. Such treatment of the poor was a common occurrence, Wisdom charged. Indeed, the police routinely jailed working men upon a wealthy person's request. Wisdom received no food in jail; authorities instead supplied him ten cents a day, a sum scarcely enough for bread, with which to negotiate his own purchases. Wisdom was reduced to playing on the pity of guards, such as it was, and begging for scraps.

The justice system was likewise woefully underfunded, deficient, and sometimes corrupt. Courtrooms were neither well-lit nor well-ventilated; when it got too warm, as it often does along the equator, judges just left work early. Only two public defenders served the poor in 1899, and neither received reimbursement from the city. Summing up the situation, Guayas Governor Martín Aviles noted in his 1903 report to Quito that "as usual, the administration of justice, with rare exception, is slow and leaves much to be desired in this province."[18]

Overlapping bureaucracy hampered effective law enforcement in Guayaquil. The city really had three police departments: the national police, who dealt with general crime; the *policía de orden y seguridad*, who took care of safety and enforced health regulations; and the *policía de aseo, ornato y salubridad*, or the municipal police, who handled traffic and other minor matters. The police chief found himself continually frustrated by the autonomy of these separate police branches and the numerous other special boards and commissions. The national government finally stepped in by 1906 to try to resolve the confusion by combining the national and municipal police forces under the police chief's authority.[19]

Guayaquil police chiefs repeatedly pointed to the urgent need to add more patrolmen, especially for the city's newer districts.[20] Guayaquil had 300 patrolmen in the 1890s, 400 to 500 in the 1900s, and more than 500 by 1926. It had more police per capita than most Ecuadorian cities. Of the twelve cities in Ecuador in the late 1920s with populations of 10,000 or more, only four had higher police-to-population ratios: Guayaquil had one policeman for about every 200 people, whereas Cuenca and Ambato had one officer for about every 500 people.[21]

The public felt ill-served by law enforcement officials and regularly decried their low standards of professionalism and chronic abuse of police power. Guayaquil police officers earned very meager wages, taking home about as much as common day laborers who had steady work. Low pay encouraged neither hard work nor honesty. Reports of police brutality, drunkenness, even mistreatment of children were not at all unusual.[22] Ecuador's minister of the interior, J. Modesto Espinosa, bluntly admitted in 1886 that all Ecuador lacked sufficient numbers of properly trained officers and that the pay was so low that only ne'er-do-wells and misfits seemed attracted to the positions.[23] Guayas Governor J. M. P. Caamaño shared this assessment and added that the problem was that "the city of Guayaquil has grown in an incredible manner," and police service simply did not keep up.[24] Police were especially slow to respond to calls in the new suburban slums zones, he noted.

While one might have anticipated a glut of crime to accompany Guayaquil's too-rapid growth, the available data suggest that was not the case (see table 6.1). Crime increased, but only modestly and not as rapidly as the population. Arrest data are only available for the period from 1889 to 1909, and therefore it is possible, although unlikely, that crime rose or fell sharply in the years before and the years after. However, supporting information also strongly suggests that Guayaquil was not suffering a crime spree proportional to its population growth.

The total number of arrests in 1890 roughly equaled the number in 1909, about seven to eight thousand, while in the same period the population nearly doubled, from about 45,000 to 80,000. For two years, in 1897 and 1898, the number of arrests fell by half, but in those years police merely stopped arresting as many people for vagrancy or disturbing the peace (see table 6.1). The period 1890 to 1909 saw a rising number of violent crimes, but the increase was not steady or gradual. More than 300 violent offenses, about 7.17 per 1,000 residents, are recorded for 1890; in 1909 there were more than 700, or 8.89 per 1,000; the peak occurred in 1903, when police recorded about 900 violent offenses, or 12.96 per thousand people. The number of thefts did not increase; there were 415 in 1890, or 9.27 per thousand residents, and 353 in 1909, or 4.41 per thousand. However, the value of property stolen increased

**Table 6.1.** Gender, marital status, and literacy of Guayaquil lawbreakers, selected years, 1890–1909

| Year | GENDER | | MARITAL STATUS OF ADULTS | | | LITERACY | | |
| --- | --- | --- | --- | --- | --- | --- | --- | --- |
| | Male | Female | Single | Married | Widowed | Lit. | Illit. | Total |
| 1890 | 7,078 88% | 992 12% | — | — | — | — | — | 8,070 |
| 1891 | 7,050 87% | 953 12% | — | — | — | — | — | 8,131 |
| | (128 gender not listed) | | | | | | | |
| 1897 | 3,046 86% | 480 14% | 2,541 72% | 985 28% | — | 2,077 59% | 1,449 41% | 3,526 |
| 1898 | 4,044 88% | 574 12% | 3,581 78% | 1,032 22% | 5 | 2,798 61% | 1,820 39% | 4,618 |
| 1903a | 8,253 91% | 816 9% | 6,983 77% | 1,995 22% | 91 1% | 5,895 65% | 3,174 35% | 9,069 |
| 1904 | 7,760 90% | 855 10% | — | — | — | — | — | 8,615 |
| 1905a | 6,984 89% | 896 11% | 6,468 82% | 1,306 17% | 106 1% | 5,146 65% | 2,734 35% | 7,880 |
| 1908 | 6,191 89% | 789 11% | 5,558 80% | 1,259 18% | 163 2% | 5,343 77% | 1,637 23% | 6,980 |
| 1909 | 6,501 88% | 862 12% | 6,111 83% | 1,146 16% | 106 1% | 5,154 70% | 2,209 30% | 7,363 |

Sources: IP, Informe, 1890, 1891, 1897, 1998, 1903, 1904, 1910.
aEstimate.

markedly (see table 6.2). The total value of all goods taken in thefts increased from a low of 25,000 to 40,000 sucres in 1901 and 1903 to 100,000 sucres or more in 1909 and 1910. Overall, thieves were stealing more of value and slightly more residents fell victim to violent criminals. As Guayaquil grew, it was became a marginally more dangerous place to live.

Despite evidence to the contrary, city officials often expressed their perception of raging lawlessness. As a matter of course, annual police reports opened with long recitations about an alarming rise in crime, a "plague" of theft, prostitution, drunkenness, rape, and juvenile delinquency.[25] Officials highlighted as key concerns the swelling ranks of homeless youths who roamed the streets, shifting easily between legal and illegal occupations of peddling papers or stealing watches and the salesmen of all ages who swarmed downtown streets and the riverbank offering stolen goods for sale.[26]

So threatened were authorities by the specter of rampant crime that police officials pushed extreme measures as solutions. Police Chief R. T. Caamaño promoted the idea of exiling habitual drunks and vagrants for three to five years on the Galápagos Islands, some 650 miles off the coast.[27] He also sought strict registration and monitoring of artisans. Police Chief Octavio S. Roca renewed this theme in 1898 with a call for tighter police regulation of workers' guilds. Roca advocated requiring all workers to register with the police and carry identification cards.[28]

But if police officials overstated the severity of Guayaquil's crime problem, their notions of who was getting arrested were not mistaken. Officials pointed to artisans and foreigners as two groups heavily represented among criminal elements. But their criminality surely had at least as much to do with enforcement practices as it did with chronic misbehavior by foreigners and artisans. Police harassed workers, particularly foreign sailors, and arrested them for minor offenses associated with drinking and carousing. Immigrants made up 14 to 21 percent of all those arrested from 1897 to 1909, figures in excess of foreigners' actual presence, roughly 10 to 15 percent of the population.[29] Similarly, artisans were overrepresented in police arrest records.

Young single men committed most of the crimes in Guayaquil (see tables 6.1 and 6.3). Men comprised 86 to 91 percent of those arrested from 1890 to 1909. Ages twenty-one to thirty were prime years for lawbreaking, accounting for 45 to 57 percent of arrests from 1897 to 1909. Minors made up no more than 4 percent of those arrested during this time. As is nearly always the case—across time, across the globe—young adult males were most responsible for crimes.[30]

Crime remains a little-studied issue for most Latin American cities of the

**Table 6.2.** Crimes committed and the value of property stolen in Guayaquil, selected years, 1890–1910

| Year | Disturbing the peace & vagrancy | Violent crime | Theft | Value of Property Stolen[a] | Other | Total |
|---|---|---|---|---|---|---|
| 1890 | 6,165 (76%) | 321 (4%) | 415 (5%) | — | 1,169 (14%) | 8,070 |
| 1891 | 6,405 (79%) | 351 (4%) | 188 (2%) | — | 1,187 (15%) | 8,131 |
| 1897 | 2,456 (70%) | 355 (10%) | 220 (6%) | 71,795 | 495 (14%) | 3,526 |
| 1898 | 2,884 (62%) | 718 (16%) | 192 (4%) | 51,824 | 824 (18%) | 4,618 |
| 1901[a] | — | — | — | 25,120 | — | — |
| 1903[a] | 6,892 (76%) | 907 (10%) | 272 (3%) | 39,899 | 998 (11%) | 9,069 |
| 1904 | 6,052 (70%) | 679 (8%) | 406 (5%) | 45,428 | 1,478 (17%) | 8,615 |
| 1905[a] | 6,388 (81%) | 522 (7%) | 354 (4%) | 43,048 | 616 (8%) | 7,880 |
| 1908 | 3,372 (48%) | 476 (7%) | 272 (4%) | 55,771 | 2,860 (41%) | 6,980 |
| 1909 | 3,226 (44%) | 711 (10%) | 353 (5%) | 116,361 | 3,073 (42%) | 7,363 |
| 1910[a] | — | — | — | 96,242 | — | — |

*Sources:* IP, *Informe,* 1890, 1891, 1897, 1898, 1901, 1903, 1904, 1905, 1910; Gallegos, Naranjo, *1900 almanaque.*
[a]Estimate.

**Table 6.3.** Age of lawbreakers in Guayaquil, selected years, 1897–1909

| Year | 0–15 | 16–20 | 21–30 | 31–40 | 40+ | 15+ total | Total |
|------|------|-------|-------|-------|-----|-----------|-------|
| 1897 | — | 545 | 1,597 | 862 | 522 | — | 3,526 |
| bracket % | — | 15 | 45 | 24 | 15 | — | |
| cum. % | — | 15 | 61 | 85 | 100 | — | |
| | | | | | | | |
| 1898 | — | 887 | 2,276 | 927 | 528 | — | 4,618 |
| bracket % | — | 19 | 49 | 20 | 11 | — | |
| cum. % | — | 19 | 68 | 89 | 100 | — | |
| | | | | | | | |
| 1903[a] | 340 | 972 | 5,140 | 2,290 | 962 | 9,364 | 9,704 |
| bracket % | 4 | 10 | 53 | 24 | 10 | 96 | |
| cum. % | 4 | 14 | 66 | 90 | 100 | | |
| | | | | | | | |
| 1905[a] | 170 | 770 | 4,480 | 1,764 | 696 | 7,710 | 7,880 |
| bracket % | 2 | 10 | 57 | 22 | 9 | 98 | |
| cum. % | 2 | 12 | 69 | 91 | 100 | | |
| | | | | | | | |
| 1909 | 238 | 1,055 | 3,403 | 1,738 | 929 | 7,125 | 7,363 |
| bracket % | 3 | 14 | 46 | 24 | 13 | 97 | |
| cum. % | 3 | 18 | 64 | 87 | 100 | | |

*Sources:* IP, *Informe, 1897–1910.*
Bracket % = percentage of all lawbreakers in age bracket.
Cum. % = cumulative percentage.
[a]Estimate.

era, thus it is only possible to compare Guayaquil's crime figures to those in the cities of Argentina; these few, at least, have been ably investigated by Julia Kirk Blackwelder and Lyman L. Johnson. Comparison against their findings places conditions in Guayaquil in better perspective. Thieves vexed Buenos Aires more than they did Guayaquil. In the Argentine capital, the value of property stolen rose from 284,146 pesos in 1887 to almost 3,000,000 pesos in 1912, a much faster increase than in Guayaquil. But while Buenos Aires was a violent city, Guayaquil was more so. Guayaquil authorities recorded 7.17 violent crimes per 1,000 people in 1890 and 8.89 per thousand in 1909, whereas crimes against persons increased in Buenos Aires from 1.46 offenses per 1,000 persons in 1885 to 3.45 per thousand in 1913.[31]

The general social patterns of crime drawn from the urbanization experience of industrial cities of the United States and western Europe do not hold for Latin American cities. As Lyman Johnson notes in *The Problem of Order:* "Increased crime rates, especially rates of property crime, are commonly associated in the literature with urbanization. More developed industrialized nations have relatively higher property crime rates and lower personal crime rates than lesser-developed nations" (x). "Violent crime . . . fell throughout Europe and North America from the late nineteenth century to the post-World War II period" (xi).[32] But in Buenos Aires, Tucumán, and Santa Fe, Argentina, violent crime did not decline, nor did property crimes increase. Such was also the case in Guayaquil.

To Johnson, the Argentine city retained "in fundamental ways the social characteristics of its less developed past" (xviii). "The arrival of large numbers of displaced rural workers, unaccustomed to the social practices and behavioral norms of the city, drove up the level of public-order arrests" (127). Again, the same circumstance applied to Guayaquil, whose new residents were rural people more prone to violent crimes than property crimes.

However, some of the experience of urban industrial cities of western Europe does have parallels in Guayaquil. Howard Zehr, in his study, *Crime and the Development of Modern Society*, identifies an initial "transition stage" in "new urban-industrial areas" during which "the novel and/or disruptive stages of that process" led to a temporary increase in violence and property crime (133–35, 138). Although not an industrial city, Guayaquil was clearly an urban center in transition. Both theft and violence rose slightly in Guayaquil as it did in other cities undergoing this disruptive process.

Finally, it is not necessary to view rising crime only as evidence of social breakdown. As Zehr argues (23, 82–83), increased theft is a reflection of society's success "in selling certain common material . . . values to the population at large while its social structure was too rigid and economic opportunities too few or unequally distributed to allow access to these values and symbols by all members of society." More thefts, then, "should not be seen as pathological" as much as "acceptance of modern society's values," using non-accepted means to attain these ends.

Newcomers from the backlands saw displayed before their eyes an array of luxury imports, and they soon learned what of it was unattainable to them. Plainly, the economy of Guayaquil failed to give most workers the means to fulfill their rising expectations. Hence many stole what they could not otherwise acquire.

Likewise, the rise of violence in the city need not be interpreted as evidence of urban social breakdown. Most acts of violence target loved ones—family and friends. Often people will physically attack only someone they know rather well. As Zehr writes in *Crime and Development* (133–35), "it can be suggested that high rates of violence in urbanising areas attest to the lack of social disorganization and impersonality in such areas." That crime rose slightly in Guayaquil during these years may be viewed as evidence of the city's growing maturity.[33]

## Education

In Ecuador, as elsewhere in Hispanic America, the Catholic Church histori-cally provided education.[34] But in keeping with late nineteenth-century trends across Latin America, Ecuadorian liberals enacted a series of anti-clerical reforms that included secularizing education, beginning in 1895. President Eloy Alfaro (1895–1901; 1906–11) placed in Ecuador's constitution of 1906 a law requiring secular education. Liberal Presidents Alfaro and Leonidas Plaza Gutiérrez (1901–6; 1912–16) oversaw the development of many state-sponsored secondary schools, normal schools, and night schools for workers and increased funding for the universities. Attendance at all lev-els of instruction in Ecuador rose from 15,000 in 1871 to 32,000 in 1875 to 92,000 in 1910 and 104,000 in 1930.[35]

Ecuador had many types of schools, nearly all segregated by gender. There were five categories of elementary schools: *fiscales,* funded mainly by the national government; *municipales,* city schools funded with city revenues; *particulares,* private schools; *beneficencias,* charity schools operated first by the Church and later by the Junta de Beneficencia; and night schools run by ar-tisan mutual-aid societies and sometimes supported with grants from the na-tional or local government. After elementary school, students attended cole-gios, or high schools. Most colegios in Guayaquil were private vocational or trade schools, but there was one general, public colegio for boys, the Colegio Nacional de San Vicente Rocafuerte del Guayas, funded by the national gov-ernment. Guayaquil also had a university, likewise supported by national funds.

The national government generally funded public rural elementary schools, while both the national and municipal governments took care of city schools. In Guayaquil, about two-thirds to three-quarters of the students at-tended nationally funded public schools (see table 6.4). The municipal gov-ernments of Guayaquil and Santa Elena operated about 10 percent of the public grade schools in Guayas during much of the period. By about 1910, the national government took greater control of education, and the role of the municipalities in Guayas province receded such that in 1916 only four of the 152 public elementary schools in Guayas were municipales.[36]

Guayas province, which generated most of the nation's tax revenues, suc-cessfully demanded a larger share of the national expenditure on primary education. That share grew from 19 to 30 percent of the national govern-ment's total primary school outlay from the 1880s up to 1920; meanwhile Guayas represented only 8 to 17 percent of the country's total population. If the funds had been allocated strictly by population, Guayas would have re-ceived about half as much as it did.[37] Yet nearly all the revenues came from the Guayaquil export economy in the first place.

**Table 6.4.** Student population in public primary schools in Guayaquil and in Guayas province, detail on municipal versus national schools and gender, selected years, 1841–1921

GUAYAS PROVINCE

| Year | Municipal | National | Boys | Girls | Total[a] |
|------|-----------|----------|------|-------|----------|
| 1841 | — | — | 1,207 | 85 | 1,292 |
| 1848 | — | — | 1,647 | 180 | 1,827 |
| 1871 | — | — | — | — | 1,248 |
| 1873 | — | — | 1,384 | 416 | 1,800 |
| 1875 | — | — | 2,345 | 955 | 3,300 |
| 1879 | — | — | 1,631 | 1,525 | 3,156 |
| 1884 | 812 | 3,883 | 2,528 | 2,167 | 4,695 |
| 1885 | 827 | 4,446 | — | — | 5,273 |
| 1889 | 1,051 | 4,646 | 3,069 | 2,628 | 5,697 |
| 1894 | 1,482 | 6,836 | 4,173 | 4,145 | 8,318 |
| 1899 | — | — | 2,524 | 3,179 | 5,703 |
| 1903 | 3,398 | 8,714 | 7,061 | 5,051 | 12,112 |
| 1905 | 2,056 | 8,048 | 4,469 | 5,635 | 10,104 |
| 1908 | 2,586 | 9,501 | 5,624 | 6,463 | 12,087 |
| 1911 | — | 8,970 | — | — | — |
| 1916 | 1,603 | 11,274 | — | — | 12,877 |
| 1919 | 1,920 | 9,381 | 5,777 | 5,524 | 11,301 |
| 1921 | 1,492 | 9,380 | 5,679 | 5,193 | 10,872 |

GUAYAQUIL

| Year | Municipal | National | Boys | Girls | Total[a] |
|------|-----------|----------|------|-------|----------|
| 1871 | — | — | — | — | 614 |
| 1873 | — | 403 | 243 | 160 | 403 |
| 1884 | 520 | 1,500 | 750 | 1,270 | 2,020 |
| 1886 | 556 | 1,584 | — | — | 2,140 |
| 1887 | 616 | 1,740 | — | — | 2,356 |
| 1890 | 587 | 2,525 | 1,289 | 1,823 | 3,112 |
| 1891 | 780 | 2,719 | 1,279 | 1,612 | 3,499 |
| 1894 | 813 | 2,801 | — | — | 3,614 |
| 1899 | 1,097 | — | — | — | — |
| 1903 | 1,432 | 2,547 | 1,432 | 2,547 | 3,979 |
| 1904 | 1,796 | 2,045 | 1,248 | 2,593 | 3,841 |
| 1905 | 2,056 | — | — | — | — |
| 1911 | — | — | 3,958 | — | — |

Sources: MI, *Informe*, *1871*, 32, *1886*, *1887*; MIP, *Informe*, *1873*, *1879*, *1885*, *1890*, *1894*, 145–54, *1899*, *1909*, *1910*, 108–48, *1911–1912*, 263, *1916*, *1919*, *1921*, 10–11; *Los andes* (Guayaquil), 13 December 1873, cited in unpublished research notes of Estrada Ycaza; *El comercio* (Guayaquil), 21 May 1875, cited in unpublished research notes of Estrada Ycaza; IP, *Informe*, *1890*, 27–28, *1891*, 42–44, *1903*, *1904*, 91–97, *1905*, 147–54.
[a]Total may exceed gender detail because some students attended coed institutions.

Of all levels of government, it was the national government that provided the largest share of revenues for public education in Guayas, relying largely on a variety of special import and export taxes on aguardiente, tobacco, juice sales, and stamps.[38] The public Colegio Nacional de San Vicente del Guayas received 11,673 sucres from the national government in 1872, 25,000 sucres in 1884, and in the years after the turn of the century over 80,000 sucres annually, chiefly from a specially earmarked 3.5 percent cacao export tax (see table 6.5).[39] The university likewise got its money exclusively from the national government, primarily from a special export tax on cacao established in 1888.[40] Support for the university grew from about 5,000 sucres in 1889, to more than 215,000 sucres in 1919 (see table 6.5).

In Guayas province, only the municipal governments of Guayaquil and Santa Elena also allotted funds for public primary schools (see table 6.5). From 1884 to 1904, municipal funds (nearly all from Guayaquil) accounted for 18 to 40 percent of all public funding for primary education in Guayas; the rest came from the national government.[41] Not all municipal education funds went to city-run schools; some of it also supported the fiscales, or national schools, and by 1907 such support was no longer optional.[42] The national government came to claim 10 percent of municipal revenue to support primary education in Ecuador.[43]

However, all levels of government in Ecuador lacked an abiding commitment to education. To be sure, in absolute terms the amount spent rose: Ecuador spent 151,189 sucres on education in 1871 and twice that, 3,089,210 sucres, in 1925.[44] But when expressed as a percentage of total regular expenditures, the numbers look far less impressive (see table 6.6). At the national level, education's share fluctuated between a low of 3 percent and a high of 18 percent of total regular expenditures. The regular national budget in most years allocated less than 10 percent to education. Military funding was easily double or triple education outlays, despite the fact that Ecuador fought no major foreign conflicts. The city was yet more miserly: it never allocated more than 4 percent of its budget to education (see table 6.5).

For Guayas province as a whole, urban and rural, from the 1880s until the 1920s, the number of public primary schools grew at a rate faster than did population (see table 6.7). The number of public elementary schools in the province rose sixfold, from 25 in 1871 to 155 in 1921, while the population only doubled. That occurred largely because the first-time placement of public schools in rural zones outpaced the rural population growth. In the city of Guayaquil, the ratio of public primary schools and students to city population also increased from 1887 to 1894. However, within ten years that promising trend slowed as government struggled to keep pace with the rapidly expanding urban population (see table 6.8).

**Table 6.5.** Public funding for education in Guayas province, selected years, 1884–1924 (in sucres)

PRIMARY EDUCATION: MUNICIPAL VERSUS NATIONAL FUNDING

| Year | Municipal | National | Total |
|------|-----------|----------|-------|
| 1884 | 9,053 (18%) | 41,145 (82%) | 50,198 |
| 1889 | 15,572 (25%) | 45,948 (75%) | 61,520 |
| 1892 | 17,218 (25%) | 50,820 (75%) | 68,038 |
| 1893 | 21,529 (25%) | 65,738 (75%) | 87,267 |
| 1894 | — | — | 76,850 |
| 1898 | 28,792 (40%) | 43,364 (60%) | 72,156 |
| 1901 | 50,401 (38%) | 82,968 (62%) | 133,369 |
| 1902 | 46,938 (24%) | 145,524 (76%) | 192,462 |
| 1903 | 54,431 (29%) | 132,880 (71%) | 187,311 |
| 1904 | 59,535 (32%) | 124,092 (68%) | 183,627 |
| 1911 | — | 299,684 | — |
| 1918 | — | 360,375 | — |
| 1920 | — | 638,940 | — |

ALL LEVELS OF EDUCATION: ALL PUBLIC FUNDING

| Year | Elementary | Colegio | University | Total |
|------|-----------|---------|------------|-------|
| 1884 | 50,198 | 25,369 | 13,056 | 88,623 |
| 1889 | 61,520 | 19,086 | 4,608 | 85,214 |
| 1894 | — | 31,068 | — | 148,973 |
| 1901 | 133,369 | 80,090 | 89,485 | 302,944 |
| 1902 | 192,462 | 86,668 | 34,745 | 313,875 |
| 1908 | — | — | 48,000 | — |
| 1919 | — | 99,600 | 215,805 | — |
| 1924 | — | 89,663 | 145,748 | — |

*Sources:* MIP, *Informe, 1885,* "Report of the Sub-director of Studies of the Province of Guayas," *1890,* "Report of the Subdirector of Studies in Guayas," *1894,* 13, 150, 155, unnumbered tables, *1899,* 235–36, unnumbered tables, *1902,* 45, 58, *1903,* 65, *1905,* *1908,* 19, *1911–1912,* 263, 264, *1919,* xxv, lvii-lviii, *1921,* 28–29, *1928,* 61, 98.

The number of students attending public schools showed a marked but uneven rise (see table 6.4). In Guayas province, the public primary school population rose from 1,248 in 1871 to more than 12,000 by 1903. The public elementary student population of 1921, though, was below the 1903 level; there were 10,872 children, fairly evenly divided between boys and girls. At the Colegio Nacional de San Vicente del Guayas, founded in 1842, attendance rose from 123 boys in 1871 to 330 by 1901, although the number of pupils slipped back below 300 by 1909.[45] University of Guayaquil students, most of them in medicine or law, numbered fifty-one in 1884, ninety-eight in 1905, seventy-eight in 1909, 151 in 1921, and rose to a total of 189 by 1924.[46]

**Table 6.6.** National government expenditures, selected years, 1870–1925 (in percentages)

| Year | % education | % military | % public debt | absolute amount in 1,000s[a] |
|------|------|------|------|------|
| 1870 | 3 | 24 | 14 | 3,003 |
| 1872 | 7 | 23 | 29 | 3,312 |
| 1875 | 12 | 32 | 29 | 2,776 |
| 1878 | 5 | 28 | — | 3,272 |
| 1884 | 5 | 22 | 21 | 4,854 |
| 1885 | 5 | 25 | — | 3,930 |
| 1886 | 4 | 29 | 12 | 4,674 |
| 1887 | 6 | 27 | 23 | 4,429 |
| 1888 | 9 | 35 | 13 | 3,629 |
| 1889 | 11 | 35 | — | 3,075 |
| 1890 | 12 | 25 | 15 | 3,936 |
| 1891 | 13 | 29 | 10 | 3,946 |
| 1892 | 13 | 26 | 7 | 4,081 |
| 1893 | 13 | 25 | 8 | 4,433 |
| 1895 | 3 | 30 | 35 | 8,780 |
| 1897 | 7 | 33 | 32 | 5,690 |
| 1898 | 7 | 38 | 15 | 5,408 |
| 1899 | 7 | 42 | 25 | 6,663 |
| 1900 | 7 | 43 | 19 | 7,375 |
| 1902 | 9 | 26 | 31 | 9,343 |
| 1903 | 11 | 32 | 25 | 7,819 |
| 1904 | 9 | 23 | 26 | 10,526 |
| 1905 | 9 | 23 | 19 | 10,156 |
| 1907 | 7 | 26 | 26 | 12,219 |
| 1908 | 10 | 30 | 9 | 12,675 |
| 1909 | 10 | 23 | 17 | 15,564 |
| 1910 | 6 | 23 | 45 | 25,810 |
| 1911 | 5 | 20 | 38 | 22,437 |
| 1912 | 9 | 19 | 38 | 20,614 |
| 1913 | 11 | 19 | 25 | 21,665 |
| 1914 | 8 | 38 | 8 | 20,221 |
| 1915 | 8 | 35 | 18 | 18,995 |
| 1916 | 12 | 33 | 19 | 15,907 |
| 1917 | 11 | 29 | — | 16,545 |
| 1918 | 14 | 25 | 22 | 17,666 |
| 1919 | 14 | 23 | 21 | 20,046 |
| 1920 | 18 | 26 | 21 | 20,357 |
| 1921 | 18 | 26 | 11 | 21,450 |
| 1922 | 15 | 22 | 19 | 26,568 |
| 1923 | 11 | 21 | 26 | 29,376 |
| 1924 | 10 | 19 | 26 | 35,002 |
| 1925 | 7 | 19 | 18 | 43,890 |

*Source:* L.A. Rodríguez, *Search for Public Policy*, 224–26.
[a]In sucres—pesos before 1886.

**Table 6.7.** Public elementary schools in Guayaquil, Guayas, and Ecuador, selected years, 1841–1928

| Year | Guayaquil | Guayas | Ecuador |
|------|-----------|--------|---------|
| 1841 | — | 18 | 164 or 229 |
| 1848 | — | 27 | 243 |
| 1867 | — | — | 343 |
| 1871 | — | 25 | — |
| 1873 | 4 | 28 | 433 |
| 1875 | — | 51 | 526 |
| 1877 | — | 58 | — |
| 1884 | 14 | 65 | — |
| 1885 | 12 | 62 | 800 |
| 1887 | 14 | — | — |
| 1889 | 15 | 90 | — |
| 1890 | 16 | — | 853 |
| 1891 | 17 | — | — |
| 1892 | — | — | 1,106 |
| 1893 | 16 | — | — |
| 1894 | 18 | 115 | 1,209 |
| 1898 | 23 | — | — |
| 1899 | — | 131 | — |
| 1900 | — | 127 | — |
| 1901 | 22 | 132 | — |
| 1902 | — | 158 | 1,317 |
| 1903 | 28 | — | — |
| 1904 | 25 | 146 | — |
| 1905 | 25 | — | — |
| 1907 | 23 | — | — |
| 1908 | — | 170 | — |
| 1909 | — | 170 | 1,355 |
| 1912 | 31 | — | — |
| 1914 | — | — | 1,411 |
| 1915 | — | — | 1,231 |
| 1916 | — | 152 | 1,400 |
| 1919 | — | 143 | 1,630 |
| 1921 | — | 155 | 1,716 |
| 1924 | — | — | 1,488 |
| 1928 | — | — | 1,771 |

*Sources:* L.A. Rodríguez, *Search for Public Policy*, 85, 91; MI, *Informe, 1871*, 32, *1886, 1887; Los andes* (Guayaquil), 13 December 1873, cited in unpublished research notes, Estrada Ycaza; *El comercio* (Guayaquil), 21 May 1875, cited in unpublished research notes, Julio Estrada Ycaza; GG, *Informe, 1877,* 12; MIP, *Informe, 1873, 1885, 1890, 1894, 1899, 1900, 1901, 1903, 1905, 1909, 1910,* 108–48, *1916, 1919, 1921;* IP, *Informe, 1890, 1891, 1903, 1904, 1905; El republicano* (Quito), 1 April 1893, cited in unpublished research notes, Estrada Ycaza; Gallegos Naranjo, *1900 fin de siglo almanaque;* Paz Ayora, *Guía de Guayaquil 1901;* Barbosa *Almanaque ilustrado; El Ecuador: guía* 329; *Guayaquil en la mano 1912; Almanaque ilustrado ecuatoriano 1914.*

**Table 6.8.** Ratio of students and schools to city population, public elementary schools, selected years, 1871–1905

| Year | School students/ratio | Schools/ratio | Population |
|------|----------------------|---------------|------------|
| 1871 | 614/1:41[a] | — | 25,000[a] |
| 1873 | 403/1:62[a] | 4/1:6, 250[a] | 25,000[a] |
| 1884 | 2,020/1:20[a] | 14/1:2, 857[a] | 40,000[a] |
| 1887 | 2,356/1:19 | 14/1:3, 104 | 43,460 |
| 1890 | 3,112/1:14 | 16/1:2, 798 | 44,772 |
| 1891 | 3,499/1:13[a] | 17/1:2, 647[a] | 45,000[a] |
| 1893 | — | 16/1:3, 125[a] | 50,000[a] |
| 1894 | 3,614/1:14[a] | 18/1:2, 778[a] | 50,000[a] |
| 1903 | 3,979/1:18[a] | 28/1:2, 500[a] | 70,000[a] |
| 1905 | — | 25/1:3, 266 | 81,650 |

*Sources:* Adapted from foregoing education tables.
[a]Estimate.

For the poor, free charity and church schools supplemented the public elementary schools. Attendance at church- and charity-funded schools in Guayas province averaged around 300 to 1,000 students in the 1880s and perhaps around 500 to 1,200 in the 1890s, but attendance, always a bit irregular in Ecuador anyway, proved especially loose at the church charitable schools.[47] The Sociedad Filantrópica, founded in 1849, did perhaps the most to help orphans and the children of the very poorest; it operated a home for children, a trade school, and later a nursery school. After the turn of the century the organization's Escuela de Letras typically worked with some 500 or more pupils, and its manual arts shop trained another 150 or more every year.[48]

More affluent Guayaquil parents sometimes elected to send their children to one of the several private elementary schools, the particulares, while working-class children went to public schools. The sons and occasionally the daughters of those with money attended the small private schools or, if especially well-off, received tutoring at home. The Instituto y Colegio Mercantil de Guayaquil advertised classes in 1880 at four sucres a month for first grade and six sucres a month for second and third, prices beyond the reach of most families. Twenty children attended.[49] Particulares were uncrowded and enjoyed ample supplies and instruction from well-trained teachers.[50] Probably something on the order of about 200 to 500 children attended particulares in Guayas in the 1880s, around 800 to 1,500 in the 1890s, perhaps 1,700 in the 1900s, and about 2,400 or so from about 1910 through the 1920s.[51]

Night schools operated by artisans to benefit union members and their families were another type of private school in Guayaquil. The Sociedad de

Artesanos Amantes del Progreso ran a night school to teach basic reading and writing skills to workers; the nightly classes had 120 to 160 in attendance by 1900. The workers' schools, of which there were three in 1907, four in 1909, and seven in 1918, received small grants of support from the city and national governments. The city budgeted 7,320 sucres in 1925 to help support the educational efforts of the eleven worker schools in operation that year.[52]

Guayaquil also had numerous private colegios, or high schools, and several charitable colegios.[53] The Colegio de los Sagrados Corazones was a high school for girls founded in 1874.[54] The national government helped support it with proceeds from a 1.5 percent customs tax that provided 1,320 sucres in 1884 and 6,120 sucres in 1889.[55] The bulk of the school's revenues came, however, from the tuition paid by the 100 to 200 students.[56]

Males greatly outnumbered females in all types of education other than public elementary schools. In part this was so because secondary and higher education, both public and private, generally required the payment of a fee. The university had few female students; only twenty-one of its 189 students in 1924 (11 percent) were female.[57] Males, especially sons of the well-to-do, got the best education in Guayaquil.

The number of public elementary schoolteachers in Guayas province grew from ninety-five in 1884 to more than 300 by 1909. By 1925, Guayaquil employed special instructors in gym, drawing, needlecraft, English, and singing.[58] But finding enough good teachers proved a continual challenge. Those hired were not always well trained. This is not surprising, considering the low pay; teachers earned little more than unskilled day laborers, a mere sucre or two a day, despite laws that mandated much higher teacher salaries. After taking note of the thirty-sucre-a-month salary of one rural teacher in 1873, school inspector Francisco Campos drew the obvious conclusion: "it is not possible that [his] . . . duties will be carried out well."[59] Sometimes teachers offered special classes that required payment of a fee, and then devoted themselves to this enterprise, ignoring nonpaying pupils. Teachers frequently went months without being paid at all. When asked why he quit, one rural parish teacher declared: "Here I was dying of hunger, because it had been five months that they hadn't paid my salary."[60] He ultimately collected only half of what was due him. Some teaching positions languished unfilled for months on end because the salary was so low that no able person wanted the job.[61]

Not often well trained, some teachers were simply not qualified. As inspector Campos reported in 1873, "Nearly all the teachers were named temporarily to their posts, and their titles conferred without going through the examinations. Those teachers who had passed the exams preferred to open private schools where they made more money."[62]

There was no normal school in the entire province until the 1890s, and even then few students took training. Colegio San Vicente's normal school had only eight students in 1894.[63] Guayas had 227 public elementary school teachers in 1918; among them, 107 had no formal degree of certification. Two years later, there were 226 teachers in Guayas, of whom ninety-three lacked formal degrees. Of the teachers without formal training, most were men: due to gender discrimination, men could often get away with teaching despite having no certification, whereas women usually could not.[64] Overall, the public elementary schools exhibited little uniformity or coherence in their instructional standards.[65]

Guayaquil schools consistently earned poor report cards. A newspaper reported that the girls colegio exams consisted of little more than a series of leading questions on religious themes, followed by empty recital of memorized phrases. The boys colegio, San Vicente Rocafuerte, did no better, as reports by the minister of public education and local newspapers made plain. Ecuador's frequent civil wars disrupted the calm of intellectual reflection, leading colegio officials to declare periods of "free study." The subdirector of education for Guayas said in 1886 that "the students became accustomed to looking upon serious and conscientious study with indifference or repugnance."[66] San Vicente earned a reputation of conferring a most shallow education; it failed to offer required courses, relied on learning by rote memorization, emphasized Latin instead of practical knowledge, and hired inferior instructors who held pupils to only the very loosest academic standards. *La nación* in 1880 likened the San Vicente approach to the medical fad of homeopathy—evidently educators had similar faith in very small doses.[67]

When the state had the resources to carry out a tour of inspection of public elementary schools in the province, the reports could be withering. Inspectors Ignacio Roca and Francisco Campos visited most Guayas elementary institutions in 1873. They commented in such terms as: "in need of complete reform," "provide[s] . . . very poor service," "not possible for only one teacher to teach effectively so many diverse subjects to so many students," "need[s] all basic supplies," "lack[s] all necessities," "cramped, dirty, without ventilation . . . [and] lacking supplies," "could not even offer a visitor a chair."[68] Because the inspectors could only report and not take action, conditions were seldom corrected, as the subsequent report in 1879 by inspector Martín Tenza made abundantly plain.[69]

Although attendance was compulsory and admission free at public elementary level institutions, many school-aged children did not go. Poorer

Colegio Vicente Rocafuerte, 1928.

families could not do without the money their children might earn at work. Classes were large, with one teacher seeking to cope with sixty to a hundred or more young pupils. In the town of Morro the sole teacher had 127 boys in his classroom. Some less accommodating teachers just turned away all new students. Existing schoolhouses were often in urgent need of repair. The subdirector of studies in Guayas, Jose M. Mateus, rated the condition of the eighty-eight fiscales in Guayas in 1894 and found only fifteen to be in good condition, forty-eight in average condition, and thirty-five in bad condition.[70] Most public elementary schools—two-thirds of them in 1893—were located in rented buildings or rooms, making it difficult to modify the structures to better suit educational purposes.[71]

Rural districts experienced the most acute problems. Like farming families everywhere, parents were often especially reluctant to send their children to school. Attendance by pupils and even the instructors lagged. Rural teachers drifted in and out of positions. Ecuador's intermittent wars further disrupted the educational process. Many rural areas of Guayas province had no schools or teachers at all, especially for girls, and in districts that opened schools, students often had to walk long distances to attend. In some places the rainy season made it impossible for children to get to school for months.

Lacking facilities, some rural teachers decided simply to hold classes in their own homes or under a large tree. Country schools generally did not have enough books, and chalkboards, desks, even chairs were a luxury. Some teachers made up for their lack of pay by putting their pupils to work performing domestic chores or farm tasks. One enterprising teacher started a handicrafts business in his home using the unpaid pupils as his labor force. In some rural districts, the only students were the teachers' offspring.[72]

In sum, education in Guayaquil and rural Guayas evidenced many serious problems. Funding rose, but more slowly than the population grew. If the percentage of regular national revenue assigned to education inched upward at times, it always slumped back to previous low levels. Even by 1925, most Guayaquil children did not go to school. Higher education continued to focus on law and medicine, leaving Ecuador undersupplied with well-trained technical experts in agriculture, engineering, or business.[73] And overall, the complaints from newspaper editors, teachers, and school inspectors about the quality of education continued without pause.

Educational reform in Guayaquil was neither economically or politically necessary. The cacao export economy did not require the training of vast new legions of black-suited employees; there were already many more applicants than jobs. For the elite, whose children attended private schools or were coached by hired tutors, any concern about the state of the public institutions was only in the abstract. The tiny middle class complained about the public schools but proved too weak to press effectively for change; middle-class parents typically resorted to sending their children to private schools. Workers well understood the sorry state of public education but could do little to build the political resources to successfully campaign for school reform. If at times government moved to give more attention to education, the reform impulse lost momentum within a few years as battling caudillos again and again plunged Ecuador into civil war.

In Guayaquil as in other fast-growing cities of the time, economic success came coupled with population growth and the emergence of social challenges. Guayaquil made some progress in dealing with these conditions, and in some respects, such as in educational opportunities, life in Guayaquil was better than life elsewhere in Ecuador. But Guayaquil did not have a great amount of money to spend on city reform, and what little it had was often wasted: some was lavished on excessive military expenditures, on poorly conceived development projects, or on outlays dear to the favored elite— such as erecting elaborate bronze statues celebrating their forebears. If Guayaquil at times took steps to address its problems, grand gestures heralding the start of new projects too frequently received preference over the more mundane task of seeing the works through to completion. But in the end, the most important cause of Guayaquil's dilemma was the city's steadily increasing numbers. In the race to extend new services, Guayaquil could not keep up.

## Chapter Seven

# Disease, Health Care, and Death
# in Guayaquil

U.S. consul Charles Weile requested a leave of absence from his post in Guayaquil in 1875 due to the rapidly approaching rainy, "sickly" Guayaquil winter. When the State Department denied Consul Weile's request, he quit. He proved difficult to replace. Richard McAllister Jr. refused the post, citing the city's poor health reputation. Alexander McLean took the job, but he too soon wanted out. In explaining he wrote, "I have had the fever here twice during my incumbency [of less than a year], and my family have all been afflicted." One new U.S. minister to Ecuador, Thomas Biddle, never made it to his post in Quito: he fell victim to a fatal fever soon after debarking in Guayaquil. Wrote the U.S. consul in Guayaquil who was sending back the body, "it was a suicidal act to come here during the sickly season."[1] Throughout its history, Guayaquil claimed notoriety as one of the most disease-infested ports of the Pacific. Travelers stayed away, and diplomats avoided assignments there. If people from other nations thought anything about Guayaquil, it was that it was a death trap that should be strictly avoided regardless of one's duties.

But while foreign visitors and sailors knew the port as the "pesthole of the Pacific," civic boosters proclaimed Guayaquil the glistening "pearl of the Pacific." Both perceptions actually contained some elements of truth. Nevertheless, if the city did make progress, it still could not overcome the daunting challenges of its health conditions; Guayaquil remained a truly dangerous place to live. Beyond the difficulties of trying to make a living, guayaquileños had the added challenge of just trying to stay alive.

## Leading Health Concerns

Hospital directors and sanitation department heads of the era regarded respiratory diseases such as tuberculosis, pneumonia, and bronchitis, and digestive disorders including dysentery and diarrhea, as the largest killers in Guayaquil. Respiratory and digestive disorders together accounted for almost four of every ten deaths in Guayaquil from 1870 through 1925.[2]

Respiratory diseases presented the more serious threat, causing more than one of every five deaths in the city. The number rose from just over 400 in 1893—one of every six deaths in Guayaquil that year, to about 1,500 in 1925—one of every three deaths. Respiratory illnesses principally claimed adults and thus left many families destitute. Tuberculosis alone caused roughly half of all respiratory-related deaths; more than eight in ten tuberculosis victims were adults. The annual report of the sanitation service noted in 1913 that tuberculosis was the single leading cause of death in Guayaquil.[3] The city's high risk of respiratory illness stemmed from several factors, beginning with its housing deficiency. The dirty and crowded homes of the poor provided conditions well suited to pass the tubercle bacilli to new hosts.

Digestive illnesses, particularly dysentery and the various disorders that led to acute diarrhea, caused one of every seven deaths in Guayaquil for most of the period. The ratio had increased by 1925 to one of every three deaths. Unlike respiratory-related illnesses, digestive diseases mainly killed children; they made up nearly eight of every ten victims.

Certainly the habits of migrants contributed to the substantial threat of enteric illnesses. In their previous homes in the thinly populated countryside, people followed the practice of disposing of garbage and wastewater wherever convenient. One might get away with this in the country; in the crowded city such habits were deadly. But the main source of danger from digestive diseases was that the city quickly outgrew its existing sanitation and water services.[4]

After 1859, city workers dug a ten-mile open channel to drain human waste into the adjacent Laguna Salada. This measure did not meet the city's needs, however, and the Guayaquil dung heaps piled higher and higher. Papers ran editorials, citizens complained, but the problem only grew worse. As resident Marcos Avellan wrote in his 1876 petition to the city council, "our streets are always filthy."[5]

In 1881 the city began construction of its first sewer lines, a project not completed until 1892. Even then, the sewer lines rarely reached the poorer districts where the newcomers from the countryside crowded together. In these working-class neighborhoods, families lived packed together in foul surroundings, and the crooked, narrow trails between their shacks too often served more as sewers than streets. Winter rains would flush out the slum roads and distribute their contents throughout the city.[6]

Existing sewer lines needed repair by 1896, and by 1903 the system had all but completely broken down. The city continued to rely on colonial-era systems for sewerage disposal: open carts collected human feces from homes in open carts, hauled their loads through the streets to the piers, loaded them on lanchas, took them to the middle of the river, and dumped them. A visitor in 1914 wrote that filth continued to "accumulate . . . in the houses and patios, or courtyards, especially those of the poorer classes," and wastewater from taverns, factories, laundries, and homes slopped out all over Guayaquil.[7]

The absence of public latrines meant people away from their homes had no choice but to urinate and defecate wherever they might. Typical was the complaint of Antonio Elizalde Najar, who wrote the city council in 1893 demanding police action to stop people from using his yard as a toilet every evening after dark.[8] The Plaza Bolívar functioned as a giant open latrine. When the Colegio de San Vicente burned down, its charred remains were quickly utilized as a public toilet.[9]

In colonial times, people traveled long distances just to bathe in or drink of the supposedly salubrious waters of the Guayas River.[10] In the late nineteenth century, the poor still drank from the river during the winter, when heavy rains drove seawater downstream from the city. But as Guayaquil grew and people polluted the Guayas, the water became much less usable. Although even in the 1860s newspapers discussed how illnesses came from bad drinking water, in the 1880s poor people still hauled muddy drinking water out of the Guayas from the very piers that also served as toilets. Some got their water upstream (good water could also be found in the Río Boliche south of Guayaquil) or purchased barrels from those who did. The rich avoided the problem and favored bottled beverages.

By 1880 the city was totally dependent on water haulers, "*aguadores*," but there was widespread displeasure with their service. In an attempt to augment the city's inadequate supply of fresh water—too often fouled with garbage, offal, animal waste, or sewage—in 1886 the city council president, Dr. Francisco Campos, directed the newly created public works department to undertake construction of an aqueduct. Several foreign construction firms participated in building the line, but the project went forward haltingly, fraught with ruptured pipes, extended delays, and a great deal of bickering and bitter accusations by all involved. Piped water first flowed in 1891, and by 1902 the Agua Clara spring about fifty-six miles away began supplying fresh drinking water directly to Guayaquil.[11]

The new lines quickly proved insufficient for the steadily multiplying population. Privileged homes with indoor plumbing (by 1893, 150 homes had service) found that the water ran infrequently, usually only a few hours a day. Most people had little choice but to keep drawing on the polluted waters of the Guayas. Worse, raw sewerage seeped into poorly constructed water lines. Sanitation director L. F. Cornejo Gomez said in 1911 that Guayaquil suffered a constant lack of potable water and due to a lack of funds was utterly powerless to do anything about it.[12] The city again faced how to expand potable water supplies by 1918, when the idea gained support of pumping water directly from the nearby Río Daule and treating it with chlorine. The city sent Drs. Miguel Martínez Serrano and Ricardo Aguirre Aparicio to Lima to study a similar program there. Yet by 1921 Guayaquil still received but a fifth of the water supplies it needed. As one observer put it, "Guayaquil, surrounded by water nevertheless finds itself short."[13]

Inadequate supplies of pure water and improper sewage disposal contributed greatly to the high incidence of enteric disorders. Other water-borne maladies, especially cholera and typhoid fever, also posed grave health hazards. Cholera was rarer, if deadlier when contracted, than typhoid fever, which afflicted more people but whose victims stood a better chance of recovery. Typhoid fever was one of Guayaquil's leading health risks, twice causing 200 deaths in a year and accounting for one of every twenty deaths in the city; it claimed adults and children evenly.[14] Intestinal worms, also associated with tainted water supplies and improper waste disposal, probably lived in most guayaquileños. Worms seldom killed their hosts but left some weakened and vulnerable to other maladies that would.

The death toll from respiratory and digestive diseases, Guayaquil's leading killers, never really declined, and residents tended to view their presence as almost inevitable. Guayaquileños expressed much more concern over the periodic epidemics. Probably the most dreaded was yellow fever, which slipped into the city aboard ships from contaminated ports (often Panamá), or sometimes from the surrounding lowlands. Either way, it was devastating. Spread by the bite of *Aedes aegypti* mosquitoes, yellow fever probably first hit Guayaquil in 1842, when half the population fled in terror and more than 4,000 died.[15] Another serious epidemic appeared in 1903, when yellow fever caused more than one in ten deaths in the city and killed a third to a half of those infected. Guayaquil suffered repeated epidemics (1877, 1878, 1880, 1890–91, 1883, 1884, 1886, 1902, 1909, 1911, 1912, and 1913). Surprisingly, nearly all victims were adult males; urban yellow fever (as distinct from jungle yellow fever) is generally not considered gender-selective (see table 7.4).[16] It is possible that the typical outdoor occupations of men in the

Guayaquil—as construction workers, vendors, cacao handlers, and long-shoremen—placed them outdoors near greater concentrations of mosquitoes and consequently at greater risk.

An outbreak of yellow fever could startle the city council into action, but until the origins and spread of the disease were discovered in 1900, governments everywhere found themselves powerless to do much to stop it. The 1880–81 epidemic that claimed 472 lives was known as the *"aduanera* fever" or customhouse fever because workers there were most heavily afflicted; city health officials and others reasoned that because the epidemic seemed to cluster along the waterfront, the trouble likely came from the prevalent piles of rotting ship cargo. But many also believed at the time that the disease came from cigar smoke, or from any decaying organic matter, such as table scraps. The Guayaquil city council ordered a special religious ceremony (at taxpayer expense) and repeatedly fired cannons into the air, hoping to drive off foul airs but succeeding only in driving the community into panic. However, the Junta Sanitaria (sanitation commission), under city council authority, also recommended a vigorous sanitation campaign that encompassed ventilating storehouses, organizing better trash pick up, and disposing of dead animals by burning them or by depositing the carcasses in the middle of the river rather than along the shore.[17]

A better understanding of the cause of yellow fever began to develop after the turn of the century but did not assure effective action against it in Guayaquil. The sanitation director, in his 1910 report, explained with singular lucidity what had to be done to halt the spread of yellow fever. He knew what to do, but, he added, "we need money, without which a sanitation campaign is impossible."[18]

Guayaquil was one of the few cities on the South American continent where yellow fever still manifested a serious threat in 1909, and by 1916, it was perhaps the only such city. Ultimately, the Rockefeller Yellow Fever Commission helped Guayaquil eradicate the disease in 1919. Guayaquil's scant reserve of fresh drinking water had led people to store their supplies in tanks, cisterns, and barrels; by doing so, they unwittingly furnished the yellow fever vector, the *Aedes aegypti* mosquito, with plentiful and ideal breeding grounds. Guayaquil became the first city to use fish in its anti-yellow fever campaign: people covered their fresh-water containers and released minnows, or *chalacos,* in the tanks. The fish ate the mosquito larvae, thereby consuming the source of Guayaquil's yellow fever.[19]

Another mosquito-borne disease, malaria, spread by *anopheles* mosquitoes, hit hardest when heat and rains peaked. While hospital and cemetery records might seem to indicate that malaria became more prevalent after the turn of the century, it was almost certainly present before then. Prior to 1900, medical authorities did not keep separate tallies on malaria but simply grouped it with various maladies under the heading "other fevers." Although not highly lethal—for every victim who died of malaria, another twenty-five recovered—the threat from malaria never completely ebbed; the yearly death toll seldom fell much below 200 lives and often reached 500. Some years malaria accounted for more than one of every nine deaths in the city. Children made up three-fourths of its victims, a pattern typical for regions where malaria is endemic. City sanitation director L. Becerra noted in 1912 that "the [undrained] streets of the city offered very good conditions for breeding different species of mosquitoes."[20]

Guayaquil's tropical equatorial climate provided excellent opportunities for illnesses to take hold and spread, and finding near-perfect breeding conditions, the disease-carrying mosquitoes flourished. The homes of Guayaquil's poor typically lacked glass or screen coverings over windows. Moreover, most guayaquileños had but slight natural immunity to disease. The many newcomers from isolated rural hamlets had in moving to a crowded city incurred a very high risk of contracting novel sicknesses. Yellow fever, which imparts immunity to previously exposed populations, never spread to the sierra; the disease-carrying mosquitoes only live in coastal regions. Malaria likewise concentrated in lowland regions and killed a higher percentage among populations that had not yet experienced the disease.[21]

As a port city, Guayaquil took in travelers from other lands every day, placing the city in constant danger of infection with diseases from all over the globe. Thus bubonic plague came from Asia and arrived in Guayaquil in 1908. Instantly, it swept through the city, and again, the city's response was essentially ineffectual. The sanitation department dispatched workmen to homes where someone had died of the plague, and there the laborers would set their efforts on tearing the roof off the house. The theory was that the sun's rays would disinfect and purify the dwelling. Sanitation workers also poisoned all the rats they could find, but this too was of little avail, for Guayaquil's rat population was just too large. The city sanitation director said, "Their number increases geometrically."[22] But some good came from the various city efforts, as workers ripped down many substandard, ramshackle buildings. Police conducted door-to-door inspections to enforce sanitation orders, in a campaign that the public generally supported.

Sanitation workers also tried to inspect everything transported out of Guayaquil in an effort to keep other parts of Ecuador from becoming infected. However, by 1909 the epidemic had spread inland. When the national government learned that plague had advanced inland to Huigra, it ordered the town completely leveled. The plague progressed onward nevertheless, working its way up the railway line. As the epidemic approached the highlands, the North American physician stationed there by the U.S.–owned railway company, Dr. Max Meitzner, fled for his life; he had only shortly before been named by the Ecuadorian government subdirector of sanitation for the sierra.[23]

Guayaquil established a vaccination service, but the program met only limited success. In 1913, when plague again struck, nearly 20,000 people took the Linfa Haffkine anti–bubonic plague vaccine. The shot, however, afforded protection for only a few months, and 2 percent of those inoculated contracted the disease.[24] Up to 1917, bubonic plague often claimed more than three hundred lives a year—one-tenth of all deaths in the city; it then gradually subsided but did not disappear. Unlike yellow fever, plague affected both genders evenly, but it did afflict more adults than children. A particularly lethal disease, the plague usually killed one-third or more of those infected (see table 7.1).[25]

Given bubonic plague's reputation, it is not surprising that officials tried either to deny its existence or, in the face its undeniable presence, shift blame for the problem onto other towns. In 1910, for example, the police chief stressed that many plague victims came into the city from the surrounding rural districts.[26] While no doubt true, this obscured the fact that the miserable sanitary conditions of Guayaquil and the generally dirty living circumstances of the poor allowed bubonic plague to develop and spread within the city. In 1919, officials declared that bubonic plague no longer was a health concern in Guayaquil.[27] This claim was simply not true, as fifty-nine plague victims in 1920 might have attested had they survived.

Two highly communicable childhood diseases, measles and smallpox, also took many lives. Measles, although not usually lethal, could at times pose a threat, as in 1888 when more than 550 fell victim to it. It reappeared periodically and in 1920 claimed the lives of more than 200 children—one of every twenty-five deaths in the city that year. Smallpox was likewise a sporadic disease that reached epidemic rates among children every few years. Deadlier than measles, the worst smallpox outbreak hit in 1890; more than 400 children died that year, and their deaths accounted for one of every seven in Guayaquil.[28]

The city had a longstanding smallpox prevention program, but immunization campaigns frequently began only after the disease had started to spread.[29] The Ecuadorian medical community increasingly recognized by the 1890s that the old "arm-to-arm" immunization method had drawbacks; it was still employed, though, because vaccine was scarce. Moreover, authorities typically found that when they needed the vaccine, the supplies had

**Table 7.1.** Patient care at Guayaquil's public health facilities, selected years, 1818–1925

| Year | Hospital Civil | | | Insane Asylum | | | Military Hospital | | |
|---|---|---|---|---|---|---|---|---|---|
| | *treated* | *died* | *%* | *treated* | *died* | *%* | *treated* | *died* | *%* |
| 1818 | — | — | 17 | — | — | — | — | — | — |
| 1819 | 3,640[a] | 514 | 14 | — | — | — | — | — | — |
| 1874 | — | — | — | — | — | 503 | 3 | 1 | |
| 1875 | 5,391 | 672 | 12 | — | — | — | — | — | — |
| 1881[b] | 3,728 | 634 | 17 | 91 | 6 | 7 | — | 38 | — |
| 1883[b] | 4,371 | 741 | 17 | 139 | 12 | 9 | — | — | — |
| 1884[b] | 4,738 | 647 | 14 | 160 | 18 | 11 | — | — | — |
| 1885[b] | 4,511 | 503 | 11 | 126 | 9 | 7 | — | — | — |
| 1886[b] | 5,778 | 646 | 11 | 141 | 10 | 7 | — | — | — |
| 1887[b] | 5,861 | 849 | 15 | 154 | 11 | 7 | — | — | — |
| 1888[b] | 6,639 | — | — | — | — | — | — | — | — |
| 1889[b] | 7,541 | 975 | 13 | 610 | 81 | 13 | — | 73 | — |
| 1890 | 6,852 | 742 | 11 | 199 | 20 | 10 | — | 64 | — |
| 1891 | 7,780 | 895 | 12 | 413 | 47 | 11 | 2,767 | 59 | 2 |
| 1892 | 5,097 | 678 | 13 | 348 | 41 | 12 | — | — | — |
| 1893 | 6,100 | 656 | 11 | 342 | 37 | 11 | — | 46 | — |
| 1894 | 7,003 | 700 | 10 | 264 | 24 | 9 | — | 78 | — |
| 1895 | 9,010 | 878 | 10 | 297 | 20 | 7 | — | 60 | — |
| 1897 | 11,119 | 989 | 9 | 287 | 28 | 10 | 3,551 | 102 | 3 |
| 1898 | 9,113 | 604 | 7 | 296 | 16 | 5 | 2,749 | 24 | 1 |
| 1899 | 9,282 | 600 | 6 | 298 | 31 | 10 | — | 27 | — |
| 1900 | 9,411 | 654 | 7 | 280 | 48 | 17 | — | — | — |
| 1901 | 9,923 | 704 | 7 | — | — | — | — | — | — |
| 1902 | 7,711 | 544 | 7 | 296 | 36 | 12 | — | — | — |
| 1903 | 5,076 | 525 | 10 | 275 | 61 | 22 | 1,018[a] | 32 | — |
| 1904[b] | 6,361 | 431 | 7 | 274 | 24 | 8 | 699[a] | 21 | — |
| 1905[b] | 7,643 | 488 | 6 | 265 | 32 | 12 | 1,336[a] | 36 | — |
| 1906 | 8,337 | 587 | 7 | — | — | — | — | — | — |
| 1908 | 5,414 | 426 | 8 | 218 | 33 | 15 | 1,401 | 9 | 1 |
| 1909 | 6,289 | 523 | 8 | 242 | 15 | 6 | 991 | 17 | 2 |
| 1910 | 6,084 | 390 | 6 | 265 | 18 | 7 | — | — | — |
| 1911 | 7,308 | 426 | 6 | 283 | 25 | 9 | — | — | — |
| 1914 | 7,093 | 503 | 7 | 332 | 30 | 9 | — | 34 | — |
| 1917 | 8,623 | 305 | 4 | 295 | 21 | 7 | — | 12 | — |
| 1919 | 10,757 | 542 | 5 | 290 | 28 | 10 | — | 7 | — |
| 1920 | 11,137 | 561 | 5 | 275 | 16 | 6 | — | 4 | — |
| 1922 | 12,727 | 540 | 4 | 317 | 44 | 14 | — | 2 | — |
| 1924 | 15,595 | 556 | 4 | 295 | 20 | 7 | — | 4 | — |
| 1925 | 17,393 | 634 | 4 | 304 | 36 | 12 | — | — | — |

**Table 7.1.** continued

| Year | HOSPICIO DEL CORAZÓN DE JESUS | | | ASILO MANN/HOSPITAL CENTRAL (ANNEX) | | | TB ASYLUM CORONEL/ C. ROMERO | | |
|---|---|---|---|---|---|---|---|---|---|
| | treated | died | % | treated | died | % | treated | died | % |
| 1892 | 123 | 6 | 5 | — | — | — | — | — | — |
| 1893 | 260 | 33 | 13 | — | — | — | — | — | — |
| 1894 | 351 | 32 | 9 | — | — | — | — | — | — |
| 1895 | 312 | 42 | 13 | — | — | — | — | — | — |
| 1897 | 577 | 56 | 10 | — | — | — | — | — | — |
| 1898 | 668 | 65 | 10 | — | — | — | — | — | — |
| 1899 | 722 | 53 | 7 | — | — | — | — | — | — |
| 1900 | 929 | 85 | 9 | — | — | — | — | — | — |
| 1901 | 1,014 | 68 | 7 | — | — | — | — | — | — |
| 1902 | 739 | 84 | 11 | — | — | — | 315 | 168 | 53 |
| 1903 | 340 | 44 | 13 | — | — | — | 391 | 202 | 52 |
| 1904[b] | 356 | 38 | 11 | 1,490[a] | 86 | — | 331 | 144 | 44 |
| 1905[b] | 411 | 50 | 12 | 1,640[a] | 72 | — | 419 | 172 | 41 |
| 1906 | 395 | 43 | 11 | — | — | — | 339 | 186 | 55 |
| 1908 | 304 | 28 | 9 | 1,125 | 46 | 4 | 221 | 119 | 54 |
| 1909 | 268 | 22 | 8 | 1,118 | 61 | 5 | 105 | 62 | 59 |
| 1910 | 248 | 19 | 8 | — | — | — | 295 | 118 | 40 |
| 1911 | 223 | 30 | 13 | — | — | — | 401 | 157 | 39 |
| 1914 | 254 | 35 | 14 | 3,083 | 154 | 5 | 680[b] | 163 | 24 |
| 1917 | 350 | 49 | 14 | 3,386 | 132 | 4 | 520 | 258 | 50 |
| 1919[b] | 377 | 94 | 25 | 8,283 | 278 | 3 | 673 | 324 | 48 |
| 1920[b] | 342 | 46 | 13 | 8,415 | 330 | 4 | 530 | 286 | 54 |
| 1922[b] | 324 | 62 | 19 | 5,047 | 150 | 3 | 468 | 245 | 52 |
| 1924[b] | 327 | 48 | 15 | 9,086 | 215 | 2 | 477 | 265 | 56 |
| 1925[b] | 361 | 65 | 18 | 5,805 | 173 | 3 | 585 | 329 | 56 |

| Year | YELLOW FEVER QUARANTINE | | | BUBONIC PLAGUE QUARANTINE | | | SMALLPOX QUARANTINE | | |
|---|---|---|---|---|---|---|---|---|---|
| | treated | died | % | treated | died | % | treated | died | % |
| 1905[b] | 176[a] | 60 | | (combined quarantine) | | | — | — | — |
| 1908 | 54 | 33 | 61 | 588 | 274 | 47 | — | — | — |
| 1909 | 480 | 221 | 46 | 912 | 320 | 35 | 16 | 1 | 6 |
| 1910 | 320 | 114 | 36 | 731 | 266 | 36 | — | — | — |
| 1911 | 369 | 152 | 41 | 524 | 202 | 39 | — | — | — |
| 1912 | 565 | 263 | 47 | 504 | 188 | 37 | — | — | — |
| 1913 | 342 | 186 | 54 | 774 | 304 | 39 | — | — | — |
| 1914 | 67 | 23 | 34 | 459 | 155 | 34 | — | — | — |
| 1915 | 3 | 3 | — | 178 | 58 | 33 | — | — | — |
| 1917 | 231 | 67 | 29 | 428 | 136 | 32 | 72 | 11 | 15 |
| 1918 | 480 | — | — | — | — | — | — | — | — |
| 1919 | 266 | 87 | 33 | 79 | 20 | 25 | — | — | — |

**Table 7.1.** continued

| | YELLOW FEVER QUARANTINE | | | BUBONIC PLAGUE QUARANTINE | | | SMALLPOX QUARANTINE | | |
|------|---------|------|---|---------|------|----|---------|------|---|
| Year | treated | died | % | treated | died | % | treated | died | % |
| 1920 | — | — | — | 240 | 62 | 26 | 78 | 3 | 4 |
| 1922 | — | — | — | — | 17 | — | — | — | — |
| 1924 | — | — | — | 176 | 54 | 31 | — | 1 | — |
| 1925 | — | — | — | 128 | 52 | 41 | — | — | — |

*Sources:* PCC, *Informes, 1881–1892;* IP, *Informes, 1890–1910;* JB, *Memorias, 1893–1925;* GG, *Informe, 1901;* SS, *Informe, 1911, 1913, 1914; El Ecuador: guía comercial, agrícola e industrial de la república,* 681–737; Ecuador, Consulate of Ecuador, New York. *Republic of Ecuador* (1921), 30, reprinted in GBFO, "Report," January 1922; Estrada Ycaza, *El hospital,* 88, 113, 149, 159; Estrada Ycaza, "Apuntes para la historia del Hospital Militar," 42.
[a]New entrants only, preexisting population unknown.
[b]Estimate

all lost potency. Guayaquil then had to wait several months for new serum from Lima or Europe; meanwhile, epidemics such as those of 1893, 1905, and 1908 already had run their course. After 1910, the vaccination program finally began to reach more people, and the director of sanitation closed the facility that had served as a quarantine. The disease did not again return to Guayaquil in force, although it continued to kill children elsewhere in coastal Ecuador.[30]

Another disease that represented a fairly steady low-level threat in Guayaquil was tetanus, or lockjaw, which frequently claimed more than one hundred lives a year and particularly afflicted the young. Newborns were at high risk if unsterile instruments were used during delivery, and older children faced danger because they were apt to go barefoot. It is probable that deaths from tetany—often confused with tetanus—may also have been added in the records to those caused by tetanus. Tetany, the severe muscle convulsions caused by extreme calcium and vitamin D deficiencies, often appeared at weaning. In any case, Guayaquil made practically no progress in quelling tetanus: it was still a significant health hazard in 1925.

Finally, deaths by accidental or violent causes also became a greater concern. More street traffic, especially trolley cars, inevitably brought more collisions. Murder rates also rose. Only fifteen people died from violence or accidents in 1892; by 1911, 115 did, and many more suffered serious injuries. Most victims were men. Accidents or violence crippled or maimed about 500 people in 1904, and among them, more than eight of ten were men.[31]

In all, then, from dysentery and tuberculosis to yellow fever, malaria, and murder, chances for an early grave abounded in Guayaquil.

## Medicine

Even in the most advanced nations, let alone Ecuador, conventional thinking about the origin, spread, and treatment of disease continued to rely until the late 1800s upon centuries-old medical wisdom little improved by time.[32] Prevailing opinion had held that disease spread either by contagion or infested airs, miasmas, tainted by putrefying organic material. Physicians commonly believed that all disease stemmed from a single cause—poisons in the system—and thus mandated the use of heroic measures to rid toxins from the body. The measures included blistering, daily bleedings of twelve or more ounces, enemas (and if bleeding from the anus resulted from repeated applications, so much the better), and harsh drugs to promote purging and sweating. Accepted theories of medicine consisted of little more than attempts to rationalize such procedures. For much of the nineteenth century, then, medical care everywhere continued to be based upon serious misconceptions; treatment too often proved to be ineffective or even harmful. Of course, some patients recovered despite the ministrations of doctors.

Even prior to the development of modern scientific understanding of the origin and spread of disease, some public health care measures were still effective. Quarantining and early forms of vaccination proved fairly successful in combating such illnesses as bubonic plague and smallpox. In Guayaquil, as elsewhere, the prevailing notion that disease stemmed from evil miasmas led officials to call for cleanup campaigns to rid the city of the sources of the foul winds. Obviously such measures could be beneficial. Draining pools of water shrank mosquito breeding areas, thereby reducing the risk of malaria and yellow fever. Hauling away human waste, offal, and garbage reduced the chance that drinking water and food would be contaminated, thereby lowering the threat from enteric disorders, cholera, and typhoid fever. Cleaning and disinfecting living quarters reduced the risk of tuberculosis, and controlling the flea population in dwellings helped lower the threat from bubonic plague and typhus.

Nevertheless, in the days when physicians and health care officials lacked a complete understanding of the origin and spread of many of these afflictions, most public sanitation efforts still had a hit-or-miss quality. Cleaning all the belongings of bubonic plague victims in an autoclave was costly and not really necessary. There was no benefit from fumigating all the letters that arrived from infected ports. Firing cannons into the air just spread alarm. And special city expenditures for religious ceremonies benefited presumably only the souls, not the bodies, of the pious.

Then, in nineteenth-century western Europe, several vitally important medical breakthroughs led to new understanding of the origins and prevention of disease. The application of this knowledge in Europe and the United States soon fostered improvements in medicine and public health, bringing an end to the use of time-honored orthodox medical practices and a decline in the appeal of pseudo-scientific fads. Research won wider acceptance for the germ theory of disease. Advances came in surgery, as developments in the use of anesthesia—ether and later chloroform—allowed surgeons to control pain during operations. U.S. and European hospitals adopted sterile methods. With the introduction of asepsis and anesthesia, surgical death rates fell and physicians could attempt new types of operations. Further progress in techniques and apparatus brought the stethoscope, thermometer, and microscope into widespread usage in the United States and western Europe. X-rays, discovered in 1895, were used in U.S. hospitals before 1900. After the early years of the twentieth century, chemical examination of blood and urine also became common in the United States. The age of modern medicine had begun.

But news of this progress spread unevenly in the western world, and outdated notions of treatment lingered in places like Ecuador that were removed from the centers of intellectual and scientific advancement. In time, most medical advances found their way south, but the pace of change was slow and understanding and acceptance of new methods often incomplete.

Medical education in Ecuador centered in Quito, which had produced physicians since the seventeenth century. The coast opened its first medical school in 1867 at the University of Guayaquil; the seven faculty members were not actually inducted until 1877, however, and the dedication of a permanent building did not take place until 1888. By 1892, the Guayaquil medical faculty had grown to thirteen; the faculty did not expand after that. The university opened a dentistry department in 1904, but it produced no graduates until 1922. Still, the medical profession in Guayaquil gradually progressed, as evidenced by the emergence of at least four medical societies, the publication of five medical journals, and the hosting of the first national medical congress in 1915. The doctor-patient ratio in Ecuador also improved. There were eighty-one licensed doctors in 1863 to serve a population of about 893,000, for a ratio of one physician for 11,025 people; by 1909, there were 236 doctors in a population of 1,643,000, a ratio of one to about 7,000.[33]

However, not all practicing physicians in Ecuador had formal training or licenses; many fakes dispensed dubious cure-alls, and some pharmacists sold tainted or impure drugs. Even medical school graduates were not always well prepared. Ecuador's constant civil strife frequently led to the closure of the universities and the declaration of "free study." And when in session the universities did not always provide a sound education. Students encountered a dearth of medical reference material; the public library had the only real collection in the late nineteenth century, and it numbered but 266 books on medicine.[34] The national government in 1889 contracted a leading German medical bacteriologist, Dr. Gustavo von Lagerheim of Hamburg, to train Quito doctors in the latest European advances and the path-breaking work of Robert Koch and Louis Pasteur. Lagerheim brought the first microscope to Ecuador. It got little use, as Lagerheim received a chilly reception from the highlands medical community. Exasperated by the lack of interest in his work and upset by the hostility to his Protestantism, he packed and left in a huff in 1892.[35]

Knowledge of new developments eventually arrived, notably to the port city, which was historically less isolated and traditional than Quito, and medical practice began to modernize. Most leading Ecuadorian physicians traveled abroad to receive advanced medical schooling. The national government gave scholarships for foreign study toward the end of the nineteenth century; more scholarships went to students from Quito than from Guayaquil. Most students went to western Europe, though some chose to go to the United States—at the time a very poor second choice.[36] By the 1890s, Ecuador's universities offered instruction in bacteriology and required hands-on training at the hospital as well as formal classroom lectures. In the field of surgery, physicians first used ether in Guayaquil in 1894 and aseptic surgical methods by 1898. X-rays were in use in Guayaquil in 1908. Ecuadorian surgeons performed hysterectomies by 1907; by 1912 they performed Cesarean sections on living mothers (such operations on mothers who died in delivery had been used for some time); and in Guayaquil in 1919, the first blood transfusion in Ecuador took place. As medicine was conducted on a more scientific and rational basis in Ecuador, formally trained and licensed doctors gained prestige.[37]

## Public Medical Facilities

In Guayaquil and elsewhere, the traditional role of hospitals was that of workhouse and warehouse for the aged, mentally retarded, insane, blind, or lame. By the late nineteenth century, the mission of the hospitals had evolved into one more singularly medical. Guayaquil hospitals overflowed with groaning, suffering, soon-to-die patients. Many of the poor avoided the public health facilities although the services were usually free of charge. Rather than risk treatment at one of the city institutions, many preferred to take their chances with traditional folk remedies or, increasingly, medicated themselves with imported patented medicines.

There were many medicines from which to pick. Asthmatics could try tar and eucalyptus syrup or Grimault cigarettes. Fosters Pills and La Urotropina Schering were said to cure all manner of urinary-tract disorders and dysfunction. Better still, Mallen Pills cured everything, according to the company's ads. If they did not, Dr. T. Frank Lynott of Chicago would send, for a small fee, a pamphlet that explained how to cure oneself.[38]

Those who could afford the rising fees of private doctors received professional medical attention at home. Public hospitals did not have rooms for paying customers, and private clinics were few—three in 1900 and six in 1925.[39] Among the privileged, even major surgery was often done at home or, if not too urgent, in Europe. Though stricken with a contagious epidemic disease, a wealthy patient could generally make arrangements with his or her private physician to prevent being sent to a city quarantine, as the law otherwise required.

The public health care facilities almost exclusively served the poor, and then, perhaps, as a desperate last resort. Only as modern practices were gradually introduced in the twentieth century and conditions slowly improved did the popular image of hospital-as-death-house began to change. In time, the introduction of modern medical machinery, often expensive and immobile, meant that wealthy patients for the first time also had to consider going to the hospitals to receive care.[40]

Despite greater use of hospitals, more than two-thirds of deaths still occurred at home. About 2,500 of the 3,500 deaths in the city in 1914 occurred in private dwellings. Interestingly, in that year 90 percent of the child deaths took place at home, while 50 percent of adult deaths occurred at home. A practice among working-class parents probably accounts for the difference: they hired doctors to come to their homes to treat their gravely ill children, but if they got sick themselves, they would submit themselves to hospital care.

In 1887, the city council authorized the newly formed Junta de Beneficencia to run most of the city's health care facilities and provide burials for those who died destitute. Junta members included women of the elite families and such leading men of the area as José Luís Tamayo, who became president of Ecuador, and Efren Aspiazu of the fabulously wealthy cacao-growing Aspiazus of Los Ríos province. Funds for the city's charity organization came from the municipal and national governments, lotteries, charitable grants, and rents from donated properties. Those sources did not provide enough money to cover costs, however, and after only five years, the junta lapsed deeply into permanent state of debt.[41]

Despite its limited resources, the Junta sought to respond to the health concerns of Guayaquil by opening several new facilities. Before the 1880s, Guayaquil had only two health care centers, the Hospital Caridad, operated by the city, and the military hospital, run by the provincial government. Soon the Junta added a maternity hospital, insane asylum, tuberculosis center, quarantines for bubonic plague, yellow fever, and smallpox, a vaccination facility, and several orphanages. Catholic nuns working in the institutions, the Hermanas de la Caridad, won praise for their patient care. The expansion of services brought benefits: more people received treatment, and city mortality rates showed a slow, if uneven, decline. Yet despite all efforts, very serious problems remained.[42]

The busiest facility was the city hospital, known at different times as the Hospital Caridad, Hospital Civil, and Hospital General. The total annual number of patients rose from about 4,000 in 1881 to more than 17,000 in 1925; the gain, however, owed more to rapid handling of patients than to an increase in the number of beds (see table 7.1). At the end of 1875, the hospital had 255 patients. Fifty years later, the hospital counted 622 patients at the end of the year (see table 7.2). Thus while the annual number of people treated at the hospital quadrupled, the ordinary, daily patient population roughly doubled. Doctors treated patients with greater alacrity.

City council president José María Urvina Jado wrote in 1881 that the hospital was in need of substantial renovation. The facility had particular need for special operating rooms, as doctors had to perform surgery in full view of other patients.[43] A fire at the military hospital in 1887 forced the transfer of patients to the Hospital Civil, which resulted in extreme crowding.[44] As the hospital filled up, administrators had little recourse but to send the overflow to be housed at the insane asylum. The chief of the Hospital Civil, Dr. D. Frederico Mateus, wrote an exceptionally scathing report in 1893, complaining that the building was hot, crowded, and understaffed, and had foul, disease-ridden air throughout. He called for the building of a special wing for those with infectious illnesses. Contagious diseases had spread rapidly among the already weakened population, and many patients who arrived suffering relatively mild complaints soon caught yellow fever and died while at the hospital.[45]

The citywide blaze of 1902 gutted the hospital, and patients had to be shifted to the already full Asilo de Maternidad Alejandro Mann, the maternity annex. The Junta de Beneficencia quickly arranged a loan from the Banco del Ecuador (plunging the Junta yet deeper into debt) to build a new facility; two years later it opened the new Hospital General. With the gradual adoption of modern medical practices, mortality rates began at last to fall. In its 1905 report to Congress, the justice and welfare ministry singled out the hospital—unique in that it was supported almost entirely with city and not national funds—as the best in Ecuador.[46] Its record continued to improve: in

**Table 7.2.** Daily patient population at Guayaquil health care facilities, selected years, 1874–1925 (patients present at the end of each year)

| Year | Hospital civil | Insane asylum | Military hospital | Hospicio del C. de Jesus | Asilo Mann/ Annex |
|------|------|------|------|------|------|
| 1874 | 306 | — | 81 | — | — |
| 1875 | 255 | — | — | — | — |
| 1880 | 252 | — | — | — | — |
| 1881 | 305 | 47 | — | — | — |
| 1886 | — | 88 | — | — | — |
| 1888 | 404 | 126 | — | — | — |
| 1889 | 356 | 131 | — | — | — |
| 1890 | 418 | 112 | 131 | — | — |
| 1891 | 419 | 122 | 221 | — | — |
| 1892 | 328 | 122 | — | 81 | — |
| 1893 | 395 | 130 | — | 122 | — |
| 1894 | 371 | 139 | — | 126 | — |
| 1895 | 368 | 166 | — | 128 | — |
| 1896 | 404 | 182 | 114 | 186 | — |
| 1897 | 396 | 178 | 111 | 215 | — |
| 1898 | 373 | 198 | 72 | 275 | — |
| 1899 | 386 | 169 | — | 301 | — |
| 1900 | 419 | 157 | — | 374 | — |
| 1901 | 380 | 156 | — | 316 | — |
| 1902 | 252 | 154 | — | 208 | — |
| 1905 | 313 | — | — | 233 | — |
| 1906 | 349 | — | — | 282 | — |
| 1908 | 378 | 127 | 114 | 195 | 69 |
| 1909 | 214 | 138 | 71 | 194 | 95 |
| 1910 | 458 | 170 | — | 174 | 86 |
| 1911 | 484 | 173 | — | 169 | 59 |
| 1912 | — | — | — | — | — |
| 1913 | 455 | 169 | — | 169 | — |
| 1914 | 470 | 226 | — | 171 | — |
| 1916 | 343 | 169 | — | 231 | — |
| 1917 | 442 | 185 | — | 234 | 132 |
| 1918 | 500 | 192 | — | 248 | — |
| 1919 | 564 | 185 | — | 233 | — |
| 1920 | 512 | 168 | — | 240 | — |
| 1921 | 521 | 170 | — | 207 | — |
| 1922 | 475 | 155 | — | 230 | — |
| 1923 | 506 | 165 | — | 230 | — |
| 1924 | 860 | 178 | — | 240 | — |
| 1925 | 622 | 166 | — | 244 | — |

**Table 7.2.** continued

| Year | TB asylum | Yellow Fever Quarantine | Bubonic Plague Quarantine | Smallpox Quarantine |
|------|-----------|-------------------------|---------------------------|---------------------|
| 1902 | 40 | — | — | — |
| 1905 | 42 | — | — | — |
| 1906 | 28 | — | — | — |
| 1908 | 15 | 1 | 9 | — |
| 1909 | 18 | 14 | 46 | — |
| 1910 | 29 | 2 | 11 | — |
| 1911 | 30 | 13 | 19 | — |
| 1912 | — | 6 | 47 | — |
| 1913 | — | 3 | 49 | — |
| 1914 | — | 0 | 45 | — |
| 1916 | 31 | 5 | 57 | 0 |
| 1917 | 53 | 2 | 55 | 4 |
| 1918 | 56 | 18 | 3 | — |
| 1919 | 67 | 0 | 1 | 0 |
| 1920 | 60 | — | 49 | 18 |
| 1921 | 43 | — | — | — |
| 1922 | 34 | — | — | — |
| 1923 | 47 | — | 24 | — |
| 1924 | 55 | — | 2 | — |
| 1925 | 52 | — | 11 | — |

*Sources:* Samaniego, *Cronología médica ecuatoriana,* 211, 212; Mauro Madero, *Historia de la medicina,* 274; PCC, *Informes, 1881–1892;* IP, *Informes, 1890–1910;* JB, *Memorias, 1893–1925;* GG, *Informe, 1901;* SS, *Informe, 1913, 1914; El Ecuador: guía comercial,* 681–737; Estrada Ycaza, *El hospital Guayaquil,* 159.
Note: The Hospital Civil was also known as the Hospital General.

1881 and again in 1883 almost one in five of those treated at the old hospital had died, but by the 1920s only one in twenty at the new facility died.

The military hospital was one of Guayaquil's oldest health care institutions, although one of declining importance. When the new building opened in 1891, following a fire, almost 3,000 men yearly received treatment at the military hospital; by 1909 it handled fewer than 1,000. Its usual daily patient population fell from 200-plus at the end of 1891 to about seventy in 1909 (see tables 7.2 and 7.3).[47]

As the provincial government phased out the military hospital, Guayaquil opened several small hospitals, auxiliaries, and annexes. One was the Hospicio del Corazón de Jesus, founded in 1892, and at the time probably the most modern medical institution in the city.[48] However, as with Guayaquil's other hospitals, it soon became crowded. The staff treated about 120 people the year the hospital opened and more than 1,000 just nine years later. Eventually, as other facilities appeared, the annual patient load fell to about 300.

The number of patients in the facility at the end of each year rose from eighty in 1892 to a peak of over 370 in 1900, and then leveled out at about 200 during the 1920s (see table 7.2). Death rates jumped sharply at the hospital over the period, probably because it was asked to care for more of the city's sickest patients. In its first year of operation only 5 percent of patients died, but soon the institution was losing more than 10 percent in most years and in 1919 lost 25 percent of those under its care (see table 7.1).

The Asilo de Maternidad Alejandro Mann, an annex to the Hospital Civil, operated primarily as a maternity and children's hospital beginning in 1903. Built with 25,000 sucres from the Junta de Beneficencia and a 25,000-sucre donation from Guayaquil philanthropist Alejandro Mann, the institution handled more than 3,000 patients in 1914 and between 5,000 and 9,000 patients annually by the 1920s (see tables 7.2 and 7.3). Hospital directors frequently declared the facility sorely deficient and compiled long lists of specific shortcomings. The director in 1914 noted in a report that the entire building needed immediate repair: the annex lacked electric lights, adequate plumbing, private rooms for operations, separate quarters for contagious diseases, and a place to bathe patients.[49]

The city also operated special tuberculosis centers, though the facilities could have done very little to help patients; doctors the world over at that time could offer almost no positive treatment for tuberculosis. What the institutions really provided was community protection by isolating the highly contagious victims. The first tuberculosis hospital, Asilo Coronel, opened in 1902, but the city soon had to use the building as a quarantine for bubonic plague and yellow fever victims. The city opened a new tuberculosis asylum, Asilo Calixto Romero, in 1910.[50] It was no real improvement. Sanitation director L. F. Cornejo Gomez called the new facility little more than a warehouse.[51] The city tuberculosis asylums treated about 300 people in 1902 and handled about 400 to 700 victims annually over the following two decades. It typically housed about thirty patients at a time, the majority of them men (see table 7.4). Only with the deepest reluctance could one have entered these institutions, for in most years more than half of all patients died (see table 7.1).

The yellow fever and bubonic plague quarantines, set up as permanent establishments in 1905, had perhaps the darkest reputation of all city institutions. Guayaquileños called them "death's waiting rooms."[52] The yellow fever quarantine often had more than 200 patients a year and as many as 560 in 1912 (see table 7.1).[53] Doctors could do nothing to help victims; even today there is no known cure for yellow fever. Hoping for the best was all doctor and patient could do. Busier was the bubonic plague quarantine, which often handled more than 400 patients a year and in 1909 treated more than

Hospicio del Corazón de Jesus, 1925.

900 (see table 7.2). The mortality rates at the quarantines rivaled those of the tuberculosis asylum; in most years at least a third died, in bad years more than half. Director L. Becerra said of the quarantines in his 1912 report, "these establishments need substantial reform"—and "right away."[54]

The plague quarantine certainly needed improvement. It had no electricity, and rooms lacked water, blankets, and bedding. The doctor in charge of the yellow fever asylum, W. Pareja, felt that his facility was beyond repair. It should be burned down and a new one built, he recommended. Given the facilities' conditions, it is easy to understand people's desperate efforts to evade the law and avoid being sent to quarantine.

The city also made efforts to provide care for the insane, but modern practices came slowly to this field of medicine in Ecuador as elsewhere.[55] The dominant view of the era was that treatment would probably not help; the insane were incurable. Therefore, while mental patients usually did not suffer the cruelties of earlier times—being chained and beaten, for example—they still received little actual treatment.

Before 1881, Guayaquil either kept mentally disturbed people in jail or housed them with the general patient population at the Hospital Civil. That year, Guayaquil opened its first insane asylum, the Manicomio Velez. The new institution soon met with difficulties. City council president Urvina Jado noted shortly after the asylum opened that it required a special area for

**Table 7.3.** Estimated death rate and total deaths in Guayaquil, selected years, 1841–1925 (death rate is per 1,000 people)

| Year | Deaths | Death rate |
|------|--------|------------|
| 1841 | 460[a] | 35[a] |
| 1842 | 1,506[a] | 155[a] |
| 1843 | 1,044 | 71[a] |
| 1857 | 1,122 | 48 |
| 1876 | 1,784 | 70[a] |
| 1877 | 2,518 | 99[a] |
| 1878 | 2,510 | 98[a] |
| 1879 | 3,718 | 144[a] |
| 1880 | 2,872 | 111 |
| 1881 | 2,058 | 67[a] |
| 1882 | 2,140 | 59 |
| 1883 | 3,173 | 85[a] |
| 1884 | 2,288 | 59[a] |
| 1885 | 2,109[a] | 52[a] |
| 1886 | 2,394[a] | 57[a] |
| 1887 | 2,402[a] | 55[a] |
| 1889 | 3,568[a] | 80[a] |
| 1890 | 3,130 | 70 |
| 1891 | 2,882 | 64[a] |
| 1892 | 2,355 | 52 |
| 1893 | 2,485 | 52[a] |
| 1894 | 2,907 | 58 |
| 1895 | 3,153 | 63[a] |
| 1897 | 3,806 | 75 |
| 1898 | 2,576 | 46[a] |
| 1899 | 2,771 | 46 |
| 1900 | 3,012 | 48[a] |
| 1901 | 3,402 | 52[a] |
| 1903 | 3,174[a] | 45[a] |
| 1904 | 2,860 | 40[a] |
| 1905 | 3,103 | 42[a] |
| 1906 | 4,424 | 58[a] |
| 1907 | 3,702 | 47[a] |
| 1908 | 3,510 | 44 |
| 1909 | 3,631 | 45[a] |
| 1910 | 3,177 | 39 |
| 1911 | 3,368 | 41[a] |
| 1912 | 5,300 | 63[a] |
| 1913 | 3,981 | 47[a] |
| 1914 | 3,573 | 41[a] |
| 1915 | 3,950 | 45[a] |
| 1916 | 3,614 | 41[a] |
| 1917 | 3,639 | 41[a] |

**Table 7.3.** continued

| Year | Deaths | Death rate |
|------|--------|------------|
| 1918 | 4,200[a] | 46[a] |
| 1919 | 4,565 | 50 |
| 1920 | 4,961 | 51[a] |
| 1921 | 3,813[a] | 38[a] |
| 1922 | 3,690 | 35[a] |
| 1923 | 4,500[a] | 41[a] |
| 1924 | 4,390 | 38[a] |
| 1925 | 4,825 | 40 |

*Sources:* PCC, *Informes, 1879–1892;* IP, *Informes, 1890–1910;* JB, *Memorias, 1893–1925;* GG, *Informe, 1901, 1907;* SS, *Informe, 1911, 1913, 1914; El Ecuador: guía;* Estrada Ycaza, *El Hospital,* 142; Matamoros, *Almanaque;* Linke, *Ecuador,* 4–8; Gallegos Naranja, *1883 almanaque, 1900 almanaque;* Quintero Lopez, *El mito del populismo* 360; L. F. Carbo, *El Ecuador, en el centenario* 43; Estrada Ycaza, *Regionalismo y migracion* 265; Paz, *Guía 1901;* Barbosa, *Almanaque 1906, Almanaque 1907; Guayaquil 1912: directorio; América libre; 1925 almanaque;* USCD, Reinberg, "Report," 10 March 1887; Ecuador, Consulate of Ecuador, New York, *The Republic of Ecuador* (1921), 25, reprinted in GBFO, "Report," January 1922, "Report 1923," 12, 31 December 1923; and adapted from table 1.1.
[a]Extrapolated.

the violently insane, a need underscored when several disturbed patients murdered a guard. Despite its limited space, the insane asylum also frequently doubled as a treatment center for overflow contagious patients from other facilities, which contributed greatly to the high asylum death rates. The Manicomio lost about one in ten patients each year, but in 1903 more than one of every five patients at the insane asylum died. At last, in 1910, the city moved the patients to a new facility, the Manicomio Lorenzo Ponce, and conditions improved.[56] The patient population in city asylums held remarkably steady given Guayaquil's rapid population growth; no doubt only the most visibly or violently insane were admitted to the Manicomio.

The Junta de Beneficencia operated several smaller special facilities. A leper quarantine, opened in 1880 in the hills by Guayaquil, had five rooms and beds for sixty. The Junta also maintained three orphanages and a house of temperance. There was probably more philanthropic giving in commercially vibrant Guayaquil than in Quito or elsewhere in Ecuador, and a few small private charitable societies emerged in the city: the Sociedad Filantrópica del Guayas, founded 1849; the Sociedad Humanitaria del Guayas; the Sociedad Protectora de la Infancia, founded in 1905, which gave out free drugs; the Sociedad de Puericultura, which took in orphans and sometimes gave needy mothers free milk; the Sociedad Belén del Huérfano which sought to help orphans; and the Red Cross.[57]

**Table 7.4.** Patient gender health care facilities in Guayaguil, selected years, 1875–1925

| Year | Males | Females | Total |
|---|---|---|---|
| 1875[a] | 3,835 (71%) | 1,556 (29%) | 5,391 |
| 1881[a] | 2,518 (68%) | 1,210 (32%) | 3,728 |
| 1883[a] | 2,841 (65%) | 1,530 (35%) | 4,371 |
| 1884[a] | 3,295 (70%) | 1,443 (30%) | 4,738 |
| 1885[a] | 3,024 (67%) | 1,487 (33%) | 4,511 |
| 1886[a] | 3,865 (67%) | 1,913 (33%) | 5,778 |
| 1887[a] | 4,044 (69%) | 1,817 (31%) | 5,861 |
| 1888[a] | — | — | 6,639 |
| 1889[a] | — | — | 7,541 |
| 1890 | 4,594 (67%) | 2,258 (33%) | 6,852 |
| 1891 | 5,211 (67%) | 2,569 (33%) | 7,780 |
| 1893 | 4,090 (67%) | 2,010 (33%) | 6,100 |
| 1894 | 4,610 (66%) | 2,393 (34%) | 7,003 |
| 1895 | 5,704 (63%) | 3,306 (37%) | 9,010 |
| 1897 | 7,207 (65%) | 3,912 (35%) | 11,119 |
| 1898 | 5,933 (65%) | 3,180 (35%) | 9,113 |
| 1899 | 6,179 (67%) | 3,101 (33%) | 9,282 |
| 1900 | 6,351 (67%) | 3,060 (33%) | 9,411 |
| 1901 | 6,799 (69%) | 3,124 (31%) | 9,923 |
| 1902 | 5,061 (66%) | 2,650 (34%) | 7,711 |
| 1903[a] | 3,582 (71%) | 1,494 (29%) | 5,076 |
| 1906 | 5,400 (65%) | 2,937 (35%) | 8,337 |
| 1910[a] | 4,046 (67%) | 2,038 (33%) | 6,084 |
| 1911 | 4,943 (68%) | 2,365 (32%) | 7,308 |
| 1914 | 4,928 (69%) | 2,165 (31%) | 7,093 |
| 1917 | 5,656 (66%) | 2,967 (34%) | 8,623 |
| 1919 | 7,117 (66%) | 3,640 (34%) | 10,757 |
| 1920 | 7,063 (63%) | 4,074 (37%) | 11,137 |
| 1922 | 8,400 (66%) | 4,327 (34%) | 12,727 |
| 1924 | 10,817 (69%) | 4,778 (31%) | 15,595 |
| 1925 | 12,192 (70%) | 5,201 (30%) | 17,393 |

INSANE ASYLUM

| Year | Males | Females | Total |
|---|---|---|---|
| 1881[a] | 54 (59%) | 37 (41%) | 91 |
| 1883[a] | 86 (62%) | 53 (38%) | 139 |
| 1884[a] | 104 (65%) | 56 (35%) | 160 |
| 1885[a] | 78 (62%) | 48 (38%) | 126 |
| 1886[a] | 69 (49%) | 72 (51%) | 141 |
| 1887[a] | 91 (59%) | 63 (41%) | 154 |
| 1890 | 94 (47%) | 105 (53%) | 199 |

**Table 7.4.** continued

INSANE ASYLUM

| Year | Males | Females | Total |
|---|---|---|---|
| 1891 | 309 (75%) | 104 (25%) | 413 |
| 1892 | 266 (76%) | 82 (24%) | 348 |
| 1893[a] | 263 (77%) | 79 (23%) | 342 |
| 1894 | 155 (59%) | 109 (41%) | 264 |
| 1895 | 187 (63%) | 110 (37%) | 297 |
| 1897 | 170 (59%) | 117 (41%) | 287 |
| 1898 | 163 (55%) | 133 (45%) | 296 |
| 1899 | 167 (56%) | 131 (44%) | 298 |
| 1900 | 153 (55%) | 127 (45%) | 280 |
| 1902 | 168 (57%) | 128 (43%) | 296 |
| 1903[a] | 173 (63%) | 102 (37%) | 275 |
| 1909[a] | 108 (45%) | 134 (55%) | 242 |
| 1910 | 137 (52%) | 128 (48%) | 265 |
| 1911 | 136 (48%) | 147 (52%) | 283 |
| 1914 | 176 (53%) | 156 (47%) | 332 |
| 1917 | — | — | 295 |
| 1919 | 134 (46%) | 156 (54%) | 290 |
| 1920 | 125 (45%) | 150 (55%) | 275 |
| 1922 | 152 (48%) | 165 (52%) | 317 |
| 1924 | 130 (44%) | 165 (56%) | 295 |
| 1925 | 133 (44%) | 171 (56%) | 304 |

HOSPICIO DEL CORAZÓN DE JESUS

| Year | Males | Females | Total |
|---|---|---|---|
| 1892 | 52 (42%) | 71 (58%) | 123 |
| 1893 | 115 (44%) | 145 (56%) | 260 |
| 1894 | 158 (45%) | 193 (55%) | 351 |
| 1895 | 160 (51%) | 152 (49%) | 312 |
| 1897 | 243 (42%) | 334 (58%) | 577 |
| 1898 | 260 (39%) | 408 (61%) | 668 |
| 1899 | 281 (39%) | 441 (61%) | 722 |
| 1900 | 351 (38%) | 578 (62%) | 929 |
| 1901 | 404 (40%) | 610 (60%) | 1,014 |
| 1902 | 348 (47%) | 391 (53%) | 739 |
| 1903[a] | 121 (36%) | 219 (64%) | 340 |
| 1906 | 135 (34%) | 260 (66%) | 395 |
| 1910 | 74 (30%) | 174 (70%) | 248 |
| 1911 | 61 (27%) | 162 (73%) | 223 |
| 1914 | 77 (30%) | 177 (70%) | 254 |

**Table 7.4.** continued

HOSPICIO DEL CORAZÓN DE JESUS

| Year | Males | Females | Total |
|------|-------|---------|-------|
| 1917 | 127 (36%) | 223 (64%) | 350 |
| 1919 | 145 (38%) | 232 (62%) | 377 |
| 1920 | 130 (38%) | 212 (62%) | 342 |
| 1922 | 115 (35%) | 209 (65%) | 324 |
| 1924 | 113 (35%) | 214 (65%) | 327 |
| 1925 | 133 (37%) | 228 (63%) | 361 |

TUBERCULOSIS ASYLUM

| Year | Males | Females | Total |
|------|-------|---------|-------|
| 1902 | 191 (61%) | 124 (39%) | 315 |
| 1903[a] | 217 (55%) | 174 (45%) | 391 |
| 1906 | 216 (64%) | 123 (36%) | 339 |
| 1911 | 262 (65%) | 139 (35%) | 401 |
| 1914[a] | 468 (69%) | 212 (31%) | 680 |
| 1917 | 292 (56%) | 228 (44%) | 520 |
| 1919 | 399 (59%) | 274 (41%) | 673 |
| 1920 | 296 (56%) | 234 (44%) | 530 |
| 1922 | 249 (53%) | 219 (47%) | 468 |
| 1924 | 274 (57%) | 203 (43%) | 477 |
| 1925 | 347 (59%) | 238 (41%) | 585 |

YELLOW FEVER QUARANTINE

| Year | Males | Females | Total |
|------|-------|---------|-------|
| 1914 | 48 (72%) | 19 (28%) | 67 |
| 1917 | 171 (74%) | 60 (26%) | 231 |
| 1919 | 201 (76%) | 65 (24%) | 266 |

BUBONIC PLAGUE QUARANTINE

| Year | Males | Females | Total |
|------|-------|---------|-------|
| 1914 | 213 (46%) | 246 (54%) | 459 |
| 1917 | 190 (44%) | 238 (56%) | 428 |
| 1919 | 50 (63%) | 29 (37%) | 79 |
| 1920 | 139 (58%) | 101 (42%) | 240 |
| 1924 | 97 (55%) | 79 (45%) | 176 |
| 1925 | 75 (59%) | 53 (41%) | 128 |

*Sources:* PCC, *Informes, 1881–1892;* IP *Informes, 1890–1910;* JB, *Memorias, 1893–1925;* GG, *Informe, 1901;* SS, *Informe, 1913, 1914; El Ecuador: quía,* 681–737; Estrada Ycaza, *El Hospital,* 149, 159.
[a]Estimate.

Chemical testing facilities accompanied medical progress in Guayaquil. Given the need for a reliable source of vaccines as well the desire to accurately test foods and drugs, the city operated a chemical laboratory that was first set up in 1905 at the Colegio Vicente Rocafuerte. The city opened its new Laboratorio Quimico Municipal in 1909 under the directorship of Dr. Ramon Flores Ontaneda, who previously had operated a private lab in the city. Flores Ontaneda himself died in the battle against disease; he got infected with bubonic plague as a result of an accident while he prepared a vaccine.[58] By 1907 the city had four hygiene inspectors, with four assistants, to examine conditions at markets, factories, bakeries, and breweries. Dr. Roberto Levi, director of the municipal lab, conducted a citywide inspection in 1912 and visited many of the places where food was processed and sold.[59]

The sanitation department, administered as a branch of the police department, was created in 1908 to handle other city hygiene matters including most vaccinations. It had a staff of seventy-one by 1920. The department stayed busy. It inoculated 1,348 against plague and 148 against smallpox in 1911 and 2,953 against plague and 187 against smallpox in 1912. Department agents annually inspected and fumigated more than 2,000 vessels arriving in port, sprayed insecticide in 400 to 600 houses, disinfected 3,000 to 4,000 other homes, cleaned up 6,000 to 8,000 patios, exterminated 60,000 to 70,000 rats, and washed 40,000 to 80,000 pieces of clothing in the autoclave. The department also handled public health care education, at times distributing free pamphlets printed at government expense (although probably one in three guayaquileño adults could not read).[60]

Overall, the various activities brought about improvements in Guayaquil's public health care, yet much remained to be done. The city sanitation service noted in its 1914 report that Ecuador lagged behind most Latin American nations in its public sanitation services. Health facilities for the city's poor offered only minimal care.[61] For sick and dying working people in Guayaquil, options were grim indeed.[62]

### Death

Death rates for Guayaquil are difficult to determine, for while the dead could be accurately counted, it proved much more difficult to number the living. People in Guayaquil moved so frequently, both within and to and from the city, that officials could merely estimate the total population. They completed very few census tallies. However, the Junta de Beneficencia carefully noted death totals in the burial records at the Catholic cemetery. Of course, not everyone was Catholic, and some deceased were buried elsewhere, perhaps their hometowns, while some nonresidents from the surrounding countryside who came to the city seeking medical assistance subsequently died in and were buried in Guayaquil. Thus, the available data furnish a general sense, not an exact count, of city death rates.[63]

It is clear enough that death rates in Guayaquil followed a downward drift. Guayaquil's death rate in 1879 was roughly 140 per 1,000 (see table 7.3). The rate declined after 1880 and fluctuated between fifty and eighty per 1,000 until the turn of the century. After that time, the death rate averaged about forty per 1,000. The worst year of death was 1912, a year of war and its attendant epidemics, when Guayaquil lost more than 5,000 lives.

**Table 7.5.** Deaths in Guayaquil, by gender, selected years, 1881–1925

| Year | Males | Females | Total |
|------|-------|---------|-------|
| 1881[a] | 1,293 (63%) | 765 (37%) | 2,058 |
| 1884 | 1,386 (61%) | 902 (39%) | 2,288 |
| 1885[a] | 1,168 (55%) | 941 (45%) | 2,109 |
| 1886[a] | 1,363 (57%) | 1,031 (43%) | 2,394 |
| 1890 | 1,791 (57%) | 1,339 (43%) | 3,130 |
| 1891 | 1,682 (58%) | 1,200 (42%) | 2,882 |
| 1893 | 1,428 (57%) | 1,057 (43%) | 2,485 |
| 1894 | 1,620 (56%) | 1,287 (44%) | 2,907 |
| 1897 | 2,142 (56%) | 1,653 (43%) | 3,806[b] |
| 1898 | 1,447 (56%) | 1,129 (44%) | 2,576 |
| 1903[a] | 1,799 (57%) | 1,375 (43%) | 3,174 |
| 1904[a] | 1,591 (56%) | 1,256 (44%) | 2,860[b] |
| 1905[a] | 1,706 (55%) | 1,397 (45%) | 3,103 |
| 1909 | 1,955 (54%) | 1,676 (46%) | 3,631 |
| 1911 | 1,857 (55%) | 1,511 (45%) | 3,368 |
| 1912 | 2,881 (54%) | 2,419 (46%) | 5,300 |
| 1913 | 2,138 (54%) | 1,843 (46%) | 3,981 |
| 1914[a] | 1,908 (53%) | 1,665 (47%) | 3,573 |
| 1915[a] | 2,217 (56%) | 1,733 (44%) | 3,950 |
| 1917[a] | 1,952 (54%) | 1,687 (46%) | 3,639 |
| 1919 | 2,446 (54%) | 2,119 (46%) | 4,565 |
| 1920 | 2,671 (54%) | 2,290 (46%) | 4,961 |
| 1922 | 1,999 (54%) | 1,691 (46%) | 3,690 |
| 1924 | 2,292 (52%) | 2,098 (48%) | 4,390 |
| 1925[a] | 2,576 (53%) | 2,249 (47%) | 4,825 |
| Total | (55%) | (45%) | |

*Sources:* PCC, *Informe, 1881, 1887;* IP, *Informe, 1890, 1891, 1897, 1898, 1903, 1904, 1905, 1910;* JB, *Memoria, 1893, 1894, 1905, 1914, 1915, 1917, 1919, 1920, 1922, 1924, 1925;* SS, *Informe, 1911, 1913;* USCD, Martin Reinberg, "Report 1886," 10 March 1887; and adapted from table 7.3.
[a]Estimate.
[b]1897, 11 gender unknown; 1904, 13 gender unknown

Children were at special risk, and infant mortality rates improved little over the years (see table 7.10). A child born in Guayaquil stood only a 50 percent chance of celebrating her or his twelfth birthday. Children one year old or under accounted each year for one-fourth to one-third of all deaths in the city throughout the period. Most people in Guayaquil, women or men, did not live to the age of twenty.

Because the study of health care in turn-of-the-century urban Latin America remains in its infancy, it is difficult to compare with certainty what is known about Guayaquil against the situation in other cities. Information is often frustratingly incomplete or unavailable for 1870–1925; it is especially deficient for the cities that most resembled Guayaquil, the other tropical port cities. Accordingly, while some comparisons can be gleaned, final conclusions await further comparative research.

Guayaquil's death rates apparently compared very unfavorably to what is known of other Latin American cities of the era. Nineteenth-century Havana generally had a death rate in the thirties or forties per 1,000, though during the island's struggle for independence from 1895 to 1898 the rate rose to 72 per 1,000. In the last quarter of the nineteenth century in Guayaquil, the death rate commonly reached at least the fifties per 1,000 and was often higher, sometimes much higher. At least nine times during those years, Guayaquil's death rate equaled or surpassed the rate that Havana suffered during its worst years of chaos and war.[64]

Lima, Peru, had a death rate of forty-three per 1,000 in 1880, while Guayaquil's was 111. The death rate in Buenos Aires, Argentina, from 1908 to 1911 of 17.3 per 1,000; Rosario, Argentina, had twenty-three ; and Mexico City, where typhus claimed many lives, had a rate of 53.4 per 1,000. Guayaquil in those same years averaged forty-two deaths per 1,000 inhabitants.[65] The rate in Santiago, Chile, annually averaged about thirty-five per 1,000 in the years 1900–24, and Rio de Janeiro from 1901 to 1920 had about twenty-three deaths per 1,000 inhabitants.[66] Guayaquil in those years had an average annual death rate of about forty-five.

Even some populations seemingly at very high risk had death rates considerably lower than Guayaquil's from 1870 to 1925. Rio de Janeiro in the years 1840 to 1851, a period when waves of African slaves poured into the city, had a death rate of between twenty-eight to forty-two, averaging about thirty-seven; that was well below levels in Guayaquil.[67] In the warm, humid, North American port city of Charleston, South Carolina, the death rate among blacks, the poorest residents, averaged forty-four from 1881 to 1894.[68] During that time in Guayaquil, the rate averaged about sixty-two for the entire population, not just the underclass.

The 1912 rate for Quito was 23.7 per 1,000; the leading killers there were respiratory and digestive illnesses, and tuberculosis made up 40 percent of all deaths. That year Guayaquil's death rate was sixty-three per 1,000. Ecuador as a whole from 1915 to 1919 had an average annual death rate of thirty, whereas Guayaquil averaged about forty-five. From 1920 to 1924, Ecuador had an average rate of twenty-nine; in Guayaquil it was forty-one. Ecuador showed a higher rate than eight other Latin American countries but a lower death rate than Mexico, Guatemala, El Salvador, and Chile.[69] Therefore, it was not Ecuador that was exceptionally unwholesome, just Guayaquil.

Multiple factors compounded to render Guayaquil's gloomy statistics. Unlike other Latin American cities that had some or many of the conditions that spawned deadly diseases, Guayaquil had nearly all of them, and many in the extreme. Climate was the most obvious single factor. The tropical environment is friendly to microorganisms, and killing diseases can linger a long time outside of a host, waiting for a new victim to happen by. Some diseases, such as yellow fever, malaria, and cholera, are more prevalent in tropical regions though by no means unknown elsewhere. Guayaquil also grew faster than most Latin American cities; it grew from 1870 to 1920 at an annual rate of 3.19 percent, which made it all the more difficult for health and other services to keep up with population.[70] Additionally, the people in other Latin American cities generally inherited stronger natural immunity against disease than did the residents of Guayaquil. African descendants in such places as Rio de Janeiro enjoyed comparatively stronger biological defenses against yellow fever, typhoid fever, and malaria than did the mestizo and Indian underclass of Guayaquil.[71]

But other circumstances in Guayaquil further contributed to the depressing state of its health conditions. The all-too-frequent civil wars of Ecuador brought highland soldiers trooping down to the hot, steamy coastal lowlands. Epidemic diseases followed. Quito, for example, sent highland troops to quell a revolt that broke out in Guayaquil in 1911–12. An observer wrote that "a violent yellow fever epidemic in Guayaquil is . . . inevitable, as the city is full of unacclimated hill people, troops and camp followers. All other diseases are also already prevalent."[72] Government and rebel troops clashed at Yaguachi, a town just east of Guayaquil, and soon "yellow fever had broken out at several of the intermediate station where the troops from the highlands had camped."[73] Again, in 1913 and 1914, during the civil war centered in Esmeraldas, dysentery, typhoid fever, malaria, and yellow fever quickly spread around the squalid army camps, traveled to other coastal cities, and ultimately arrived in Guayaquil.

The busy port of Guayaquil was faster-growing than most Latin Ameri-

**Table 7.6.** Age at death in Guayaquil, selected years, 1890–1925 (cumulative totals)

| Year | 0–1 | 2–3 | 4–6 | 7–12 | 13–15 | 16–20 | Total |
|---|---|---|---|---|---|---|---|
| 1890 | — | — | — | — | 1,717 55% | 1,800 58% | 3,130 |
| 1891 | — | — | — | — | 1,340 46% | 1,426 51% | 2,882 |
| 1897 | 847 22% | — | — | — | — | 2,140 56% | 3,806 |
| 1898 | 674 26% | — | — | — | — | 1,394 54% | 2,576 |
| 1905[a] | 1,096 35% | — | — | — | — | 1,838 59% | 3,103 |
| 1907 | 1,104 30% | — | — | — | — | — | 3,702 |
| 1909 | 960 26% | — | — | — | 1,767 49% | 2,004 55% | 3,631 |
| 1911 | | | 1,266 (to five years) 49% | | | | 3,368 |
| 1912 | | | 2,128 (to five years) 40% | | | | 5,300 |
| 1914 | 1,125 31% | — | — | — | 1,804 50% | 1,992 56% | 3,573 |
| 1915 | 1,258 32% | 1,538 39% | 1,770 45% | 1,995 51% | 2,061 52% | 2,292 58% | 3,950 |
| 1916 | — | — | — | 1,864 52% | — | — | 3,614 |
| 1917 | 1,209 33% | 1,542 42% | 1,771 49% | 2,004 55% | 2,057 57% | 2,265 62% | 3,639 |
| 1919 | 1,212 27% | 1,712 38% | 1,993 44% | 2,268 50% | 2,345 51% | 2,621 57% | 4,565 |
| 1920 | 1,562 31% | 2,164 44% | 2,581 52% | 2,906 59% | 2,984 60% | 3,200 65% | 4,961 |
| 1922 | 1,265 34% | 1,522 41% | 1,649 46% | 1,820 49% | 1,865 51% | 2,057 56% | 3,690 |
| 1924 | 1,562 36% | 1,933 44% | 2,201 50% | 2,425 55% | 2,490 57% | 2,703 62% | 4,390 |
| 1925 | 1,574 33% | 1,889 39% | 2,137 44% | 2,328 48% | 2,410 50% | 2,707 56% | 4,825 |

MINORS (0–12) VERSUS ADULTS, SELECTED YEARS, 1881–1925

| Year | Minors | Adults | Total |
|---|---|---|---|
| 1881[a] | 970 (47%) | 1,088 (53%) | 2,058 |
| 1884 | 1,119 (49%) | 1,169 (51%) | 2,288 |
| 1885[a] | 1,147 (54%) | 962 (46%) | 2,109 |
| 1886[a] | 1,293 (54%) | 1,101 (46%) | 2,394 |
| 1892[a] | 966 (41%) | 1,389 (59%) | 2,355 |

**Table 7.6.** continued

Minors (0–12) versus adults, selected years, 1881–1925

| Year | Minors | Adults | Total |
|------|--------|--------|-------|
| 1893 | 1,277 (51%) | 1,208 (49%) | 2,485 |
| 1894 | 1,584 (54%) | 1,323 (46%) | 2,907 |
| 1895 | 1,496 (47%) | 1,657 (53%) | 3,153 |
| 1897 | 1,882 (49%) | 1,924 (51%) | 3,806 |
| 1898 | 1,312 (51%) | 1,264 (49%) | 2,576 |
| 1899 | 1,343 (48%) | 1,428 (52%) | 2,771 |
| 1900 | 1,294 (43%) | 1,718 (57%) | 3,012 |
| 1901 | 1,644 (48%) | 1,757 (52%) | 3,402 |
| 1903[a] | 1,286 (41%) | 1,888 (59%) | 3,174 |
| 1904 | 1,250 (44%) | 1,610 (56%) | 2,860 |
| 1906 | 2,396 (54%) | 2,028 (46%) | 4,424 |
| 1910 | 1,632 (49%) | 1,729 (51%) | 3,361 |
| 1911 | 1,436 (44%) | 1,832 (56%) | 3,268 |
| 1914 | 1,737 (49%) | 1,836 (51%) | 3,573 |
| 1915 | 1,995 (51%) | 1,955 (49%) | 3,950 |
| 1916 | 1,864 (52%) | 1,750 (48%) | 3,614 |
| 1917 | 2,004 (55%) | 1,635 (45%) | 3,639 |
| 1919 | 2,268 (50%) | 2,297 (50%) | 4,565 |
| 1920 | 2,906 (59%) | 2,055 (41%) | 4,961 |
| 1922 | 1,820 (49%) | 1,870 (51%) | 3,690 |
| 1924 | 2,425 (55%) | 1,965 (45%) | 4,390 |
| 1925 | 2,328 (48%) | 2,497 (52%) | 4,825 |

*Sources:* PCC, *Informe, 1881–1892;* IP, *Informe, 1890–1910;* JB, *Memoria, 1893–1925;* SS, *1912, 1913;* USCD, Reinberg, "Report," 10 March 1887; GG, *Informe, 1907;* and adapted from table 7.3.
[a]Estimate.

can cities, as well as particularly unsanitary and unusually warm and humid; unaccustomed newcomers with little natural disease resistance formed the largest share of the population; and the city had to share locally generated tax revenues with the rest of Ecuador: these factors, then, might go a long way toward explaining the severity of Guayaquil's health care problems.

Whether one condemns or praises Guayaquil's health record for the late nineteenth and early twentieth centuries depends upon one's frame of reference. In an absolute sense—that is, Guayaquil in 1870 compared to Guayaquil in 1925—there was notable improvement, as seen in the decline in the city's death rate. However, in a relative sense—when compared to what is known about similar cities of the era—Guayaquil was a disgrace. While it is true that essential elements in determining a city's health conditions—climate, geography, the natural immunities of the population—were beyond

**Table 7.7.** Leading causes of death in Guayaquil, selected years, 1889–1925 (percentage of all causes of death)

| Year | Respiratory illnesses | Digestive illnesses | Violence/accidents | Yellow fever |
|------|------|------|------|------|
| 1889[a] | 700 (20%) | 507 (14%) | 39 (1%) | 72 (2%) |
| 1890 | 571 (18%) | 282 (9%) | 38 (1%) | — |
| 1891 | 414 (14%) | 246 (9%) | 29 (1%) | 142 (5%) |
| 1892 | 486 (21%) | 187 (8%) | 15 (1%) | 145 (6%) |
| 1893 | 415 (17%) | 148 (6%) | 41 (2%) | 65 (3%) |
| 1897 | 504 (13%) | 258 (7%) | 57 (1%) | — |
| 1898 | 429 (17%) | 352 (14%) | 49 (2%) | 1 |
| 1903[a] | 680 (21%) | 346 (11%) | 46 (1%) | 382 (12%) |
| 1904 | 527 (18%) | 374 (13%) | 78 (3%) | 190 (7%) |
| 1905[a] | 572 (18%) | 469 (15%) | 41 (1%) | 175 (6%) |
| 1908 | 439 (13%) | — | — | 109 (3%) |
| 1909 | 786 (22%) | 400 (11%) | 107 (3%) | 255 (7%) |
| 1910 | — | — | — | 160 (10%) |
| 1911 | 312 (10%) | 540 (17%) | 115 (4%) | 221 (7%) |
| 1912 | 782 (15%) | 641 (12%) | 157 (3%) | 403 (8%) |
| 1913 | 697 (18%) | 595 (15%) | 94 (2%) | 232 (6%) |
| 1914 | 669 (19%) | 1001 (28%) | 78 (2%) | 29 (1%) |
| 1915 | 815 (21%) | 995 (25%) | 84 (2%) | 18 |
| 1916 | 801 (22%) | 689 (19%) | 86 (2%) | 166 (5%) |
| 1917 | 1056 (29%) | 831 (23%) | 66 (2%) | 79 (2%) |
| 1919 | 1212 (27%) | 800 (18%) | 95 (2%) | 99 (2%) |
| 1920 | 1471 (30%) | 777 (16%) | 86 (2%) | — |
| 1922 | 1087 (29%) | 815 (22%) | 101 (3%) | — |
| 1924 | 1421 (32%) | 1175 (27%) | 64 (1%) | — |
| 1925 | 1561 (32%) | 1387 (29%) | 96 (2%) | — |
| Total | (21%) | (15%) | (2%) | (3%) |

| Year | Bubonic plague | Malaria | Typhoid fever | Typhus |
|------|------|------|------|------|
| 1889[a] | — | 104 (3%) | 16 | — |
| 1890 | — | — | — | — |
| 1891 | — | — | — | — |
| 1892 | — | — | — | — |
| 1893 | — | — | — | 16 (1%) |
| 1897 | — | 13 | — | — |
| 1898 | — | 2 | — | — |
| 1903[a] | — | 260 (8%) | 7 | — |
| 1904 | — | 175 (6%) | 6 | 6 |
| 1905[a] | — | 83 (3%) | — | 4 |
| 1908 | 332 (9%) | 322 (9%) | 32 (1%) | — |
| 1909 | 398 (11%) | 219 (6%) | 15 | 8 |
| 1910 | 311 (9%) | 194 (6%) | 40 (1%) | |

**Table 7.7.** continued

| Year | Bubonic plague | Malaria | Typhoid fever | Typhus |
|------|----------------|---------|---------------|--------|
| 1911 | 260 (8%) | 171 (5%) | 37 (1%) | 10 |
| 1912 | 236 (4%) | 512 (10%) | 242 (5%) | 4 |
| 1913 | 339 (9%) | 312 (8%) | 91 (2%) | 2 |
| 1914 | 179 (5%) | 263 (7%) | 97 (3%) | — |
| 1915 | 117 (3%) | 475 (12%) | 209 (5%) | — |
| 1916 | 345 (10%) | 358 (10%) | 94 (3%) | — |
| 1917 | 161 (4%) | 424 (12%) | 81 (2%) | — |
| 1919 | 23 (1%) | 529 (12%) | 102 (2%) | — |
| 1920 | 59 (1%) | 532 (11%) | 136 (3%) | — |
| 1922 | 19 (1%) | 331 (9%) | 147 (4%) | — |
| 1924 | 45 (1%) | 317 (7%) | 85 (2%) | — |
| 1925 | 55 (1%) | 356 (7%) | 162 (3%) | — |
| Total | (3%) | (7%) | (2%) | |

| Year | Cholera | Measles | Smallpox | Tetanus |
|------|---------|---------|----------|---------|
| 1889[a] | 26 (1%) | 119 (3%) | — | 172 (5%) |
| 1890 | — | 29 (1%) | 437 (14%) | 67 (2%) |
| 1891 | — | — | 122 (4%) | — |
| 1892 | — | — | 1 | 36 (2%) |
| 1893 | 20 (1%) | — | 289 (12%) | 153 (6%) |
| 1897 | 10 | 2 | 13 | 50 (1%) |
| 1898 | — | 10 | 3 | 41 (2%) |
| 1903[a] | — | — | 8 | 105 (3%) |
| 1904 | 5 | 1 | 9 | 126 (4%) |
| 1905[a] | 2 | 4 | 85 (3%) | 112 (4%) |
| 1908 | 10 | 30 (1%) | 130 (4%) | — |
| 1909 | 39 (1%) | 1 | 3 | 76 (2%) |
| 1910 | 17 | 0 | 0 | |
| 1911 | 39 (1%) | 22 (1%) | — | — |
| 1912 | 37 (1%) | 98 (2%) | — | — |
| 1913 | 28 (1%) | 48 (1%) | — | — |
| 1914 | 45 (1%) | 7 | — | 47 (1%) |
| 1915 | 51 (1%) | 37 (1%) | 1 | 143 (4%) |
| 1916 | 33 (1%) | 56 (2%) | 4 | 99 (3%) |
| 1917 | 24 (1%) | 23 (1%) | 14 | 34 (1%) |
| 1919 | 33 (1%) | 17 | — | 51 (1%) |
| 1920 | 40 (1%) | 215 (4%) | 5 | 50 (1%) |
| 1922 | 19 (1%) | — | — | 90 (2%) |
| 1924 | 13 | 69 (2%) | 1 | 91 (2%) |
| 1925 | 18 | — | — | 108 (2%) |
| Total | (1%) | (1%) | (1%) | (2%) |

**Table 7.7.** continued

| Year | Other fevers | Unknown or other | Total |
|------|-------------|------------------|-------|
| 1889[a] | 1,264 (35%) | 549 (15%) | 3,568 |
| 1890 | 825 (26%) | 882 (28%) | 3,130 |
| 1891 | 1,025 (36%) | 904 (31%) | 2,882 |
| 1892 | 760 (32%) | 725 (31%) | 2,355 |
| 1893 | 852 (34%) | 486 (20%) | 2,485 |
| 1897 | 2,281 (60%) | 618 (16%) | 3,806 |
| 1898 | 1,126 (44%) | 562 (22%) | 2,576 |
| 1903[a] | 688 (22%) | 652 (21%) | 3,174 |
| 1904 | 623 (22%) | 740 (26%) | 2,860 |
| 1905[a] | 678 (22%) | 878 (28%) | 3,103 |
| 1908 | 31 (1%) | 2,075 (59%) | 3,510 |
| 1909 | 556 (15%) | 768 (21%) | 3,631 |
| 1911 | 284 (9%) | 1,257 (38%) | 3,268 |
| 1912 | 54 (1%) | 3,017 (57%) | 5,300 |
| 1913 | 23 (1%) | 1,520 (38%) | 3,981 |
| 1914 | 61 (2%) | 1,097 (31%) | 3,573 |
| 1915 | 71 (2%) | 934 (24%) | 3,950 |
| 1916 | 49 (1%) | 834 (23%) | 3,614 |
| 1917 | 29 (1%) | 817 (23%) | 3,639 |
| 1919 | 339 (7%) | 1,265 (28%) | 4,565 |
| 1920 | 177 (4%) | 1,413 (28%) | 4,961 |
| 1922 | 104 (3%) | 977 (26%) | 3,690 |
| 1924 | 87 (2%) | 1,022 (23%) | 4,290 |
| 1925 | 123 (3%) | 959 (20%) | 4,825 |
| Total | (14%) | (28%) | |

*Sources:* PCC, *Informe, 1889, 1892;* IP, *Informe, 1890, 1891, 1897, 1898, 1903, 1904, 1905, 1910;* JB, *Memoria, 1893, 1905, 1911, 1914, 1915, 1916, 1917, 1919, 1920, 1922, 1924, 1925;* SS, *Informe, 1911, 1912, 1913.*
[a]Estimate.

the immediate control of government, it is important to ask not only if death rates fell, but if they fell as far as was possible, whether everything that might be done was being done.

In Guayaquil it was not. If the city expanded existing hospitals and added new ones, these steps did not nearly accompany needs, as administrators from the city health care institutions emphatically and repeatedly stressed. If some sanitation measures were taken, the city still remained appallingly filthy, as the reports of city officials and observations of foreign visitors abundantly and vividly detailed.[74]

Many in Guayaquil well understood the disease implications of failing to fund needed sanitation programs. University dean A. Lascane of the medical faculty noted in 1879, "never has Guayaquil been as filthy."[75] He urged

**Table 7.8.** Major causes of death in Guayaquil, by age and gender, selected years, 1911–1925

RESPIRATORY ILLNESSES

| Year | Adult males | Adult females | Adult total | Children (0–12) | Total |
|------|-------------|---------------|-------------|------------------|-------|
| 1911 | 69 | 65 | 134 (43%) | 178 (57%) | 312 |
| 1914 | 261 | 237 | 498 (74%) | 171 (26%) | 669 |
| 1915 | — | — | 594 (73%) | 221 (27%) | 815 |
| 1916 | — | — | 520 (65%) | 281 (35%) | 801 |
| 1917[a] | — | — | 579 (55%) | 477 (45%) | 1,056 |
| 1919[b] | — | — | 821 (68%) | 391 (32%) | 1,212 |
| 1920 | — | — | 811 (55%) | 660 (45%) | 1,471 |
| Total | | | (62%) | (38%) | |

DIGESTIVE ILLNESSES

| Year | Adult males | Adult females | Adult total | Children (0–12) | Total |
|------|-------------|---------------|-------------|------------------|-------|
| 1911 | 102 | 65 | 167 (31%) | 373 (69%) | 540 |
| 1914 | 182 | 128 | 310 (31%) | 691 (69%) | 1,001 |
| 1915 | — | — | 239 (24%) | 756 (76%) | 995 |
| 1916 | — | — | 123 (18%) | 566 (82%) | 689 |
| 1917[a] | — | — | 166 (20%) | 665 (80%) | 831 |
| 1919 | — | — | 155 (19%) | 645 (81%) | 800 |
| 1920 | — | — | 160 (21%) | 617 (79%) | 777 |
| Total | | | (23%) | (77%) | |

ACCIDENTS OR VIOLENCE

| Year | Adult males | Adult females | Adult total | Children (0–12) | Total |
|------|-------------|---------------|-------------|------------------|-------|
| 1911 | 72 | 16 | 88 (77%) | 27 (23%) | 115 |
| 1914 | 57 | 7 | 64 (82%) | 14 (18%) | 78 |
| 1915 | — | — | 72 (86%) | 12 (14%) | 84 |
| 1916 | — | — | 75 (87%) | 11 (13%) | 86 |
| 1917[b] | — | — | 45 (68%) | 21 (32%) | 66 |
| 1919 | — | — | — | — | 95 |
| 1920 | 71 | 4 | 75 (87%) | 11 (13%) | 86 |
| Total | | | (81%) | (19%) | |

YELLOW FEVER

| Year | Adult males | Adult females | Adult total | Children (0–12) | Total |
|------|-------------|---------------|-------------|------------------|-------|
| 1911 | 168 | 42 | 210 (95%) | 11 (5%) | 221 |
| 1914 | 22 | 5 | 27 (93%) | 2 (7%) | 29 |
| 1915 | — | — | 15 (83%) | 3 (17%) | 18 |
| 1916 | — | — | 149 (90%) | 17 (10%) | 166 |
| 1917[a] | — | — | 64 (81%) | 15 (19%) | 79 |
| 1919 | — | — | 88 (89%) | 11 (11%) | 99 |
| Total | | | (88%) | (12%) | |

**Table 7.8.** continued

BUBONIC PLAGUE

| Year | Adult males | Adult females | Adult total | Children (0–12) | Total |
|------|-------------|---------------|-------------|-----------------|-------|
| 1911 | 79 | 80 | 159 (61%) | 101 (39%) | 260 |
| 1914 | 52 | 59 | 111 (62%) | 68 (38%) | 179 |
| 1915 | — | — | 76 (65%) | 41 (35%) | 117 |
| 1916 | — | — | 196 (57%) | 149 (43%) | 345 |
| 1917[a] | — | — | 98 (61%) | 63 (39%) | 161 |
| 1919 | — | — | — | — | 23 |
| 1920 | — | — | 35 (59%) | 24 (41%) | 59 |
| Total | | | (60%) | (40%) | |

MALARIA

| Year | Adult males | Adult females | Adult total | Children (0–12) | Total |
|------|-------------|---------------|-------------|-----------------|-------|
| 1911 | 32 | 19 | 51 (30%) | 120 (70%) | 171 |
| 1914 | 49 | 37 | 86 (33%) | 177 (67%) | 263 |
| 1915 | — | — | 121 (25%) | 354 (75%) | 475 |
| 1916 | — | — | 82 (23%) | 276 (77%) | 358 |
| 1917[a] | — | — | 77 (18%) | 347 (82%) | 424 |
| 1919 | — | — | 154 (29%) | 375 (71%) | 529 |
| 1920 | — | — | 111 (21%) | 421 (79%) | 532 |
| Total | | | (25%) | (75%) | |

TYPHOID FEVER

| Year | Adult males | Adult females | Adult total | Children (0–12) | Total |
|------|-------------|---------------|-------------|-----------------|-------|
| 1911 | 6 | 22 | 28 (76%) | 9 (24%) | 37 |
| 1914 | 27 | 32 | 59 (61%) | 38 (39%) | 97 |
| 1915 | — | — | 126 (60%) | 83 (40%) | 209 |
| 1916 | — | — | 53 (56%) | 41 (44%) | 94 |
| 1917[a] | — | — | 35 (43%) | 46 (57%) | 81 |
| 1919 | — | — | 57 (56%) | 45 (44%) | 102 |
| 1920 | — | — | 42 (31%) | 94 (69%) | 136 |
| Total | | | (53%) | (47%) | |

CHOLERA

| Year | Adult males | Adult females | Adult total | Children (0–12) | Total |
|------|-------------|---------------|-------------|-----------------|-------|
| 1911 | 2 | 6 | 8 (21%) | 31 (79%) | 39 |
| 1914 | 13 | 5 | 18 (40%) | 27 (60%) | 45 |
| 1915 | — | — | 47 (92%) | 4 (8%) | 51 |
| 1916 | — | — | 24 (73%) | 9 (27%) | 33 |
| 1917[a] | — | — | 21 (88%) | 3 (13%) | 24 |
| Total | | | (61%) | (39%) | |

**Table 7.8.** continued

MEASLES

| Year | Adult males | Adult females | Adult total | Children (0–12) | Total |
|------|-------------|---------------|-------------|------------------|-------|
| 1911 | 2 | 2 | 4 (18%) | 18 (82%) | 22 |
| 1914 | 0 | 0 | 0 | 7 (100%) | 7 |
| 1915 | — | — | 0 | 37 (100%) | 37 |
| 1916 | — | — | 1 (2%) | 55 (98%) | 56 |
| 1917[a] | — | — | 0 | 23 (100%) | 23 |
| 1920 | — | — | 3 (1%) | 212 (99%) | 215 |
| Total | | | (2%) | (98%) | |

VICTIMS OF TETANUS

| Year | Adult males | Adult females | Adult total | Children (0–12) | Total |
|------|-------------|---------------|-------------|------------------|-------|
| 1914 | 10 | 4 | 14 (30%) | 33 (70%) | 47 |
| 1915 | — | — | 9 (6%) | 134 (94%) | 143 |
| 1916 | — | — | 9 (9%) | 90 (91%) | 99 |
| 1917[a] | — | — | 3 (9%) | 31 (91%) | 34 |
| 1919 | — | — | 6 (12%) | 45 (88%) | 51 |
| 1920 | — | — | 6 (12%) | 44 (88%) | 50 |
| Total | | | (11%) | (89%) | |

TUBERCULOSIS

| Year | Adults | Children | Total |
|------|--------|----------|-------|
| 1910 | — | — | 478 |
| 1911 | — | — | 471 |
| 1912 | — | — | 548 |
| 1914 | 400 (90%) | 42 (10%) | 442 |
| 1919 | 602 (83%) | 125 (17%) | 727 |
| 1920 | 550 (83%) | 113 (17%) | 663 |
| 1922 | — | — | 572 |
| 1924 | — | — | 646 |
| 1925 | — | — | 739 |
| Total | (85%) | (15%) | |

Sources: JB, Memoria, 1911, 1914, 1915, 1916, 1917, 1919, 1920, 1922, 1924, 1925; SS, Informe, 1911, 1912, 1913; and adapted from table 7.7.
[a]1917: children (0–15).
[b]Estimate.

**Table 7.9.** Morbidity rates of major causes of death in Guayaquil, selected years, 1893–1900: Illness and death at the Hospital Civil.

|  | 1893 | | 1894 | | 1900 | |
|---|---|---|---|---|---|---|
|  | *Treated* | *Died* | *Treated* | *Died* | *Treated* | *Died* |
| Respiratory illnesses | 453 | 164 | 2,064 | 225 | 891 | 141 |
|  |  | (36%) |  | (11%) |  | (16%) |
| Digestive illnesses | 888 | 99 | 1,009 | 132 | 1,568 | 193 |
|  |  | (11%) |  | (13%) |  | (12%) |
| Accidents or violence | 654 | 11 | 266 | 7 | 285 | 7 |
|  |  | (2%) |  | (3%) |  | (2%) |
| Yellow Fever | 553 | 184 | 589 | 237 | 6 | 2 |
|  |  | (33%) |  | (40%) |  | (33%) |
| Malaria | 934 | 57 | 57 | 4 | 2,092 | 90 |
|  |  | (6%) |  | (7%) |  | (4%) |
| Smallpox | 141 | 35 | 61 | 26 | 97 | 20 |
|  |  | (25%) |  | (43%) |  | (21%) |

*Sources:* JB, *Memoria, 1893, 1894, 1900* (yearly, title varies).

the governor to take action: "Today [the city is] . . . a true focal point for spreading infection . . . and if active measures . . . [a]re not taken immediately without losing a day, we fear that the city will suffer yet more than it did in 1842 [from a severe yellow fever outbreak]."[76] Ecuador's interior minister, J. Modesto Espinosa, made an important connection in 1886 toward understanding the spread of disease: "the increase in the number of newcomers that are coming to our active port and the unhealthful climate there make it indispensable to increase greatly the expenditures [on public health care and sanitation]."[77] Sanitation director L. Becerra echoed those thoughts in 1912, when he observed that Guayaquil needed sewers, paving, street filling, and potable water. "If Guayaquil were a city that was fairly hygienic, if it had a sufficient quantity of water to meet the needs of the population, if the city gov-

**Table 7.10.** Infant mortality in Guayaquil, selected years, 1898–1914

| Year | Births | Deaths | Infant mortality rate |
|---|---|---|---|
| 1898 | 3,102 | 674 | 217 |
| 1905[a] | 3,324 | 1,096 | 330 |
| 1907 | 3,161 | 1,104 | 349 |
| 1909 | 3,586 | 960 | 268 |
| 1914 | 5,720 | 1,125 | 197 |

*Sources:* Adapted from tables 5.2 and 7.6.
[a]Estimate.

ernment occupied itself in some manner in the service of hygiene as do other city governments in the world," then, and only then, would health improvements follow, Becerra said.[78] Summing up the problem, sanitation director L. F. Cornejo Gomez pointed out that Guayaquil's spending on sanitation and health was quite parsimonious compared to that in cities of other nations.[79]

All cities of the age faced challenges in providing sanitation and health care as their cities grew. Health officials in New York City explained that almost "no sanitary measures, however simple, can be enforced without compelling individuals to yield something of pecuniary interest or of personal convenience to the general welfare."[80] That Guayaquil sanitary laws aroused neither anger nor opposition from business interests reveals how little was attempted.

Other cities attempted more. The public health care program in New York City is instructive in this regard, although New York was obviously a very different city than Guayaquil. Its temperate climate posed less daunting environmental hazards; it had more wealth to spend; and its economy fostered a sizable middle class, historically among the most active segments in pushing for reform. But its example demonstrates what others found it possible to do and hence what Guayaquil failed to do.[81] With the New York Board of Health taking the lead, authorities aggressively closed down rank polluters such as meat-rendering plants; ordered removal of manure heaps; shut down unsewered privies; constructed a sufficient sewer system; fined companies that dumped offal into the rivers; supplied enough clean water; forced slumlords to clean up their tenements or risk condemnation of their properties; enforced a tough building code; sanitized city marketplaces; made concerted drives against tuberculosis and diphtheria; aggressively policed the city's milk and food supplies; provided school nurses; subsidized school lunches; sought to stop child labor; offered government-sponsored child care education programs for parents; administered free vaccines door to door; and launched extensive summer health care inspections of slum districts. In Guayaquil, none of these things happened.

Guayaquil made some efforts to meet the challenge of its adverse natural circumstances, but ultimately it did not do enough. The private nature of its economy could not emphasize providing for public needs. In Guayaquil, "everybody's business" was still mostly "nobody's business."[82] Thus, the city earned and richly deserved its foul reputation.

## Chapter Eight

# Collective Popular Action

### Unions, the Collapse of the Export Economy, and the General Strike of 1922

Day to day, ordinary women and men sought to cope with death and life in Guayaquil. As people sought to improve their circumstances, they typically turned first to individualistic strategies, hoping to succeed where most failed, to win within the existing system. Following the colonial custom of the Andes, some workers and their families would tie their fortunes to a protector, a patron. By forging client/patron linkages, workers could gain occasional benefits, such as help getting a job, or assistance with the government bureaucracy. In return, the patron could call in favors from his clients; the patron also gained in status—he got to look, act, and feel like somebody important. Although the approach at times yielded material results for individuals or families, such a strategy could not produce collective advancement for workers as a whole.

Workers sometimes did act collectively to try to better their lives. In other cities, unions provided a key organizing point for united action. But in Guayaquil, the socioeconomic conditions were not at all conducive to unionization. Except for a few privileged workers, most Guayaquil laboring people neither took part in nor benefited from union action.

On rare occasions, if the right conditions came together, workers could join in collective action. Such a mass action could be dramatic and vent popular discontent but achieved little in the way of lasting results. Ultimately, none of the strategies employed by workers in Guayaquil would do much to improve their circumstances.

## Labor Organizations

Ordinary working people had long employed irregular methods to express their political concerns in Ecuador, for formal politics were closed to them. Most adults were not permitted to vote; Ecuador restricted the franchise to literate males, twenty-one or older. This meant that in Guayaquil in 1894, for example, with a population of over 50,000, it took only 2,000 votes to win a seat on the city council. Moreover, the elections were so brazenly corrupt that the few potential voters often saw little point in bothering to cast ballots. Employees felt compelled to vote as directed by their employers. Voting was not generally secret; the military watched over the proceedings and sometimes played an active role. Said one foreign critic, "Soldiers . . . [did] the voting in Ecuador," and they were most "industrious voters."[1] Only 3 percent of the population could vote in 1888; by 1933 that figure had risen to only 3.1 percent.[2]

But if the urban poor tended to ignore and be ignored by conventional politics, they would at times take advantage of the sporadic political unrest by launching popular protests and punctuating some with acts of extreme violence. Workers in Guayaquil had a long tradition of urban confrontation, and rural peasants brought with them a history of occasional mass protests when they moved to the city.[3]

Some workers sought to expand their political role and improve their economic situation by organizing labor unions. However, the union movement that developed in Ecuador was both very small and very dependent upon the government. The earliest groups, during the nineteenth century, were mutual-aid societies of artisans.[4] These organizations functioned chiefly as burial societies, collecting dues from members to pay funeral expenses of fallen members and see to their widows and orphans. Guayaquil had four such aid societies in 1895; about twenty more appeared between 1896 and 1914. The organizations included the Sociedad de Artesanos Amantes de Progreso (1875), followed by typesetters (1884), food suppliers (1896), carpenters (1896), bakers (1898), market vendors (1904), tailors (1905), barbers (1905), pharmacy workers (1916), and others. Some groups soon expanded their mission by opening night schools and reading rooms. The Hijos de Trabajo (1896) operated three such schools for its more than 500 members.

Government backing, which began in the late nineteenth century, was crucial to the early formation of artisan and worker organizations. President Eloy Alfaro, the caudillo who dominated Ecuador national politics from 1895 to 1912, took an especially active role in encouraging the development of artisan and worker associations as supports for his governing Liberal Party. Alfaro's help was tangible. In 1906 he gave the Sociedad Hijos de Trabajo a plot of land for their new building. When the entire Guayaquil city council resigned in protest, Alfaro named all new members. La Confederación Obrera del Guayas (COG) (founded in 1905 with some 1,000 members) and other artisan associations also received cash grants from the government to fund their night schools.

The link between organized labor and the government had practical advantages for both. Observing events elsewhere in South America, Ecuadorian political leaders like Alfaro understood the explosive potential of organized labor; he saw obvious advantages to having organized labor closely tied to the government. On the other side, artisans and workers perceived that they were too few in number and too disorganized to worry about their unions' independence. At the time, government help appeared to be a blessing.[5]

Nurtured by government support, Ecuadorian workers held their first congress in 1909, led by the Quito-based Sociedad Artística e Industrial del Pichincha (founded 1892). Twenty-eight organizations attended, including seventeen labor organizations—most of them conservative Catholic labor associations from the highlands—and eleven other delegations representing town councils from various Ecuadorian cities. Many of the delegates were not workers at all, but shopkeepers, small businessmen, writers, and middle-class intellectuals. Among other topics, they discussed government help in securing payment for job-related injuries, retirement homes for workers, a ban on import taxes placed on materials used in manufacturing, more government support for education, and suffrage for all workers. The congress ended, however, without a clear consensus on the issues. Four years later, artisan groups of the coast held their first conference, the 1913 Guayas Assembly, which brought together nineteen local organizations. The meeting issued a call for increased government support for education and for workmen's compensation laws.[6]

In time, labor's friends in the Liberal Party responded by placing assorted reform laws on the books. Congress passed several labor reforms in 1916, including a law that reaffirmed the eight-hour workday (a measure first enacted in 1906, if forgotten thereafter). In 1921 Ecuador approved assistance for those who suffered work-related accidents. These statutes continued to be honored mostly in their breech, but they did at least represent a first step and demonstrate to some labor groups the value of patient collaboration with government.[7]

Some worker groups pressed their claims directly upon employers. Railway workers were the most aggressive, striking five times from 1906 to 1919 (see table 8.1). Unions in Guayaquil used the strike as a weapon particularly to fight for enforcement of the eight-hour workday law. Trolley, railway, and sanitation workers all walked out in a concerted effort in 1916 to force their employers to comply with the law. The workers held a general rally on October 3, 1916; the protest turned ugly when strikers attacked trolley cars and chased away customers, and police and military arrived and disbanded the crowd. The 1916 movement broke up in defeat.[8]

Ecuador held its second national labor conference, the Congreso Obrero, in Guayaquil in 1920. In charge of arranging the affair was the COG, the nation's leading labor federation, if a rather tame one; it received the bulk of its financial support from the national government and from the municipal government of Guayaquil.[9] The city council even helped pay for the 1920 congress. Clearly, the purpose of the convention was to cement the relationship between emerging labor groups and the Liberal Party. Seventy-eight delegates representing about fifty organizations from all over the nation attended. Twenty-six came from Guayaquil, including typesetters, carpenters, plumbers, barbers, shoemakers, bakers, hatmakers, bricklayers, jewelers, cacao handlers, leather workers, potassium nitrate workers, pharmacy workers, tailors, market vendors, and others.

Given the COG's close ties with the government and its traditional artisan membership, the Congreso Obrero proved to be a rather nonconfrontational meeting. Artisans, whose old way of life was quickly giving way to new technology, did not often have the same interests as new workers who operated the machines (and hence obviated the need for crafts workers). Guayaquil artisans joined together and dug in their heels against the steady pull of economic modernity.[10] The Congreso Obrero's list of desired reforms underscored its moderate orientation. Among the requests: increased government support for education, a minimum wage law, pay raises, enforcement of the eight-hour workday law, legislation requiring one day off a week, a government compensation program for work-related injuries, laws restricting female and child labor, government inspection of working conditions, price controls on basic necessities, government subsidies for decent low-cost housing, government help in establishing worker savings funds, a special tax on unused farmland, and the prohibition of alcohol.

But in Guayaquil, the ranks of nonartisan workers was growing, and several small, anticapitalist unions began to emerge. Soon the moderate workers' organizations had radical enemies. A new socialist publication, the *Bandera roja*, appeared in Guayaquil and began bitterly assailing the 1920 labor congress as a gathering of petty bourgeois shopkeepers. This charge was not entirely untrue, although it perhaps would have been more accurate to say that self-employed artisans constituted the bulk of the 1920 labor congress. The *Bandera roja* was just one of several anticapitalist publications that appeared in the city at the time; also starting up were *Luz y acción, Alba roja, El*

**Table 8.1.** Strikes in Guayaquil, 1889–1920

| Year | Group/issue |
| --- | --- |
| 1889 | bakers/pay |
| 1896 | carpenters/shorter workday (9 hours daily) and pay |
| 1897 | typesetters |
| 1898 | bakers/pay |
| 1906 | railway workers (Duran?)/working conditions |
| 1907 | railway workers (Duran?)/late paychecks |
| 1908 | rubber workers/pay |
| 1908 | railway workers (Duran)/pay, protection from mosquitoes |
| 1908 | cacao handlers/pay |
| 1913 | carpenters (and others?)/compliance with 8-hour workday law |
| 1915 | carpenters and others/8-hour workday |
| 1916 | trolley workers/8-hour workday |
| 1916 | cacao handlers, pharmacy workers, day workers/pay and 8-hour day |
| 1916 | railway workers (Duran?) |
| 1918 | barbers/pay |
| 1919 | railway workers (Duran)/wages |
| 1919 | widespread protest (light and power workers, plumbers, streetcar workers, pier workers, bakers)/taxes and opposition to government lists of union memberships |
| 1920 | drugstore workers/benefits |

*Sources:* Milk, "Growth and Development"; González Casanova, *Historia del movimiento obrero en América Latina: Colombia, Venezuela, Ecuador, Peru, Bolivia, Paraguay;* Naranjo, *I international;* Robalino Bolle, *El sindicalismo en el Ecuador;* Ycaza, *Historia del movimiento obrero ecuatoriano.*

*cacahuero, El proletario, Tribuna obrera, El hambriento, Germinal,* and *La revuelta,* some of which disappeared after only a few issues.

Some publications and radical worker organizations may have been socialist in orientation, but most were probably anarcho-syndicalist. However, Guayaquil was unlike Argentina or Brazil, where mass immigration from Spain or Italy brought many potential anarcho-syndicalist organizers. Radical notions arrived in Guayaquil mostly in the form of printed material. While it is impossible to know precisely how far anticapitalist philosophies spread in Guayaquil, it is safe to conclude that their influence was limited. The market vendors union was possibly anarchist in orientation, and the Sociedad Cosmopolita de Cacahueros Tomas Briones favored anarcho-syndicalism, as their publication makes plain enough. At the same time, a secretive, radical workers' federation, the Asociación Gremial del Astillero, probably also anarcho-syndicalist in orientation, emerged in southern Guayaquil, the newer section of town. And the Liga Obrera, formed as an alternative to the COG, was radical enough. In 1922 the Sociedad Cosmopólita de

Cacahueros Tomas Briones helped to form the Federación de Trabajadores Regional Ecuatoriana (FTRE), Guayaquil's largest radical labor association, with thirty-six or so member groups that comprised anarcho-syndicalist barbers, tailors, leather workers, dock workers, and others.[11]

So by 1920 Guayaquil had seen the beginnings of worker organization. The COG spoke for the two dozen or so skilled artisan groups. Moderate and reform-oriented, this group depended on government aid. Its advantaged workers focused their energies on petitioning their benefactors in the Liberal Party for the redress of grievances. Government passed favorable legislation, but gave no effort to enforcement. At the same time, a few laborers including some unskilled dock workers and cacao handlers had joined small—indeed very small—anticapitalist unions. However, it is unclear what impact, if any, such radical associations might have had. Certainly they did not have the power to launch strike waves or to confront the government. In fact, it would be a mistake to exaggerate the influence of either grouping of organized workers, the moderates or the radicals. Most people in Guayaquil remained unemployed a good deal of the time, and when they found work, it was usually for just a day or two. Only a small fraction had steady jobs, and of these, a much smaller fraction belonged to labor unions. In Guayaquil, nearly no one belonged to unions.

There are many reasons why this was so. Labor historians have long identified the key factors that tended to foster the development of powerful worker groups in a variety of contexts, but none of these conditions obtained in Guayaquil. One factor is geographic proximity. If workers are grouped together in a factory or a cluster of factories (or sometimes in an isolated mining district) it is easier to spread ideas and to organize. Shared conditions encourage empathy. The interconnectedness of factory labor and unions has long been recognized. Guayaquil had neither.

As Charles Bergquist has shown in his study, *Labor in Latin America*, xenophobia can be a vitally important tool for labor.[12] For turn-of-the-century Latin America, the development of the export economy sometimes required heavy capital investment beyond the means of the domestic elite, and in such cases foreign capital stepped in. Export workers could rally against what might be depicted as foreign exploitation of both the workers and the nation. However, in other instances relatively little capital outlay was needed to produce and process the export item. In these cases domestic ownership was more likely. In such cases, the working class could not use the nationalist themes of foreign exploitation. The exploiters were not foreign.

Cacao production in Ecuador required comparatively little capital investment. Land could be acquired fairly inexpensively along the thinly settled coast, and cacao required very little processing prior to shipment—workers spread it out in the sun to dry, covered it with palm leaves to sweat and open the beans, then bagged it and loaded it aboard ship. Local businessmen had the means to produce cacao. Moreover, nationalism was not very strong in Ecuador. The people of the coast and the sierra regarded one another with mutual contempt and suspicion. Ecuadorians, like other people, could and did hate foreigners, but that did not keep them from hating one another even more. Nationalism, then, generally did not serve as a protest strategy for workers in Ecuador. Significantly, the most militant group of workers in Ecuador, the railway men, found ample popular and even governmental support as they clashed with the railway company, one of the few firms in the nation that foreigners owned and operated.

### Crisis

For a time, especially from the late 1890s until World War I, the price of cacao stayed high, at around twenty sucres per quintal, and the exchange value of the sucre remained solid at roughly two to a dollar. World consumption of cacao rose eight times over between 1894 and 1924. But trouble loomed, for Guayaquil's reliance upon cacao to supply nearly all of its export earnings placed it in a vulnerable position of dependence upon capricious world markets. Even during this era of prosperity, energetic new competitors challenged Ecuador's position as the world's principal cacao supplier. After 1912, Ghana, then a British colony on the African Gold Coast, emerged as the world's main cacao producer, and Sao Tomé, Brazil, the Dominican Republic, and Trinidad also pushed for shares of the world market. Cacao became much more abundant; world production increased from 69,097 metric tons in 1894 to 126,513 in 1903, 300,000 in 1916, and 500,000 in 1924. Consumption could not keep pace with the ever higher levels of production, and prices fell. In response, Ecuadorian cacao growers in 1911 formed a national cartel, the Agriculturalists Association. But this group lacked the power to significantly affect world prices. If Ecuador had in 1898 controlled 28 percent of the world's cacao production, by 1923 its share had fallen to but 7 percent. Worse, sugar prices were rising, and other nations' cacao required less sugar for processing than did Ecuador's.[13]

Market conditions worsened during World War I. Ecuador could not reach key buyers, such as Germany and the Netherlands; other major purchasers reordered their priorities for war and purchased far less chocolate. By 1917 the Agriculturalists Association sold 70 percent of Ecuador's cacao, nearly all of it on consignment, while waiting for prices to improve. But in

1921 world market conditions for cacao took an even sharper turn for the worse. Global production levels soared and demand slumped.[14]

Ecuador's troubles were part of the post–World War I recession in the international economy; a broad trend toward overproduction of primary products combined with weakening world demand as population growth slowed in North America and Europe. Prices for primary products like cacao began a steady downward slide. As export earnings dwindled, foreign currency became scarce in Ecuador. The sucre plummeted in value from 47 cents (U.S.) in 1920 to 16 cents (U.S.) by 1923. The price for cacao hit bottom in 1923; its dollar price dropped to half of what it had averaged in years from 1900 to 1913 and to only one-fourth of what it had been just three years earlier.[15]

Incredibly, not one but two exceptionally virulent plant blights appeared at that time in Ecuador, further exacerbating Guayaquil and coastal Ecuador's dilemma. Cacao had previously flourished so easily in the Guayas River Basin that major producers seldom saw much point in caring for the trees. Their haphazard approach to agriculture brought stiff penalties when monilia fungus (in 1914) and then witchbroom disease (in 1922) swept through the untended groves, reducing healthy green trees to dry sticks. Spraying might have helped, but workers found it too hard to reach all the afflicted areas. Most of the trees in some places died within a year. Ecuadorian cacao harvests fell markedly in 1923 and 1924.[16]

The cacao crisis rocked government finances with extreme force at a time when Ecuador was not in good fiscal condition. Ecuador had borrowed heavily against the future during the cacao boom years, betting on continued good prices and heavy sales. But as Linda Alexander Rodríguez has shown in her study of Ecuadorian government finances, *The Search for Public Policy*, the "unorthodox fiscal arrangements" could work only "as long as cacao exports remained high."[17] As the economic crisis broadened in the 1920s, the national government continued to depend on loans from the banks of Guayaquil, principally the Banco Comercial y Agrícola. But the banks no longer had the resources to support high levels of government borrowing. The government decided to allow banks to issue currency in proportion to the amount of government debt and gold reserves held. This policy quickly proved inflationary and further eroded the value of the sucre.

The Ecuadorian government attempted to respond to the crisis by experimenting with fixed official rates of exchange, beginning in 1914 with the Ley Moratoria, which froze the exchange rate. A crisis atmosphere developed as people who had previously displayed little interest in monetary policy now expressed concern. Alarm spread among workers and in the small middle class. The government's control over currency exchange and its efforts to prop the sagging value of the sucre became one of the most important political issues of the day.

Even large nations faced extreme difficulties when they attempted to mitigate the impact of adverse changes in the world economy. For a small nation like Ecuador, little could help matters when a global economic storm hit; the small Ecuadorian national government did not have the power to alter the situation. N. Clemente Ponce, Ecuadorian Minister of Foreign Relations, recognized that Ecuador's economic collapse was caused by "the universal commercial and financial crisis," which hurt "even the governments of wealthy nations."[18]

Given the very minor role of workers in the political system, the ineffectiveness of their undirected sporadic violence, and the weakness and dependency of most small labor unions, Guayaquil workers had yet to find a good method to voice their concerns. When economic collapse came to Guayaquil after World War I, the anxieties and frustrations of working-class families multiplied. The decline in cacao exports brought an acute contraction in the earnings that Guayaquil relied upon to purchase imports. Imports declined to well below pre–World War I levels; they fell in 1921 to about a third of what they had been the year before. To ordinary people in Guayaquil that was a serious blow, given the city's dependence on imports to supply food and other necessities. Now that foreign exchange had become costly and scarce, food stocks dwindled and prices rose. Basic supplies such as flour, lard, lentils, onions, sugar, rice, potatoes, beans, butter, salt, and coffee rose steeply in price. Rents quadrupled. The Guayaquil paper, *El guante,* reported that "every article tripled in price."[19] Other observers commented, "the prices of all prime necessities of life have been triplicated and quadruplicated within the last few years."[20] And while prices rose, employment opportunities disappeared; that added to the suffering of most who lived in Guayaquil.

Railway workers took action. On October 17, 1922, they drew up a list of demands and presented them to the U.S. company that owned and managed the railroad.[21] The workers had serious complaints. In addition to basic economic demands, such as timely paychecks, workers also felt that U.S. employees in management received special advantages denied the Ecuadorian and Jamaican work crews. The men charged that North Americans received better care from the company physician, Dr. Max Meitzner. Workmen helped pay Meitzner's salary but received little medical care in return. When one Ecuadorian worker lost a hand in a dynamite accident, Meitzner refused to travel to his assistance. This episode and others like it—notably Meitzner's conduct during the plague epidemic—earned for him and the company the deep resentment of many workers. They demanded that the company hire an

Ecuadorian doctor and establish auxiliary medical posts. Workers further sought payment in gold or in dollars, like U.S. employees received. Pride in the national currency aside, the workers saw the value of the sucre slipping. Finally, workers called for fifteen days' notice prior to all future layoffs and the rehiring of dismissed union organizers. On October 19 the railroad men struck.

General Manager J. C. Dobbie refused to negotiate and brought in strike-breakers to run the railroad. But the workers stood firm. Grouped together in the town of Durán, the railroad terminus near Guayaquil, they held meetings and painted anti-American slogans on the walls. Ecuador's small organized labor movement threw its support behind the strikers. The newly formed, independent, and radical Federación de Trabajadores Regional Ecuatoriana (FTRE) issued a manifesto backing the strikers. The older, government-backed COG sent a supportive telegram and 1,000 sucres. In Guayaquil hundreds of workers held a rally to show their solidarity with the strikers. Students and workers led similar demonstrations in Riobamba.

After a tense few days, Dobbie at last agreed to negotiate and quickly accepted the railroad workers' demands. Dobbie planned to offset pay raises with a fare hike and apparently thought that President Luís Tamayo had agreed to this plan. Dobbie reasoned that he had staved off a possible revolt by settling the strike on the workers' terms. But President Tamayo did not see the matter in the same light and canceled the rate increase. The fact that foreigners owned the railway no doubt made that move easier for President Tamayo. His government took no steps to repress the workers. Indeed, to have done so would have looked like unpatriotic pandering to foreign interests. Given the severity of Ecuador's crisis, Tamayo prudently sought to avoid being cast in the role of supporting foreign exploiters against Ecuadorians.

The strike was an unmitigated victory for the workers. Dobbie promised better medical care at company expense and strict adherence to the eight-hour workday law. The company reinstated fired workers, agreed to build better housing for employees, and granted substantial raises. Across the river in Guayaquil, workers paid careful attention. To them, the railroad strike was a clear example of how people could better their lot if they held firm and acted together.[22]

## General Strike

Long-suffering workers in Guayaquil shared in the euphoria if not the material benefits of the railroad workers' victory. If workers in Durán could win raises and make fools of management, guayaquileños believed that they might do the same. On November 6–8, 1922, workers from the trolley companies (electric and mule-drawn), the electric company, and the gas and water works met in an ad hoc grand assembly in Guayaquil. After all-day sessions they issued a set of demands. They had wasted little time in following the example of the railroad men.[23]

Workers in Guayaquil were hard pressed by the economic crisis. Trolley workers were especially poor—they lived on bare subsistence wages; conductors received but 1.20 sucres a day and drivers got only 1.50. The men left for work at 4:30 A.M., and their shifts did not end until 11:00 P.M. Besides working long hours, drivers had to keep an eye on the trolley cars on Sundays, their only day off. If anything happened to the trolleys, compensation came from the drivers' wages. Finally, employees complained, they lived in constant dread of being fired.

Although they had obvious reasons for hostility, the trolley workers drew up fairly mild demands. They wanted more money, shorter hours, greater job security, safer working conditions, and to be treated with greater respect. Specifically, they asked for a pay raise of 80 cents for conductors and 1.60 sucres more daily pay for drivers. They sought an eight-hour workday with extra money for overtime. Workmen agreed to continue supplying their own uniforms—no doubt sewn by their wives or mothers—but asked that the company provide the cloth. Workers wanted to be freed of the obligation of guarding the trolleys on weekends and asked that damages to the vehicles become the company's financial responsibility. In addition, the men requested that suspensions from work never run longer than five days. Finally, they demanded strict compliance with existing safety regulations and an end to all verbal abuse. They made twenty-eight demands, all of them rather modest.[24] Management rejected the demands, and the workers struck.

Employees and management agreed to talk. The workers selected Dr. J. José Vicente Trujillo, a noted young labor lawyer from the COG, and Dr. Carlos Puig, the striking railroad workers' attorney, to represent them at the contract negotiations with the light, power, and trolley companies. Also attending the meetings were Jorge Pareja, the governor of Guayas province, General Enrique Barriga, regional military commander, and Alejo Mateus, chief of police. These government officials saw the preservation of law and order as their primary responsibility. Already workers had shut down city transport, and rumors circulated that the drivers planned to park the trolley cars across busy downtown intersections. The officials' strongest fear was that the city would be without light during the night, and that under darkness Guayaquil would erupt into worker violence. The military transferred troops into the city.[25]

Over the next few days the strike gathered momentum. People employed in manufacturing shops or factories could not work, for there was no power. The walkout became the talk of the city. Newspapers centered their editions around the strike, with editorial opinions in the major dailies stressing the reasonableness of workers' demands.[26]

But in other quarters, tempers grew short. When the railroad workers decided to go to Guayaquil and join the grand assembly—and brought with them more than 500 sucres for the strike fund—General Manager Dobbie raged. He believed he had given in to the railway workers' whims and expected his employees to get back to work. Dobbie angrily fired off a sharply worded note to the managers of the transit companies in Guayaquil, assuring them that if his men walked out in support of the strike, he would hold the companies directly responsible for any losses he incurred.[27]

As the strike gathered force, the workers' spokesmen, especially assembly president Adolfo Villacres, recognized their very limited power to restrain the emboldened strikers. The printers union, acting without direct approval from Villacres or the assembly, ran off thousands of leaflets inviting union and nonunion workers from all over the city to join in the strike. Not all who accepted the printers' invitation were well behaved. A band of drunken men wandered toward the power plant, firing off their guns and otherwise causing trouble. They apparently intended to force their way into the building to shut off the city's lights. The assembly dispatched a crew to round up the troublemakers and pack them off to jail. Still, it was clearly becoming more difficult to maintain order as popular support developed for the strike. The assembly of workers soon grew to some 3,000 members and began to stage large outdoor rallies.

After extended negotiations, and just when a settlement seemed imminent, the workers assembly raised a different and more serious issue, thus delaying an end to the strike. From the beginning, many workmen had believed that pay raises would be of little help so long as the value of the sucre continued to deteriorate. They were right, for inflation would quickly wipe out whatever pay gains they secured. What many workers and others desired was a return to the foreign exchange law of June to September 1922, the last in a series of futile attempts to artificially prop up the declining value of the sucre. Undeterred by repeated failures of such measures, the strikers helped to resurrect the idea.

Artificial exchange rate control was a notion that would not go away. Indeed, it remained a very popular idea throughout Ecuador. Supporters of the measure seized upon President Tamayo's frequently voiced but dubious assertion that unscrupulous speculators had driven down the value of the sucre, and that strict regulation of specie would easily remedy the problem. This was a major misunderstanding. The value of the sucre fell because the value of cacao exports had hit bottom. "Speculators" had little to do with it.

Countries that export one primary product routinely suffer economic depression and a decline in currency value when the price of their export falls sharply. This experience was hardly unique to Ecuador. Nonetheless, artificial exchange rate control offered a seemingly simple, if totally unrealistic, solution to the nation's economic dilemma.

*El universo,* one of the two major Guayaquil dailies, called for "attacking the problem at its origin."[28] In a front page editorial, the paper noted the close-at-hand strike settlement and called for resolution of what it saw as the real cause of labor unrest, the exchange rate problem. *El universo* held that a renewal of the exchange moratorium would slowly iron out currency fluctuations that had become completely unregulated "and controlled by a few planters without heart or conscience." Blaming speculators, the paper called on President Tamayo to end "monopoly control" over foreign exchange.[29] *El universo* demanded that precious foreign currency not be squandered on the decadent opulence of the rich but instead be used to build import substitution industries in Ecuador.

Alert to the trouble in Guayaquil, President Tamayo and his secretary of the interior departed for the coast, with reconsideration of an exchange rate moratorium ranking high on their agenda. Moreover, when white-collar workers from Guayaquil's financial district joined the walkout, they brought with them a desire to make the exchange rate issue one of the assembly's demands. The assembly soon began to consider how to obtain a reduction in the exchange rate.[30]

The more conservative COG, acting on its own initiative outside of the Grand Assembly, further propelled the exchange rate question to the forefront of discussion. It drafted a petition calling for a halt to specie speculation and asked for a moratorium on the exchange of all foreign currency. It circulated the petition and appealed to President Tamayo, arguing that the previous June to September 1922 exchange rate law had been the only effective measure in controlling specie speculation abuses. The COG felt that Ecuador had to take protective measures because of its over reliance upon cacao exports, and it called for government control over all foreign money.[31]

The fourth day of the strike was the turning point. Workers and management seemed to have a contract settlement at hand, while the president was on his way down from Quito to discuss and no doubt approve another specie exchange moratorium. Representatives Dr. Carlos Puig and Dr. J. José Vicente Trujillo returned to the assembly to gain the workers' approval of the settlement and to end the strike. However, management had added a new stipulation for settlement. The trolley companies planned to go before the city council to get formal approval for doubling fares to offset the workers' pay increase. When Puig and Trujillo told the assembly of this new condition, the men moaned with disapproval.[32]

A COG delegation also went before the assembly carrying that group's petition for a moratorium on foreign specie exchange. They argued that the workers' assembly should adopt the exchange moratorium issue as one of its main demands. Emboldened by the enthusiastic show of worker solidarity evidenced in the swelling size of the assembly, moratorium advocates urged that the workers press their advantage by demanding action on this issue. Since government and management already acceded to most of their demands, why not insist on one more? Workers were aroused and authorities appeared to be in a reasonably agreeable mood; the time seemed propitious. The assembly leadership did not agree. Dr. Puig urged the rank and file to approve the strike settlement, fare hikes and all. He pleaded for an end to the strike, which, he declared, the workers already had won. But the workers remained unswayed.[33]

Dr. Trujillo and Dr. Puig had no choice but to relate to the authorities that the assembly had rejected management's settlement proposal and that instead the strike now included a new demand: an exchange moratorium. To the officials the moratorium proposal came as no surprise. Also concerned about the exchange rate issue, Governor Pareja promised to send along the workers' moratorium demand to President Tamayo.[34]

The assembly formally presented its exchange moratorium demand to Governor Pareja and suspended discussion of pay raises and the rate hikes. It would now concentrate on the moratorium. The strikers broadened the demand to include government control of all foreign currency, a halt on payments made with foreign drafts, and government recognition of a seven-member executive committee, four of whose members the workers would select, that would be entrusted with solving the economic crisis, lowering the cost of living, and regulating the exchange rate. Workers declared that the general strike would end only after the government accepted all of these demands.[35] The strikers had decided to press their advantage.

Tuesday, November 14, 1922, brought the sixth day of the walkout and the first full day of general strike. The railroad workers struck again, most businesses closed, transportation halted, and there was no light, electricity, or gas. The strike had all but shut down the city of more than 100,000 inhabitants. With the day off, workers roamed the streets enforcing the strike. "The City Trembles," *El universo*'s headline blared.[36]

Strikers marched downtown, and some parceled out leaflets from the FTRE calling for a moratorium on foreign currency exchange, an end to regressive salt and tobacco taxes, abolition of the government sugar monopoly, protection for nascent domestic industry, creation of a program for turning over unused farm land to landless peasants, and opposition to the proposed trolley fare hikes.[37] That afternoon's giant downtown demonstrations seemed to reaffirm to participants the broad support for their cause. Beyond this, the enthusiasm of the rallies served as a profound confirmation of their shared commitment.

President Tamayo, rushing down from Quito, kept abreast of the situation via telegraph.[38] The Council of State granted him extraordinary powers to deal with the crisis, which he then delegated to Governor Pareja in Guayaquil on the morning of November 15, 1922. Tamayo also appointed a commission in Guayaquil to draw up the moratorium decree. He had issued such a decree before. He was willing to try again.

Meeting early on the morning of the fifteenth at the governor's building, the commission included government authorities as well as representatives of the workers assembly. By 1 P.M. they had drawn up the new moratorium, with the agreement of all parties. They immediately wired the text of the decree to Tamayo and waited for his assent. Meanwhile, the governor, instilled with a pressing sense of urgency, sought to regain control of Guayaquil. In view of the accord reached, Pareja wanted to end the strike. He asked for commission approval to issue a proclamation declaring that the president would soon sign the moratorium decree and forbidding strikers from staging any further marches or rallies.

Worker representatives Trujillo and Puig convinced Governor Pareja to delay issuing his proclamation so they could hurry back and inform the assembly of the settlement. At 2 P.M. the governor received a note from the Grand Assembly. It would neither cancel the rally for that afternoon nor halt the general strike until Tamayo actually signed the new law. Pareja, having heard nothing from President Tamayo, at 4 P.M. decided to go ahead and issue his proclamation anyway. By then it was too late, for events had spun completely out of control in the streets of Guayaquil.[39]

That morning, Wednesday, November 15, 1922, dawned on a situation primed for explosion. Without light since Monday, the city lacked bread, meat, milk, and other essentials. Early in the morning, workers started filtering downtown, anticipating the large rally to be held at 3 P.M. On their way into the city center, workers checked in at the shops they passed to make sure that no one was breaking the strike. Those found at labor received sharp orders to join the walkout. By 1 P.M., about the time the commission finished drawing up the moratorium decree, a sizable crowd already began filling the city's downtown area. This was by far the largest demonstration yet. The crowd of children, women, and men numbered about 20,000.[40]

The strikers exhibited great energy and excitement. At 3 P.M. the crowd jammed against the governor's building to see about the exchange decree. They raised spirited shouts of "Long live the strike!" and "Lower the exchange rate!" Seeking to restore order and control, Dr. Puig spoke to the boisterous gathering. Puig declared that they had a settlement, but the strikers had heard this from him before. He said that the moratorium decree had been drawn up, and as he read it to them, people responded with cheers. Puig told the crowd that the next morning the government would announce its agreement to their demands. The rally began to take on the air of a victory celebration. When Dr. Trujillo proclaimed that the governor had agreed to free two of the labor leaders who had previously been jailed, the crowd became exuberant. "To the police station!" they cried. And with Dr. Trujillo and the governor leading the way, they set off for the police depot a few blocks away. This was a mistake.

At the police station were army troops, brought to Guayaquil in greater numbers since the beginning of the strike. Some of the troops grew edgy; soldiers watched nervously as the swollen procession approached their post crying, "To the police station! To the police station!" A jumpy soldier fired his weapon, and then another followed. At first, perhaps, they shot into the air. But as the people screamed and pushed, panicked and tried to flee, the soldiers fired into the crowd.

Once the gunfire started, it generated a momentum of its own. The pent-up tensions so carefully restrained in the preceding days now were given full expression. The crowd ran in terror. The troops broke into packs, pursued and fired. An eyewitness involved in treating the injured said, "on each block we had to stop and mend wounds" of those who had fallen in the streets. The soldiers "shot at everything they saw." It was like a "tremendous hunting party."[41] The strikers presented clear targets in their work clothes and red bandannas. Of course, some soldiers exercised restraint. Notably, the Montufar battalion confined its efforts to restoring calm. It rounded up prisoners and escorted them to jail. But Montufar was an exception. Once the violence began, the soldiers generally behaved in a ruthless and wanton manner.

After the shooting started, a few people began breaking into stores, some seeking a place to hide, some searching for guns, and doubtless some deciding to take advantage of the chaos to steal a few items. Whatever the reason, their actions provided the principal rationale for the massacre of workers that followed. The Cazadores de Los Ríos troop trapped twenty-five people inside a store—and shot and killed everyone there. There were numerous similar episodes everywhere. One eyewitness recounted the events at another store, where soldiers chased a group of people onto the roof. "They found iron fences that prevented their descent. . . . When they struggled to separate the iron bars, the bullets arrived."[42] At another shop some looters escaped. "The store of González Rubio was left full of old shoes that the strikers left in exchange for . . . new ones."[43]

The military killed many, many innocent people. But civilians joined in slaying workers. Watching from their balconies as the strikers went by in the streets, some of the affluent decided to level a few shots at those passing below.[44] One individual at the scene told of perhaps the most hideous act of violence that day, which occurred on the riverfront. Frightened and horrified people ran and hid behind a wall by the river bank, but "soldiers rushed down with bayonets on their rifles. . . . I saw a man kneel and put up his hands . . . [but] a soldier struck him with a bayonet in the back and . . . threw him [into the river]." Many people ran into the water to escape, "but they shot them," until the river literally ran red.[45]

The gunfire began to slow around 5 P.M. Police and soldiers counseled quiet: "To your houses calmly" or "To sleep ladies, to sleep."[46] At 6 P.M., with order largely restored, the troops marched down Avenida 9 de Octubre through the center of Guayaquil. Some of the wealthier families opened the windows of their balconies and began applauding and offering cries of approval—"Long live the saviours of the city." The soldiers responded with "Long live the country!"[47] Police and soldiers patrolled the city through the night. An occasional shot could be heard, but for the most part the bloodletting had ended.

There was a great deal of damage; several stores reported near-total losses.[48] Most of the damage to property came from rifle fire. Although one store's owner claimed to have lost 150 revolvers, not one soldier had died. A soldier's horse had been killed, and ten to fifteen officials, soldiers, and policemen suffered injuries, but not one lost his life.[49]

The strikers did not fare as well. No one could calculate exactly how many people had died, for too many factors muddled the body count. There were those who were shot in the river and whose bodies had floated away. There were those who died in out-of-the-way places. Four days later, the police were still turning up bodies of those killed on the fifteenth. There were cadavers dumped by soldiers into the Guayas River at night.[50] And there was a common grave at the cemetery. A witness reported that flat cars pulled up carrying a "mountain of dead." Soldiers stacked the bodies on the street corner like "cord wood" and "threw this mountain of wounded and dead and half alive into the pit in the cemetery."[51] Later, troops had to guard the common grave to prevent people from trying to identify the nameless buried. At minimum, soldiers killed 300 people.[52]

It will always be hard to understand why the military behaved so violently. The first shots came spontaneously from the lower ranks; any possible feelings of solidarity they might have felt with the workers of Guayaquil were overshadowed by a sense of beleaguerment and fear as they faced a crowd that was vastly superior in numbers if not in arms. But the massacre went on and on that afternoon, and it is likely that the class differences and the regional jealousies of the sierra-born officers contributed to the continuing bloodshed. Most army officers came from the better-off families of the sierra, and the commanders stationed in Guayaquil were among the first cohort to graduate from the new military college in Quito.[53] This sierra military elite evidently saw it as their duty to command their troops to discipline the unruly montuvios of the coast.

The day after the tragedy, the moratorium committee sent President Tamayo the following cable: "Dr. Tamayo we are in the telegraph office. . . . The situation in Guayaquil is perfectly clear: if the order for the moratorium arrives immediately we will be able to obtain quiet in the city." Tamayo did not act. The committee sent another telegram: "Dr. Tamayo: In the name of Guayaquil we ask for the decree today, tomorrow will be too late. Yesterday cost 300 victims."[54] Finally, Tamayo indicated that he would issue the law, with a few modifications, that evening. At a few minutes before midnight he made the moratorium decree. It now seemed little more than an empty afterthought.[55]

After the massacre, the workers' assembly and the general strike broke up. Assembly leaders had never exercised effective control over their diffuse organization, and now that many workers wanted to return to their jobs, there was no stopping them. Some remaining in the assembly bravely vowed to stay on strike until management met the demands of the trolley and power employees, the original strike groups. But the protest had run out of momentum. Except for the electric and mule-drawn trolleys, all city services resumed within a couple of days.[56] Even the railroad employees gave up and went back to work. At last, on November 21, 1922, workers and management settled their strike. The workers got their pay raises, shorter hours, and other principal demands, but the trolley companies enacted the fare increases. Unlike the railroad strike, the Guayaquil general strike was at best a very limited and bittersweet victory. So many had been killed, so little had been accomplished.[57]

The moratorium, intended to help protect the workers' pay increases, failed miserably. The moratorium commission tried to hold the exchange rate at 3.80 sucres to the dollar, but that proved utterly unrealistic. The sucre's real value was closer to 5.00 to one dollar. Actually, the moratorium only got Ecuador into deeper financial trouble as foreign currency became so difficult to obtain that most major Guayaquil importers could not pay their bills.[58] No British company received payment for exports to Guayaquil after the exchange decree, due to Ecuador's governmental control of all foreign currency. Claims for payment also flooded in from French and German representatives.[59]

Whether the government handled all foreign exchange or not, Ecuador still earned too little of it, and its cost remained high.[60] Speculators in foreign currency were not, as President Tamayo frequently claimed, the cause of high foreign exchange prices. The cause was Ecuador's severe trade imbalance, primarily resulting from the world cacao market. Hence, the government could not solve the problem by instituting an official exchange rate beneath the price established on the open market, and the currency exchange regulations (enacted on November 16, 1922, amended on December 5 and again on December 9) failed to address Ecuador's foreign exchange dilemma. At last the government gave up on the idea, and even President Tamayo admitted that domestic control of specie was ineffective in stabilizing the price of currency set by world market forces.[61] On October 15, 1924, President Tamayo signed a bill abolishing foreign currency control.[62] The exchange rate remained high, inflation continued, prices soared for imports including Guayaquil's crucial food imports, and people continued to suffer. The mass action of general strike had failed to bring relief to the hard-pressed workers.

Beyond the failure of the moratorium, the meagerness of the workers' pay raises, and the heavy toll in lives, the strike wrought still other costs for the workers. It subjected many people to indiscriminate police violence, caused them great hardships, and left them with higher trolley fares. For many it was hard to see how they had benefited from the movement.[63] Moreover, after the events in Guayaquil, critics attacked the labor movement, and the government withdrew its support. The violence in Guayaquil greatly alarmed Ecuador's political leaders. The government rounded up all the major labor leaders and forced them into exile. Puig and Trujillo did not return for two years.[64]

Authorities labeled the labor movement as "bolshevik" and prone to violence. Despite clear evidence to the contrary, the government and the military tried to whitewash their roles in the Guayaquil violence. They placed the blame squarely on "bolsheviks" and "anarchist[s]."[65] The pro-government version of the massacre alluded to "certain foreign and pernicious elements" and "agents of revolution" who had led the workers' movement astray; it claimed that a "Soviet" plot existed with ties in Riobamba and Quito and charged that radical workers had attacked the soldiers with guns, rocks, and knives. Only looters and communists had been killed in the gunfire, the official version maintained.[67] "We are sure that the sane and good workers" returned to their homes, and only revolutionaries stayed out in the streets and got shot.[68] The military received credit—from Tamayo and others—for saving the nation from a "criminal furor."[69] Previously, the government had bankrolled the unions and wooed worker support. The Guayaquil bloodshed changed that policy: the government now became openly hostile to organized labor. The nascent labor movement fell apart. FTRE and the Gremial del Astillero disbanded. Organized labor grew timid and cowed and could not serve as an aggressive voice for worker interests.[70] Ecuador's labor movement became one of the most feeble in Latin America.

The movement's great popular enthusiasm meant that it could not be ignored, but its lack of formal organization meant that it was unable to monitor compliance with the concessions it won. As a political observer noted, when the government abolished the moratorium law in 1924, "not a voice was raised in its defense either in Guayaquil or elsewhere."[71] The uprising ran on energy and enthusiasm, both of which collapsed when the military massacre took the heart out of the movement. In Guayaquil, workers had responded spontaneously and democratically, if ultimately ineffectively, to the collapse of the cacao export economy.[72] From unions to mass action, all collective efforts of working-class women and men had failed to bring a meaningful improvement to their lives.

*Chapter Nine*

---

# Reflections on the Possibilities of Urban Social Reform

## Lessons from the Guayaquil Experience

In 1925 the agricultural association folded. The cacao age in Ecuador was over: average annual production fell by half from 1919–22 to 1926–30.[1] Some planters managed to shift production to bananas, sugar, coffee, tobacco, or rice, but Ecuador's total exports fell well below the level of the cacao boom years. Some owners went bankrupt, their great estates abandoned and occupied by squatters. River traffic slowed to a trickle, and the upriver region lapsed into stagnation. During the cacao years forty-six steam-powered craft had regularly worked the waters above Guayaquil; by 1939, only sixteen did.[2] Several wealthy merchant families lost the fortunes they had built. Everywhere, workers lost their jobs.

At its peak, the richness of the cacao boom granted vast treasures to a fortunate few, created opportunities for migration and employment for many, and made Guayaquil a very important city. But riches flee. Ecuador sank into economic decline and isolation—waiting, hoping for better luck, and watching for signs of a new boom that could favor the nation once again.

### Patterns in Urbanization and Social Reform

Latin America's rising export economies played a critical role in shaping the history of the region in the late nineteenth and early twentieth centuries and generated many shared experiences for South American cities. Guayaquil evidenced many of the common socioeconomic patterns. Most workers in Guayaquil, as elsewhere in urban Latin America during the era, fell into the expanding category of partially employed workers in low-paid, service-related jobs.[3] Likewise, as was the case in most Latin American cities of the time, foreigners emerged as key figures in the city's bustling commerce.

But in other regards, Guayaquil's unique circumstances put it at variance with patterns found in other Latin American cites. If, like other expanding cities, Guayaquil undertook the building of new houses, sewers, water lines, streetlights, firehouses, and schools, it grew faster than most and faced greater challenges. Some Latin American cities had less healthy settings— ports constantly exposed to exotic epidemics, tropical marshes where microorganisms might flourish, populations living in densely packed housing, or insufficient water supplies that facilitated the spread of killing diseases. Ethnicity is also a key variable, because human populations differ widely in the strength of their natural immunities to disease. Some cities suffered from all possible unhealthful natural circumstances, and Guayaquil was among them. It was a tropical port city swamped by a flood of newcomers from the sierra. Severe epidemics often attended the arrival of highland soldiers who had no previous exposure to coastal diseases. The confluence of circumstances placed the city at great risk to the spread of epidemic diseases. Among Latin American cities Guayaquil showed an uncommonly high death rate. Yet, if Guayaquil accomplished less than other cities, it had more to do.

Another special difficulty facing Guayaquil was that although the busy commerce of the coast did generate increasing tax revenues, the money had to be shared with the rest of the nation. Quito, the commercially isolated capital city, claimed a large portion. If Guayaquil often had trouble finding funds to support needed construction, social programs, and sanitation, one reason was that the sierra, especially Quito, siphoned off much of the tax money.[4]

Guayaquil enjoyed several apparent economic advantages, but these it squandered. For example, it was to the city's great economic advantage that the cacao-growing region required no massive infrastructure investment to transport export goods to port. The fluvial network made a very good transportation system—a gift from nature. Yet, with the money it saved from this, Ecuador built a railway into the Andes. Seduced by the cant of progress and the hope of spreading economic development to the sierra, Ecuador built one of the most expensive, impractical, and underused transport systems in the world.

Likewise, domestic control over its leading export could have been a great economic advantage for Ecuador. The critical economic decisions were not made by foreigners interested only in exploiting the riches of Ecuador. Further, the Ecuadorian cacao estate owners might well have been expected to reinvest more of their profits in the nation of their birth and the future home of their children. However, if dependency is hardly an advantage, domestic control is no panacea.[5] Ecuador's elite proved just as capable of doing harm as any foreign imperialist. In Ecuador, the domestic elite reaped the profits of the cacao trade, but failed to lay the economic foundation for long-term economic growth. The elite did not invest in building an economic future for Ecuador; they squandered their riches on opulent living, on European vacations and shopping sprees, gambling, imported racehorses, yachts, cars, fashions, furniture and liquor, and on four or more homes—in Guayaquil, on their estates, at the beach, and in Paris.

In the largest sense, the nature of the coastal monoculture export economy and the resulting social and political patterns that emerged played the most powerful role in shaping the prospects for urban social reform in Guayaquil. This was a city and region where the economy, society, and polity were effectively dominated by a small group of privileged elite. Upriver from Guayaquil, the great estate owners monopolized the cacao trade. In the city of Guayaquil, a handful of merchants, growers, and their families tightly controlled rising cacao riches.

Conditions favoring the development of a broad middle class of relatively well-off, educated urban professionals and small businessmen hardly existed. Guayaquil's pattern of concentrated wealth brought little "trickle down," and the dearth of industry meant there was little economic "spinoff" and hence relatively few managerial positions or opportunities for small entrepreneurs.[6] Moreover, the fact that the nation's capital was located in Quito also severely limited the size of Guayaquil's middle class; coveted white-collar jobs in the government bureaucracy were in the sierra, not in Guayaquil.

As a result, Guayaquil did not develop a large and politically powerful middle class, the very group that played such a critical role in reforming other cities, starting voluntary organizations, lobbying, voting, demanding that its needs be taken seriously, and defeating the entrenched interests that stood to lose financially from the passage of urban social reforms. As John J. Johnson concluded in his classic study, *Political Change in Latin America: The Emergence of the Middle Sectors:* "Since the middle sectors are predominantly urban, they favor . . . policies that assign a disproportionately large per capita share of public revenues to the urban centers (5)."

In addition, Guayaquil had few of the conditions which might have fostered the development of a powerful union movement: its export required no industrial processing prior to shipment; no body of workers occupied a strategic position commanding control over the flow of exports, for the cacao economy presented no such chokehold for workers to grab; and the various employers were usually Ecuadorian, making unavailable the explosive xenophobic themes used to advantage by workers elsewhere. Most importantly, Guayaquil had a glut of labor; the coastal and urban economy could not provide steady employment for the waves of migrants. Yet people kept arriving, as steady population growth in the highlands coupled with the expanding claims by hacienda owners there drove more and more peasants into landlessness. Most of those who came to Guayaquil could find but loosely arranged day-to-day jobs. Powerful worker organizations could scarcely be expected to develop in such an unfavorable socioeconomic context; unemployed jornaleros, washerwomen, cooks, and maids were unlikely union members. The call for reform in Guayaquil was faint because of the absence of union or middle-class voices to promote it. Thus, it fell to the small group of wealthy elite to tend to Guayaquil's progress, and while they cared about their city, their notions of the correct order of priorities were not seriously challenged or tempered by large, organized, and powerful competing groups or classes.

The elite had their own ideas for city improvement. "Guayaquil will soon be one of the best decorated with monuments to the national glory of any city in the Americas," said Aparicio Ortega in *La nación* of April 15, 1880. However, "Guayaquil, above everything else [needed] water, sewers, and paving." He believed "[t]he city was wealthy enough to take care of the basic public needs," but it did not. In Guayaquil, the dominant elite knew that they could safely ignore worker interests—so they did.

Guayaquil was just one South American example of early capitalist urbanization in the periphery of the international economy. During this laissez-faire stage of development, the economic system went largely unregulated and urbanization proceeded in a generally disorderly, unplanned, and uncontrolled fashion. In wealthy nations, developments associated with advanced industrialization brought into question this "night-watchman" notion of government and gave rise to the modern welfare state. This changing vision of the appropriately larger role of the state achieved its fullest expression in the successful industrialized nations. They could best afford it.

Positioned at the fringe of an international economy structured to benefit the developed nations at the center, Guayaquil and other Latin American cities found themselves at a marked disadvantage. Cities at the core had more money, and their health care, sanitation, and, most importantly, living standards improved. Prosperous nations turned their considerable resources on public health care problems. European governments funded successful health and welfare programs. Their medical schools were the best in the world, due in no small measure to relatively generous state support. Government in the United States, especially at the state or local level, had by the 1890s accepted its central role in protecting public health. True, developed nations sometimes squandered revenues, but then, they had more to waste. New York Health Director Herman Biggs commented in 1911, "disease is largely a removable evil."[7] That is, its removal could be purchased. Cities like Guayaquil could not afford to buy.

In the developed world, the socioeconomic structures gave rise to political patterns that resulted in urban reform. Lyman Johnson, in *Problem of Order* notes when discussing police reform: "It is not mere coincidence that . . . [reforms] appeared first in the most dynamic commercial and industrial nations (xi)." These developments "in Europe and North America occurred only after the appearance of new, politically assertive, propertied classes that demand increased protection and a more orderly society." The triumphant capitalism of the core nations gave rise to the development of a large middle class that joined the industrialists in pressing hard for state-funded infrastructure and state-funded social reforms. The nature of economic development in peripheral cities like Guayaquil could not create the political circumstances that might have allowed for fuller and more effective reform programs.

Of course, some Latin American cities of the time were much more livable than others, notably the Atlantic cities of recent European immigration—Buenos Aires, Argentina, Sao Paulo, Brazil, and Montevideo, Uruguay. Either these cities began this way, they were effectively reformed, or both.[8]

One major advantage that these Atlantic cities enjoyed was that they faced less severe sanitation and health challenges than did most other Latin American cities. Located in temperate climatic zones, these cities naturally possessed more salubrious health and sanitation conditions than did tropical cities like Guayaquil.

In Latin America, the possibilities for urban social reform were determined most markedly by the nature and performance of the economy. That is, certain economic circumstances created a more advantageous situation for responding to the social dilemmas of rapid urbanization. Economic prosperity, in industrializing or highly successful primary product exporting cities, meant more wealth, greater employment and investment opportunities, often a more even distribution of wealth, and more tax revenue. Economic success also brought foreign investment and loans, contributing further to the local economy. A diversified export pattern provided an added advantage, protecting the economy from inevitable price shifts and boom/bust cycles in international markets.

Accordingly, some cities had more resources for responding to urban needs, and again, in Latin America, the Atlantic cities of recent settlement were the most advantaged. They had more industry and stronger export economies, generated more tax revenue, and attracted more foreign capital.[9] These cities had more money.

Of course, having the resources to pay for urban improvements did not mean that reform automatically followed. Appropriate political conditions had to be in place. Potent groups or classes that wanted reform had to exist. The Atlantic cities of recent settlement were more likely to incubate such political conditions. More prosperous economies tend to produce more complex social structures, creating at once a broader middle class and a stronger union movement, especially where workers are relatively scarce and in greater demand. An active role by those two groups was critical in rousing the will for urban social reform.

The economic and political resources for confronting problems varied considerably in Latin America. Cities like Guayaquil were at great disadvantage; they were cities with less successful economies; they were non-primary cities that received less of the national budget; or they were cities set into a national political context of division among elites split by region, battling over tax revenue, or worse, fighting one another in costly civil wars. But ultimately, the most disadvantaged cities were those that could not develop a strong middle class and union movement to fight for reform. Richer and more complex economies commonly nurtured the formation and growth of these key groups. If in Guayaquil the pattern of economic growth could trigger rapid urbanization, it could not generate the nexus of political forces needed to force solutions to the resulting social dilemmas.

# Appendix

## People and Companies Worth 100,000 Sucres or More

| Name | Wealth (sucres) | Business ties and detail |
|------|-----------------|--------------------------|
| **1870–96** | | |
| Aspiazu Brothers | 800,000 | Exports, cacao growers, banking (BCA), Chamber of Commerce. Still present in 1920. One of the major cacao growing families in Los Ríos Province and in all Ecuador. |
| Nicolas Norero & Co. | 750,000 | Imports, cacao grower, exports, banking (BT, BE). Vice-consul for Italy. Company still present in 1909 as Alfonso Roggiero. |
| Levrary (or Lebray) Duran A. & Co., and Sixto L. Duran | 608,105 | Imports, exports, banking (BE, BI). Still present in 1909. |
| Norverto Osa & Co. | 500,000 | Colombian. Imports, banking (BI, BCH, BE). Still present in 1909 as Max Muller. |
| García and Ninci Vignolo | 500,000 | Imports. Still present in 1909. |
| Successors to Daniel López | 400,000 | Exports. From Manabí. Lived for a time in Spain. |
| Luís C. Rigail | 246,000 | Imports, urban real estate |
| M. B. Haskel (or Hassel) & Co. | 225,000 | Imports. |
| Ulpiano Bejarano & Teodoro Alvarado | 204,000 | Imports. Still present in 1909. Alavarado lived in Loja. |
| Enrique Rohde & Co. | 200,000 | Colombian. Exports, cacao grower, foreign insurance agent, rep. of German steamship line, banking (BT, BE), Chamber of Commerce. Still present in 1909. |

| Name | Wealth (sucres) | Business ties and detail |
|------|-----------------|--------------------------|
| **1870–96** | | |
| Antonio Madinya & Co. | 191,400 | Imports, exports, cacao grower, executive for the Light and Power Co., banking (BE, BT, Banco Nacional), Chamber of Comerce. Still present in 1909. |
| Successors to | | |
| E. H. Henríquez | 150,000 | Imports of machinery from the U.S., exports. Still present in 1909 as González Rubio. |
| Karl Koppel & Co. | 142,000 | Imports. |
| José Joaquin Icaza | 131,000 | Imports. One of the major cacao growing families in Ecuador. |
| Alberto S. Offner & Co. | 122,000 | Retail sales (jewelry store). |
| Barbato & Mirra | 115,000 | Imports. |
| A. and Lizardo García | 102,000 | Imports, retail sales (shoes), banking (BCA). Still present in 1909. Lizardo García was later elected President of Ecuador in 1905, but did not serve. Lizardo began by working for M. A. Luzarraga. Was an early associate of Nicholas Norero. Later, one of the founders of the Guayaquil Chamber of Commerce. Later was Minister of Hacienda, Senator from Guayas, Vice President. |
| Roberto B. Jones & Co. | 102,000 | Imports. |
| Francisco A. Ceballos | 100,000 | Imports. |
| Pedro Janer | 100,000 | Retail sales (two book stores). Still present in 1909. From Spain. Gave generously to help build hospitals in Cuenca and Quito. |
| Juan Kruger | 100,000 | German. Imports, rep. of foreign steamship line, foreign insurance agent (German). Still present in 1909. Owner of the "San Remo" hacienda. |
| Adolfo A. Reyre and Brothers & Co. | 100,000 | Exports, imports, banking, foreign insurance agent, rep. for French steamship line. In 1887 A. M. Reyre was Consul for Denmark, Greece and the Low Countries in Guayaquil. Reyre Co. still present in 1909. |
| Martin Reinberg & Co. | 100,000 | Exports, imports, Consul (the United States, Austria-Hungary, Mexico), banking (BCA), Chamber of Commerce. |
| Seminario Brothers | 100,000 | One of the major cacao growing families in Ecuador, exports, banking (BT, BI, BE, BCH). Consul (El Salvador), pier owners, reps. for foreign steamship line. |
| **1897–1908** | | |
| Aspiazu Brothers | 800,000 | One of the major cacao growing families in Ecuador. Exports, banking (Caja de Ahorros de la Sociedad de Artesanos), factory owners (a foundry), foreign insurance agents |

| Name | Weath (sucres) | Business ties and detail |
|------|---------|------------------------|
| **1897–1908** | | |
| | | (German), Chamber of Commerce. Aurelio Aspiazu was a Deputy to the Ecuadorian Congress in 1899. Lautaro was Governor of Guayas. |
| Eduardo Rickert & Co. (Hermann Moller) | 700,000 | Imports, foreign insurance rep., rep. for foreign steamship line, banking (BCH, BCA), offical for Carros Urbanos Co., Chamber of Commerce, Consul (Norway, Sweden, Germany, Switzerland, Austria-Hungary). Moller, a German, served as company manager. |
| Successors to Norvento Osa & Co., (Max Muller) | 700,000 | Colombian. Imports, foreign insurance rep. (Great Britain), retail sales (lumber), official for Carros Urbanos Co., Chamber of Commerce, Consul (Belgium), banking (BCA). |
| Levrary A. Duran & Co., (Ramon L. Mejia) | 650,000 | Imports, exports, banking (BCA), Chamber of Commerce. |
| López & Guzman, (Alfredo Cartwright) | 600,000 | Exports, river boat co. owner, foreign insurance agent (Great Britain), foreign steamship line rep., banking (BCH, BE), Consul (Great Britain), Chamber of Commerce. |
| Cesar Ninci & Co. | 600,000 | Imports, Chamber of Commerce. |
| Nicolas Noreno & Co., (Alfonso Roggiero) | 600,000 | Imports, exports, banking (BCA, BT, BCH), cacao grower, Consul (Italy), Chamber of Commerce. Roggiero was from Italy. |
| Adolfo A. Reyre & Brothers & Co. | 600,000 | Exports, imports, factory owner (rice and coffee milling), foreign steamship line rep. (France), foreign insurance agent. A.M. Reyre was a foreign consul for Denmark, Netherlands, Belgium, and Greece. Alfredo O. Reyre had been Consul for Ecuador in Buenos Aires, Argentina. Chamber of Commerce. |
| Seminario Brothers | 600,000 | Cacao growers, exports, river boat owners, imports, banking, Chamber of Commerce. One of the major cacao producing families of Ecuador. |

| Name | Wealth (sucres) | Business ties and detail |
|------|-----------------|--------------------------|
| **1897–1908** | | |
| Caamano Jijon & Co. | | |
| (Stagg) | 580,000 | Cacao grower, imports, exports, financier, factory owner (furniture and saw mill, cigarettes), foreign steamship line rep., Chamber of Commerce. One of the major cacao growing families in Ecuador. |
| Manuel Orrantia & Son (José Eduardo Molestina) | 500,000 | Colombians. Cacao growers, exports, imports, banking (BT, BE, BCH), foreign insurance agents (Great Britain), Consul (Brazil), Chamber of Commerce. |
| Successors to Julio Bunge & Co. | 500,000 | Imports, foreign insurance rep. (Great Britain, Netherlands). Julio Bunge had lived in Guayaquil and had served as German Consul. |
| Martin Reinberg & Co. | 400,000 | Exports, imports, agent for the Commercial Union Insurance Co., banking (BCA), government construction contractor, Consul (the United States, Mexico), Chamber of Commerce. Martin Reinberg was ruined in a 1901 bank panic. |
| Ernesto W. Garbe | 400,000 | Financier, banking. |
| Belisario Luque | 400,000 | Imports. Born in Guayaquil. Director of BCA. |
| Enrique Rohde & Co. | 400,000 | Exports, imports, cacao grower, cacao buyer, river boat owner, agent for the Phoenix Insurance Co., factory owner (soap and candles, cotton combing), banking (BE, BT), foreign steamship line rep. (German), Chamber of Commerce. |
| Antonio Madiaya & Co. | 350,000 | Imports, exports, banking (BE, BT), cacao grower, executive for the Light and Power Co., Chamber of Commerce. |
| Guillermo (?) Kaiser, & Co. | 250,000(?) | Importer (hardware), exports, foreign insurance agent (Great Britain), Chamber of Commerce. |
| Barbato, Mirra & Co. | 200,000 | Imports, Chamber of Commerce. |
| Heirs to Adolfo Klinger | 200,000 | Financeers, banking. |
| Rodríguez Brothers | 200,000 | Imports. |
| Successors to Rafael Valdez, (Luís A. Dillon) | 200,000 | Exports, imports, factory owners (candles), foreign insurance agents (Great Britain), rural sugar mill, banking (BCA), Chamber of Commerce. Valdez was born in Esmeraldas |

| Name | Wealth (sucres) | Business ties and detail |
|------|-----------------|--------------------------|
| **1897–1908** | | |
| | | Luís A. Dillon was born in Guayaquil and served as a Senator, Governor, and Minister of Hacienda. |
| Oscar Alexander & Co. | 150,000 | Imports, Chamber of Commerce. |
| Francisco Frugoni (or Frugone) & Co. | 150,000 | Imports, Chamber of Commerce. The Frugonis were immigrants from Italy. |
| Juan H. Kruger | 150,000 | Imports, foreign insurance agent (Germany), rep. for foreign steamship line, Chamber of Commerce, cacao grower. |
| Juan Parodi | 150,000 | Imports, Chamber of Commerce, cacao grower. Italian. (Barlolome Parodi was Ecudorian Consul in Sestri Ponente, Italy.) |
| Dario Morla | 100,000 | Financier, cacao grower. The Morlas were one of the major cacao growing families in Ecuador. |
| Homero Morla | 100,000 | Financier, banking (Caja de Ahorros de la Sociedad de Artesanos), executive for the Carros Urbanos Co., Consul (Venezuela, Bolivia), Chamber of Commerce, cacao grower. Homero Morla was Senator Suplente to Congress in 1899. Former president of the Sociedad Filantrópica. |
| Horacio Morla | 100,000 | Financier, cacao grower. |
| Jaime Puig Verdaguer & Co. | 100,000 | Imports, exports, banking (BE, BT). |
| Antonio Renella C. & Co. | 100,000 | Imports, Chamber of Commerce. |
| Carlos Stierlen & Co. | 100,000 | Imports, Chammber of Commerce. |
| San Qui & Co. | 100,000 | Imports. |
| Wo On & Co. | 100,000 | Imports. |
| Alejandro Mann | 100,000 | Factory owner (ice and beer, bricks), banking (BE, BT, Caja de Ahorros), Chamber of Commerce. |
| Ortiz & Co. | 100,000 | Retail sales (lumber), imports (lumber). |
| Rigoberto Sanchez Bruno | 100,000 | Financier, banking (BCA). |
| **1909–19** | | |
| Lisimaco Guzman & Sons (previously Lopez & Guzman) | 1,000,000 | Cacao exports, banking, (BE), factory owner (cigarettes), buyer and seller of letters of credit, sold imports into the interior, foreign steamship line rep., foreign insurance agent, urban real estate speculator, Chamber of Commerce. Lisimaco Guzmamn married Merecedes Aspiazu. |

| Name | Wealth (sucres) | Business ties and detail |
|---|---|---|
| **1909–19** | | |
| A. A. Reyre Brothers & Co. (Rodrigo Arrare) | 1,000,000 | Founded in 1877 or 1880. Cacao exporter, banking (BCA, BCH), Chamber of Commerce, rep. for foreign insurance companies, rep. for foreign steamship companies, consul for Holland and Denmark. |
| Levray A. Duran & Co. (Andres Franco) | 900,000 | Imports (cloth), retail sales (shoes, hardware), exports, Chamber of Commerce. |
| Julian Aspiazu | 800,000 | Cacao grower, banking, exports, sugar mill. |
| Lautaro Aspiazu | 800,000 | Cacao grower, banking, cacao exporter, Consul (Bolivia), Chamber of Commerce. Owner the "Santa Lucia" cacao estate and cattle ranch. Governor of Guayas. Industry: telephone, power, street cars, and matches. |
| Heirs to Jacinto I. Caamaño | 800,000 | Cacao growers, cacao exports, banking. One of the major cacao growing families. Rep. for a British steamship company. |
| Enrique Rohde & Co. (Guillermo E. Rohde Arosemena) | 800,000 | Founded 1874 or 1880. Cacao exports, banking (BE, BT), factory owner (cement, lard, flour, hardware). |
| Rickert & Co. | 700,000 | English. Imports, banking, retail sales (shoes, hardware). |
| Max Muller & Co. (formerly Norverto Osa & Co.) | 600,000 | German. Imports (especially machinery), exports, banking, retail sales (hardware), Chamber of Commerce, financial ties in Colombia. |
| Bartolome Vignolo & Son | 500,000 | Imports (hardware and cloth), retail sales, banking (BE), Chamber of Commerce, branches in interior Ecuador and in Paris. The Vignolos lived in Europe. |
| Enrique Gallardo & Co. | 500,000 | Dairy farming, banking, factory owner (beer and ice), cacao grower. |
| Cassinelli Brothers & Co. | 400,000 | Italians. Imports (wine, roofing material, hardware, liquors, shoes), retail sales (shoes), exports, and owner other branches in Ecuador. |
| Juan Kruger & Co. | 400,000 | German. Founded in 1883. Imports (from |

| Name | Wealth (sucres) | Business ties and detail |
| --- | --- | --- |
| **1909–19** | | |
| | | Germany and Spain), banking, retail sales (hardware), cacao grower, Chamber of Commerce. |
| Lorenzo Tous & Co. | 400,000 | Spanish. Founded in 1902. Cacao exports, imports (beer, liquor), retail sales (hardware), banking (BCA), cacao grower, Chamber of Commerce. Vice Consul (Spain). |
| Rodríguez Brothers | 350,000 | Imports. |
| Freres Farah | 300,000 | Syrian. Founded in 1896. Imports (cloth, clothing), retail sales, Chamber of Commerce. |
| A. & Lizardo García | 300,000 | Founded in 1889. Retail sales (shoes), Chamber of Commerce. |
| Alfonso Roggiero, (Norero & Roggiero) (formerly N. Norero & Co.) | 300,000 | Imports, retail sales (shoes), exports, banking (BCA), Consul (Italy), Chamber of Commerce. |
| Antonio Madinya L. & Co. | 300,000 | Retail sales, banking (BE, BT), Chamber of Commerce. Later became a cacao grower. |
| San Siong & Co. | 300,000 | Chinese. Owned cloth factory in Hong Kong. Imports (cloth), retail sales (cloth, clothing). Lived in Hong Kong. |
| Miguel E. Seminario | 300,000 | Cacao growers, cacao exports, banking. |
| Alvarado & Bejarano | 250,000 | Cacao experts, banking, Chamber of Commerce. Spanish. Representatives for foreign steamship lines. |
| Frugone & Co. | 250,000 | Italian. Founded in 1882. Imports (wine, liquor, crystal), exports. |
| Adolfo Poppe | 250,000 | German. Imports (clothing, perfume, hats), retail sales (hats), Chamber of Commerce. Lived in Europe. |
| Successors to B. Castagneto & Co. | 200,000 | Italians. Imports, retail sales (shoes). |
| Manuel Genaro Gomez | 200,000 | Retail sales (lumber), factory owner (saw mill). |
| Felix Gonzalez Rubio & Co. (formerly E. H. Henriguez) | 200,000 | Founded in 1878. Retail sales (shoes, hardware), imports (shoes from the United States), factory owners (mechanic's shop), Chamber of Commerce. President of the city council. |
| Caputi & Co. | 200,000 | — |
| Pedro Janer & Sons & Co. | 200,000 | Founded in 1876. Retail sales (books, stationery), imports (typewriters). From Spain. |

| Name | Wealth (sucres) | Business ties and detail |
|------|-----------------|--------------------------|
| **1909–19** | | |
| | | Gave money to help build hospital in Cuenca and Quito. President of the Sociedad Espanola de Beneficencia y Socorros. |
| Widow Sara C. Gastelu | 190,000 | — |
| Widow Adela Seminario | 175,000 | Cacao grower, boat owner. |
| Arboro & Co. | 150,000 | Imports, retail sales, Chamber of Commerce. |
| Leopoldo Mercado | 150,000 | Factory owner (cigarettes, matches, brooms), branches in Quito. |
| Juan Morilari | 150,000 | Retail sales. |
| Manuel A. Pereira | 150,000 | Retail sales (books, stationery), pawn shop owner, associated with Janer's bookstore. |
| Jaime Puig y Mir | 150,000 | Boat owner, exports, retail sales, factory owner (mechanic's shop, saw mill), banking (BT). |
| Segale Brothers & Co. (Norero) | 150,000 | Factory owners (noodles, chocolates). |
| J. José Sola & Co. | 140,000 | Retail sales (shoes, hardware), imports, Chamber of Commerce. Spanish. Vice President of the Sociedad Espanola de Beneficencia y Socorros. |
| Wo On & Co. | 130,000 | Founded in 1885. Retail sales (cloth), imports. |
| Cornelio Merchan | 128,700 | Born in Guayaquil? |
| Antonio Casas (Suarez Ruata & Co.) | 120,000 | Retail sales, imports (furniture, light fixtures). Lived in Europe. |
| Holger Glaesel (Peter Holts) | 120,000 | Founded 1895. Retail sales (drugs), imports (drugs), exports (drugs—bark, seeds), Consul (Denmark). |
| Lucas Tramontana | 120,000 | Retail sales (hardware). |
| Lorenzo Allerton | 100,000 | Cacao exports, imports. |
| Manuel E. Barrionuevo | 100,000 | Founded in 1893. Cacao exports, imports (jute for cloth bags), Chamber of Commerce. |
| Calveras & Co. | 100,000 | Barber shop, retail sales (sundries), branches in interior Ecuador. |
| Coello Brothers | 100,000 | Exports, cacao growers, imports. Founded 1883. |
| Descalzi & Co. | 100,000 | Retail sales (hardware). |
| Fayad & Co. | 100,000 | Retail sales (shoes). |
| Luís S. Garcia | 100,000 | Retail sales (shoes). |
| Khadra Brothers | 100,000 | Retail sales, Chamber of Commerce. |
| Kuon On Tay & Co. | 100,000 | Founded in 1900. Owned property and cloth factories in Hong Kong. Retail sales (two stores), imports (shoes), exports (cacao, coffee). |

| Name | Wealth (sucres) | Business ties and detail |
|------|-----------------|--------------------------|
| **1909–19** | | |
| Kuon San Lon | | |
| & Co. | 100,000 | Retail sales. |
| Manuel Man Lee & Co. | 100,000 | Chinese. Owned stores, farmms, and cloth factories in Hong Kong. Retail sales (cloth), imports. |
| Freres Najas | 100,000 | — |
| Luís Orrantina & Co. | 100,000 | Cacao and cotton export, cacao grower, banking (BE, BT) factory owner (bags), Chamber of Commerce. |
| Parodi & Juan Bruzzone | | |
| & Co. | 100,000 | Italians. Imports, cacao exports, cacao growers, retail sales, foreign steamship line rep.s (Italy), Chamber of Commerce. |
| Carlos S. Phillips | 100,000 | Retail sales (jewelry), imports. |
| Ernesto Stagg | 100,000 | Imports, retail sales (shoes), banking (Mercantile Bank of America), Chamber of Commerce, exports. |
| Vignolo Brothers | 100,000 | Factory owners (noodles, chocolates, liquor), imports, retail sales. |
| **1920–25** | | |
| Lizimaco (Lisimaco?) | | |
| Guzman and Son | 1,300,000 | Lizimaco did not live in Guayaquil. Carlos Guzman A. was in the Chamber of Commerce. Cacao exports, banking, (BE), factory owner (cigarettes), buyer and seller of letters of credit, sold imports into the interior, foreign steamship line rep., foreign insurance agents, urban real estate speculation. |
| Max Muller & Co. | 600,000 | German. Imports (especially machinery), exports, banking, retail sales (hardware), Chamber of Commerce, financial ties in Colombia. |
| Bartolo Vignolo | 550,000 | Did not reside in Guayaquil. Factory owners (noodles, chocolates, liquor), imports, retail sales. |
| Cassinello Brothers | 400,000 | Italians. Imports (wine, roofing material, hardware, liquor, shoes), retail sales (shoes), exports, other branches in Ecuador. |
| Aquiles Levray | 400,000 | — |
| Holger Glaesel | 300,000 | Retail sales (drugs), imports (drugs), export of natural drugs. Consul for Denmark. |
| Juan Kruger & Co. | 300,000 | German. Founded in 1883. Imports (from Germany and Spain), banking, retail sales (hardware), cacao grower, Chamber of Commerce. |

| Name | Wealth (sucres) | Business ties and detail |
|---|---|---|
| **1920–25** | | |
| Antonio Madinya and Co. | 300,000 | Retail sales, banking (BE, BT), Chamber of Commerce. Cacao grower. |
| Leopoldo Mercado | 300,000 | — |
| Manuel Antonio Pereira | 300,000 | Born in Babahoyo. Opened business in Guayaquil 1890. Was financeer—commission agent, made loans. Import retail sales. Hurt financially by WWI. Died 1917 in Guayaquil. Suicide? |
| Miguel E. Seminario | 300,000 | Cacao growers, cacao exports, banking. |
| Janer and Co. | 250,000 | Founded in 1876. Retail sales (books, stationery), imports (typewriters). From Spain. President of the Sociedad Espanola de Beneficencia y Socorros. |
| Felix González Rubio Co. | 230,000 | Born in Manabí. President of city council, president of Chamber of Commerce, Deputy and Senator for Guayas Province, president of BCH. Retail sales and imports of shoes. |
| Freres Farah | 220,000 | Imports. |
| Frugone and Co. | 220,000 | Imports. |
| Juan Marcos and Co. | 220,000 | Juan Francisco Marcos y Aguirre. Banking. President of City Council. Member of the Junta de Beneficencia. Member of Ecuadorian Legation in Paris. |
| Heirs of Manuel Genaro Gomez | 200,000 | — |
| Luís S. Garcia | 200,000 | Imports. |
| Levy Bros. | 200,000 | Imports. Branches in the sierra and along the coast. Felipe Levy Gildred, Theodore Levy Gildred, Alberto Levy Gildred, and E. Levy Gildred. Founded 1913 by Felipe. Exports of cacao and coffee. Sierra estate owners. Sold autos and farm equipment, etc. |
| Meloni and Co. | 200,000 | — |
| Adolfo Poppe | 200,000 | German. Imports (clothing, perfume, hats), retail sales (hats), Chamber of Commerce. Lived in Europe. |
| J. José Sola & Co. | 200,000 | Retail sales (shoes, hardware), imports, Chamber of Commerce. Spanish. Vice President of the Sociedad Espanola de Beneficencia y Socorros. |
| Won On and Co. (or Wo On) | 180,000 | Retail sales of cloth and imports, especially from the Orient. |
| Heirs of J. I. Caamaño | 150,000 | One of the major cacao growing families, cacao exports. |

| Name | Wealth (sucres) | Business ties and detail |
|---|---|---|
| **1920–25** | | |
| Evangelista Calero | 150,000 | Shoes. Founded 1895. Manufactured in Ecuador (the Fabrica Nacional de Calzado) and imported. Retail branches in the interior. |
| Descalzzi and Co. (or Descalzi Humberto) | 150,000 | Chilean. Came to Ecuador in 1922. Imports. |
| Luís Orrantia and Co. | 150,000 | President of City Council. Cacao and cotton export, cacao grower, banking (BE, BT) factory owner (bags), Chamber of Commerce. |
| San Sion (Siong?) & Co. | 150,000 | Chinese. Owned cloth factory in Hong Kong. Imports (cloth), retail sales (cloth, clothing). Lived in Hong Kong. |
| Manuel E. Barrionuevo | 150,000 | Founded 1893. Cacao exports, imports (jute for cloth bags), Chamber of Commerce. Present is 1909. |
| Hinnau Brothers | 120,000 | — |
| Manuel Man Lee & Co. | 120,000 | Chinese. Owned stores, farms, and cloth factories in Hong Kong. Retail sales (cloth), imports. |
| Kuon On Tay & Co. | 120,000 | Founded in 1900. Owned property and cloth factories in Hong Kong. Retail sales (two stores), imports (shoes), exports (cacao, coffee). |
| Juan Molinari | 120,000 | Imports. |
| Jaime Puig Mir | 120,000 | Banking (BT). Boat owners, exports, retail sales, factory owner (mechanic's shop, saw mill). |
| J. E. Bucaran | 100,000 | — |
| Luis Ferrari | 100,000 | Imports. |
| Juan Vallarino | 100,000 | — |
| Noziglia and Vallaza | 100,000 | — |
| Carlos Olivares | 100,000 | — |
| Segale Norero and Co. (Norero) | 100,000 | Owned La Universal chocolate factory. |
| Carlos S. Phillips | 100,000 | Retail sales (jewelry), imports. |

**Abbreviations:**

| | |
|---|---|
| BCA | Banco Comercial y Agricola |
| BCH | Banco de Credito Hipotecario |
| BE | Banco del Ecuador |
| BT | Banco Territorial |
| BI | Banco Internacional |

*Sources:* USMR, Wing, "Report," 30 May 1871; USCD, Guayaquil Merchants to the General Superintendent of the Panama Railway, Mosley, 8 Feb. 1879, McLean, "Report," June, 1880; *La nacion* (Guayaquil) 1880; Gallegos, *1883 almanaque; Almmanaque 1884;* L. F. Carbo, ed., *Ecuador en Chicago,* 420; MI, *Informes, 1885–1898* (yearly, title varies); *El grito del pueblo* (Guayaquil) 1–31 Oct., 1896, 1900, 1912; PCC, *Informe, 1887;* Matamoros, *Almanaque, 1892; Almanaque 1893;* IP, *Informes, 1897–1905* (yearly, title varies); CCm, *Memoria 1898–1921* (yearly, title varies); Gallegos, *1900 almanaque;* Paz, *Guía 1901;* GG, *Informe, 1901;* CU, *Memoria, 1903;* Barbosa, ed., *Almanaque 1907; El Ecuador: guía,* 335, 1151, 1277, 1278; Ceriola, *Guayaquil;* AA, *Memoria, 1915, 1916, 1921;* Enock, *Ecuador,* 86; *América libre;* MH, *Informe, 1920; 1925 almanaque; El guante* (Guayaquil) 1925; Perez, *Diccionario biográfico:* Weinman, "Ecuador and Cacao," Ph.D. diss., 52–53, 55, 67, 118, 136, 175; Maier, "Presidential," *JI-ASWA* 13 (July-Oct. 1971), 498; Estrada Ycaza, *Bancos,* 49, 58, 86, 131, 145, 238; Chiriboga, *Jornaleros;* Guerrero, *Los oligarcas;* Quintero, *Mito,* 123, 130–31, 143, 145, 214–16.

# Notes

## Abbreviations

| | |
|---|---|
| AA | Asociación de Agricultores, Guayaquil |
| *Ams* | *The Americas* |
| *BLAR* | *Bulletin of Latin American Research* |
| *BNYAM* | *Bulletin of the New York Academy of Medicine* |
| CC | Concejo Cantonal, Guayaquil |
| CCm | Cámara de Comercio, Guayaquil |
| *CSSH* | *Comparative Studies in Society and History* |
| CU | Empresa de Carros Urbanos |
| GBFO | Foreign Office, British Legation in Ecuador, Record Group 371 |
| GG | Gobernador del Guayas |
| *HAHR* | *Hispanic American Historical Review* |
| *I-AEA* | *Inter-American Economic Affairs* |
| IP | Intendencia de Policía del Guayas |
| JB | Junta de Beneficencia, Guayaquil |
| *JI-ASWA* | *Journal of Inter-American Studies and World Affairs* |
| *JIH* | *Journal of Interdisciplinary History* |
| *JLAS* | *Journal of Latin American Studies* |
| *JUH* | *Journal of Urban History* |
| *LAP* | *Latin American Perspectives* |
| *LARR* | *Latin American Research Review* |
| *L-BR* | *The Luso-Brazilian Review* |
| MH | Ministro de Hacienda |
| MI | Ministro de lo Interior |
| MIP | Ministro de Instrucción Pública |
| *MP* | *Marxist Perspectives* |
| MRE | Ministro de Relaciones Exteriores |
| OP | Oficina de Pesquisas, Guayaquil |
| PCC | Presidente del Concejo Cantonal, Guayaquil |
| *RAHG* | *Revista del archivo histórico del Guayas* |

| RC | Registro Civil |
|---|---|
| *RS* | *Rural Sociology* |
| SS | Servicio Sanidad, Guayaquil |
| TM | Tesorería Municipal, Guayaquil |
| USCD | Department of State, Despatches from United States Consuls in Guayaquil, 1826–1909, Record Group 59 |
| USGR | Department of State, General Records Relating to the Political Affairs in Ecuador, 1910–29, Record Group 59 |
| USMR | Department of State, Despatches from United States Ministers to Ecuador, 1848–1906, Record Group 59 |

**Introduction**

I would like to acknowledge the contributions of James Baer, coeditor of the manuscript "The Condition of the City: Urbanization in Latin America, 1870–1930, Daily Life and the Patterns of Working Class Politics," who suggested many of the ideas offered in this introduction.

1. Scobie, "Growth of Latin American Cities," 237.

2. Glade, *Latin American Economies*, 215–16; Platt, *Latin America and British Trade*, chapter 4; Furtado, *Economic Development*, chapter 4; Sanchez-Albornoz, *Population of Latin America*, 168, 178–79; Lewis, *Evolution of the International Economic Order*.

3. Scobie, "Growth of Latin American Cities." See also J. Johnson, *Political Change*, 32.

4. In "New Perspectives" (213) Greenfield writes, "The field of Latin American urban history remains relatively unexplored." In "Recent Works" (205), Walter writes, "Latin American . . . urban histories have been rather few and far between." Chance, in "Recent Trends" (183–88), calls for more study of the relationships between cities and their hinterlands, secondary cities, national politics, and the international economy, as does Morse in "Trends and Patterns."

5. Sofer and Szuchman comment in "City and Society," 119–20, that "earlier historians wrote biographies of cities . . . but lacked the interest, techniques, or desire to examine closely the people who lived in the city." They observe that "sociologists frequently conducted their investigations in ways that made it difficult to gauge historical change." Several have noted the lack of urban social history for the nineteenth century and the narrow and often technical nature of many studies from other fields. See Greenfield, "New Perspectives."

Historians of immigration also have voiced concern over "the need to bring . . . research together in a more synchronized and concerted fashion," Morawaska writes in "Sociology and Historiography," 198. Morawaska also offers a good discussion on the differences in the approaches of historians and sociologists to urbanization.

On Latin American urban historiography see Morse, "Recent Research" and "Trends and Issues," part 2. Works on the urban history of Latin America include Scobie, *Secondary Cities;* Mörner, *Adventurers and Proletarians;* Query, "Private Interests"; Roweis, "Urban Planning"; Moore, "Urban Poor"; Cross, *Urbanization;*

Browning, "Some Problematics"; Urquidi, "Underdeveloped City"; Morse, *From Community to Metropolis;* Schaedel, "Anthropological Study"; Harris, *Growth of Latin American Cities;* Morse, *Urban Development;* and Beyer, *Urban Explosion.*

6. This point is suggested in Greenfield, "Development of the Underdeveloped City," 107.

7. Cortes-Conde and Stein, *Latin America: A Guide to Economic History.* On the evolution of writing on the social history of Latin America from 1870 to 1930, see J. Johnson, "One Hundred Years of Historical Writing"; Barraclough, *Main Trends,* 117; Sofer, "Recent Trends," 167; and K. Erickson, Peppe, and Spalding, "Dependency vs Working Class History," 177–81.

8. See L. Johnson, *Problem of Order.* On these themes Johnson laments "the thinness of the current literature," concluding that "there is much work to be done" (ix, xix). "The related topics of crime and policing are among the least-studied areas of Latin American social history" (117). See also Blackwelder and Johnson, "Changing Criminal Patterns," 359, 372.

9. In "Three Contributions to Latin American Social History," 235, Socolow writes of Guayaquil: "What is really needed is a good discussion of the city's population, including occupational . . . structure, and changes within this population over the period under study." Szaszdi, in "Historiography of the Republic of Ecuador," 503–50, fully discusses the problems within Ecuadorian historiography up to 1964. See also Robalino Davila, *Orígines de Ecuador,* and Rodríguez-O., "New Research Opportunities in Ecuador," 95–100. Rodríguez-O., in "Research into the National Period," suggests the obligation of contemporary historians to augment the scholarly infrastructure of Ecuadorian history so that future historians may build on present work.

Studies of Ecuadorian social and economic history include Estrada Ycaza, *Regionalismo y migración* and *Los bancos del siglo XIX,* among many other fine contributions; L. A. Carbo, *Historia monetaria;* Conniff, "Guayaquil Through Independence"; and Peñaherrera de Costales and Costales Samaniego, *Historia social.*

10. For an assessment of new studies see Pineo, "Recent Contributions." Works that consider Ecuadorian political history include Albornoz Peralta, *Ecuador: luces y sombras;* Schodt, *Ecuador: An Andean Enigma;* Spindler, *Nineteenth-Century Ecuador;* Mörner, *Andean Past;* Hurtado, *Political Power;* L. A. Rodríguez, *Search for Public Policy;* Quintero López, *El mito del populismo;* Cueva, *Process of Political Domination;* Kasza, "Regional Conflict"; Milk, "Growth and Development of Ecuador's Worker Organizations"; Pike, *United States and the Andean Republics;* Martz, *Ecuador: Conflicting Culture;* Mills, "Liberal Opposition"; Maier, "Presidential Succession"; Weinman, "Ecuador and Cacao"; E. Erickson et al., *Area Handbook;* and Enock, *Ecuador.*

11. See Hahner, *Poverty and Politics,* xii, 168.

12. Blackwelder and Johnson, "Changing Criminal Patterns," 370–71. The Ministry of Labor and Social Welfare in Ecuador started collecting such information only after 1925. Middleton, "Division and Cohesion," 185.

13. The Archivo Nacional in the Casa de la Cultura in Quito is an example of this problem.

## Chapter One: Urbanization in a Nonindustrial, Nonprimary City

1. Wolf, *Geography and Geology*, 575.

2. Scobie, "Growth of Latin American Cities." During this era Latin America's population increased from 30.5 million in 1850 to 61 million by 1900 and nearly doubled again by 1930 to 104 million. Latin American population grew at a rate faster than that of Europe or North America from 1900 to 1930. Glade, *Latin American Economies*, 215–16; Platt, *Latin America and British Trade*; Furtado, *Economic Development of Latin America*; Sanchez-Albornoz, *Population*, 168, 178–79; J. Johnson, *Political Change*, 32.

## Chapter Two: Economic Geography

This chapter on the geography of Guayaquil and its hinterland is drawn principally from Wolf, *Geography and Geology*; Wiles, "Land Transportation"; Whitbeck et al., *Economic Geography*; Weinman, "Ecuador and Cacao"; E. Erickson et al., *Area Handbook*; Compañía Guía del Ecuador, *El Ecuador: guía*; Franklin, *Ecuador: Portrait of a People*; Enock, *Ecuador*; Ayala Mora, *Epoca republicana*, 1:136–37; *El comercio* November 13, 1877 (Guayaquil), cited in unpublished research notes of Estrada Ycaza.

The discussion of coastal land tenure and labor is drawn from Conniff, "Guayaquil Through Independence," 385–410; Hamerly, *Historia social*; Franklin, *Ecuador*; Phillips, "Gender, Class and Cultural Politics"; Redclift, *Agrarian Reform*; Peñaherrera de Costales and Costales Samaniego, *Historia social*, vols. 1 and 4; Weinman, "Ecuador and Cacao"; Paredes Ramirez, "Económica y sociedad"; and Saunders, "Man-Land Relations," 57–69.

1. Eilif V. Miller, "Ecuadorean Soils and Some of their Fertility Properties," Ph.D. diss., Cornell University, 1948, cited in Weinman, 12; Wolf, *Geography and Geology*; Franklin, *Ecuador*, 9.

2. MIP, *Memoria, 1905*, 14.

3. GG, *Informe, 1901*, 95; MIP, *Memoria, 1905*, 7–14; Compañía Guía, *El Ecuador: guía*, 1261–1303; Chiriboga, *Jornaleros y gran proprietarios*, 153, 161; MH, *Informe, 1920*; Chiriboga, *Jornaleros*, 133.

4. This section is drawn from Compañía Guía, *El Ecuador: guía*, 1261–1303; MIP, *Memoria, 1905*, 7–9. L. F. Carbo, *El Ecuador en Chicago*, 65.

5. GG, *Informe, 1877*, 3; L. F. Carbo, *El Ecuador en Chicago*, 50–57; MIP, *Memoria, 1905*, 4; Compañía Guía, *El Ecuador: guía*, 581–613.

6. MI, *Informe, 1902*; MIP, *Memoria, 1905*, 5; Compañía Guía, *El Ecuador: guía*, 761–76.

7. GG, *Informe, 1901*, 117.

8. This discussion is drawn from the following: GG, *Informe, 1901*, 95; Compañía Guía, *El Ecuador: guía*, 1166, for information on Alvarez, and 453–558, 1134–1255; and MIP, *Memoria, 1905*, 9–14.

9. MIP, *Memoria, 1905.*

10. Tyrer, "Demographic and Economic History"; Browne, "Effects of Epidemic Disease," iii, 114, 125; Browne, "Effects of Epidemic Disease," 127–28; Hamerly, "Social and Economic History," 26–27, 82; M. Redclift, *Agrarian Reform,* 41; Hurtado, *Political Power,* 95, 31; Rojas, *La novela,* 24; Estrada Ycaza, *Regionalismo y migración,* 265.

11. Peñaherrera de Costales and Costales Samaniego, *Historia social,* vol. 1; Redclift, *Agrarian Reform,* 11; L. A. Rodríguez, *Search for Public Policy,* 28; Rojas, *La novela,* 24; and Weinman, "Ecuador and Cacao," 89–91; Pike, *U.S. and the Andean Republics,* 149. Perhaps the best work on the *huasipungaje* is the novel by Jorge Icaza, *The Villagers.*

12. Jaramillo, "Ecuadorian Family," 399.

13. GBFO, "Annual Report for 1923," December 31, 1923; GG, *Informe, 1901,* 54, 103–14; USCD, Horatio N. Beach, "Report," July 8, 1885; PCC, *Informe, 1889,* 15.

14. Hassaurek, *Four Years,* 246; USMR, Rumsey Wing, "Report," August 11, 1870; Peñherrera de Costales and Costales Samaniego, *Historia social,* vol. 1; Redclift, *Agrarian Reform,* 11; L. A. Rodríguez, *Search for Public Policy,* 28, 65; Rojas, *La novela,* 24; Weinman, "Ecuador and Cacao," 89–91; *La nación,* March 6, 1880.

15. Cisneros Cisneros, "Indian Migrations," 227, 230; Jaramillo, "Ecuadorian Family," 399.

16. Compañía Guía, *El Ecuador: guía,* 340.

17. *Diario Oficial,* Quito, September 12, 1893, cited in unpublished research notes of Estrada Ycaza. Phillips, "Gender, Class, and Cultural Politics," 36. On the independent small landholders see Redclift, *Agrarian Reform,* 39. Another advantage for coastal workers was that cacao production was probably less physically demanding than other types of agricultural labor. Mason notes in "Demography, Disease and Medical Care," 111–12, that mortality rates were lower when slaves in the Caribbean worked cacao than when they worked sugar, coffee, and other crops. For a different interpretation of coastal relations of production stressing the importance of debt peonage, see Guerrero, *Los oligarcas del cacao;* and Chiriboga, *Jornaleros.*

**Chapter Three: The Performance of a Primary Product Export**

1. Conniff, "Guayaquil Through Independence," 389, 399; Hurtado, *Political Power,* 28; and Clayton, *Caulkers and Carpenters.* This section on the economic history of the coast draws also from Hamerly, *Historia social;* Conniff, 388–96; L. A. Rodríguez, *Search for Public Policy,* 59; Clayton; and Tyrer, "Demographic and Economic History."

2. For further discussion of Guayaquil's exports and imports in the eighteenth century, see Tyrer, "Demographic and Economic History," 254. In the 1780s, "the assessed value of total exports from Guayaquil . . . was around 400,000 pesos annually, 200,000 of which came from cacao" (268). See also Clayton, *Caulkers and Carpenters.*

3. See Rodríguez-O., *Down From Colonialism.*

4. See R. Graham, *Great Britain and Modernization in Brazil;* and Platt, *Latin America and British Trade.*

5. Lewis, *Evolution of the International Economic Order*, 6 and passim. On the expansion of Latin America's trade see Kenwood and Lougheed, *Growth of the International Economy*. International trade, the authors write, "trebled and may have nearly quadrupled" from 1850 to 1880 (79). Also see Hobsbawm, *Industry and Empire;* Wallerstein, *Modern World System*, vols. 1 and 2; Furtado, *Economic Development of Latin America;* Platt, *Latin America and British Trade;* Perez Brignoli, "Economic Cycle in Latin American Agricultural Export Economies"; L. A. Carbo, *Historia monetaria;* and Sanchez-Albornoz, *Population*, 153.

6. Hamerly, "Social and Economic History," 104, 144; Wiles, "Land Transportation Within Ecuador," 55; and see Clayton, *Caulkers and Carpenters*. See Kenwood and Lougheed, *Growth of the International Economy*, 144. Discussing the growth of the international economy in the nineteenth century, the authors write: "Outside the industrializing countries economic growth was primarily a reflex action to the steady and persistent rise in the world *demand* for primary products" [emphasis added]. Also see Glade, *Latin American Economies*, chapter 7. Glade writes that "it was during the sixty or seventy years following 1850 that modern economic development had its real inception in Latin America" and that "the pull of forces generated in the world market became well-nigh irresistible" (211). Also see Bergquist, *Labor in Latin America*, 1. Bergquist writes that Latin American historiography suffers from "neglect of the full social implications of the ways Latin American economies were integrated into an evolving world capitalist system in the century after 1880."

7. Scobie writes in "Growth of Latin American Cities" that "steam navigation doubled the capacity of ships in the two decades before 1870 and halved the time needed to cross the Atlantic (234)." Chiriboga, *Jornaleros*, 363, 364, 44. Daniel Peter hit on the idea of milk chocolate in 1860.

8. This section on exports is drawn from tables 2.1, 2.3, 2.4, and 2.6, and on Ecuadorian cacao in the 1880s, from *La nación*, April 22, 1880.

9. Ayala Mora, *Epoca republicana*, 137.

10. *Bulletin of the Imperial Institute* 19, no. 3 (1921), cited in Ecuador, Consulate of Ecuador, New York. *The Republic of Ecuador* (July 1922), 26, reprinted in, GBFO, "Report," January 1922; Niles, *Casual Wanderings in Ecuador*, 42.

11. Guayaquil handled nearly all of Ecuador's export trade. Therefore, even though data on the destination of Guayaquil's exports alone, excluding the rest of Ecuador, is not always available, total figures for all of Ecuador's exports still offer a very good idea of what the export situation was for Guayaquil and the surrounding cacao-producing country. Compañía Guía, *El Ecuador: guía*, 891–97.

12. See GG, *Informe, 1901;* USCD, Shanon M. Eder, "Report on Ecuador's Commerce in 1878," March 15, 1879; and Gallegos Naranjo, *1883 almanaque*, 305.

13. This section on imports is drawn from tables 2.7 and 2.8. Discussion of British shipping is drawn from: USMR, Rumsey Wing, "Report," May 30, 1871; USCD, Charles Weile, "General Review for 1869," February 2, 1870; George Bragdon, "Report," November 14, 1870; Weile, "Report," June 24, 1875, "Report," October 24, 1875; Guayaquil Merchants to the General Superintendent of the Panamá Railway,

Brandon Mosley, Esq., February 8, 1879; Mosley to the Merchants of Guayaquil, March 4, 1879, in Alexander McLean, "Report," June 1880; McLean, "Report for 1879," January 24, 1880, "Report," April 3, 1880, and "Report," June 1880. USCD, Weile, "Report on Ecuador's Commerce," January 17, 1872. GBFO, J. A. P. Edgecumbe, "Memorandum," January 16, 1922. The British company had complete control over the Panamá-to-Guayaquil trade but only about half the southern Pacific trade with Peru and Chile. Weinman, "Ecuador and Cacao," 186. Also see USMR, Wing, "Report," January 31, 1871; and USCD, McLean, "Report for 1879," January 24, 1880.

14. USCD, Bragdon, "Report," November 14, 1870, Martin Reinberg, "Report of Ecuador and Commerce of Guayaquil for the Year 1886," March 10, 1887; GBFO, R. Mitchell, "Report on the Economic Conditions in Ecuador," September 25, 1923.

15. See: GG, *Informe, 1901;* V. E. Estrada, *Balanza económica;* CCm, *Memoria, 1900, 1902, 1903, 1904,* and *1919;* and *El Ecuador: guía,* 941. Figures for Guayaquil's imports (as distinct from all of Ecuador's imports) are not always available. However, because Guayaquil received more than 90 percent of Ecuador's total imports during this era, Ecuadorian import totals can be used to gain a good idea of Guayaquil's import situation. Also see Franklin, *Ecuador,* 47.

16. GBFO, Mitchell, "Report," September 25, 1923.

17. Chiriboga, *Jornaleros,* 223–24; Wiles, "Land Transportation," 64; Weinman, "Ecuador and Cacao," 99, 191, 215, 311. The city was at variance with the import pattern for most other South American monocultural export economies. Guayaquil did not primarily import luxuries for elites' use. However, traders sometimes brought in expensive items clandestinely in order to avoid import taxes. See Weinman, "Ecuador and Cacao," 123–24; and MI, *Informe, 1899,* 12–13. Until the 1920s, when some light industry began to appear in Guayaquil, the city imported more wine and liquor than machinery. Total imports of nonconsumer goods, lumber, machines, chemicals, boats, and so forth, rarely reached more than 8 percent of Ecuador's imports.

18. L. A. Rodríguez, *Search for Public Policy,* 20, 22, 27. USCD, Horatio N. Beach, "Description of Travel from Guayaquil to Quito," September 25, 1885. USMR, Archibald Sampson, "Report," November 19, 1898.

19. Ecuador had hoped that the railroad would offer the long-desired transportation link to the markets of the highland cites. The Guayaquil Chamber of Commerce announced in 1900 that "the opening of the railway to the interior will operate a revolution in the production and consumption of the inter-andine provinces." CCm, *Report 1901,* 21. On the problems of land transportation, see the comments provided in "Consul Letter to Minister Wing," February 1870, in USMR, Wing, "Report to the State Department," February 19, 1870. On the problems with the railway once completed, see the comments in GBFO, Beauclerk, "Report of the British Minister on His Visit to Ecuador," January 13, 1908, Mitchell, "Report," May 29, 1923. For background on the causes of the failure of this railroad, see Wiles, "Land Transportation," and L. A. Rodríguez, *Search for Public Policy.* Rodríguez shows that the money spent on the railway was generally money wasted.

20. *El grito del pueblo,* January 19, 1912.

21. L. A. Rodríguez, *Search for Public Policy,* 1; Kasza, "Regional Conflict," 38.

22. DeShazo, *Urban Workers,* 6.

### Chapter Four: The Political Economy of Regionalism

1. This discussion of Ecuadorian politics is drawn from: L. A. Rodríguez, *Search for Public Policy;* Schodt, *Ecuador;* Spindler, *Nineteenth-Century Ecuador;* Maier, "Presidential Succession"; Hurtado, *Political Power;* Pike, *U.S. and the Andean Republics;* Mörner, *Andean Past;* Weinman, "Ecuador and Cacao"; Milk, "Growth and Development"; Cueva, *Process of Political Domination;* Quintero López, *El mito del populismo;* Albornoz Peralta, *Luces y sombras;* Enock, *Ecuador;* and E. Erickson et al., *Area Handbook.*

2. Cueva, *Process of Political Domination,* 18.

3. Ibid.; Chiriboga, *Jornaleros;* Quintero López, *El mito del populismo.*

4. Hurtado, *Political Power,* 128.

5. L. A. Rodríguez, *Search for Public Policy,* xiii.

6. This discussion of Ecuadorian government finance is drawn from: L. A. Rodríguez, *Search for Public Policy;* Schodt, *Ecuador;* Spindler, *Nineteenth-Century Ecuador;* Maier, "Presidential Succession"; Hurtado, *Political Power;* Pike, *U.S. and the Andean Republics;* Mörner, *Andean Past;* Weinman, "Ecuador and Cacao"; Quintero López, *El mito del populismo.*

7. L. A. Rodríguez, *Search for Public Policy,* 95.

8. Estrada Ycaza, *Los bancos.*

9. L. A. Rodríguez, *Search for Public Policy,* 29, 34.

10. Kasza, "Regional Conflict," 20, 15, 16; Hamerly, "Social and Economic History," 4–5.

11. Kasza, "Regional Conflict," 21, 14, 19, 22; *Patria,* 1917–18; IP, *Informe, 1897, 1898;* E. Erickson et al., *Area Handbook,* 149.

12. L. A. Rodríguez, *Search for Public Policy,* 54, 45; Kasza, "Regional Conflict."

13. Guayaquil's situation was not entirely unique in Latin America. In Brazil, for example, São Paulo was clearly economically dominant, but received less from the central government than it paid in. It was "incontestably the only [city] . . . giving to the imperial government without receiving," writes Alberto Sales in *Ideologo da República* (São Paulo: Companhía Editora Nacional, 1965), 193, quoted in Hahner, *Poverty and Politics,* 39. And while Sao Paulo's commerce filled Brazil's coffers, most jobs in the national bureaucracy could only be found in rival Rio de Janeiro (5,967 government jobs in Rio compared to 984 in São Paulo in the 1890s), writes Hahner in *Poverty and Politics,* 145.

14. The Guayaquil daily, *La nación,* on March 6, 1880, employed supply-side arguments to justify ending the tithe tax: it contended that ending the tax would stimulate economic activity and result in more, not less, revenue overall.

15. L. A. Rodríguez, *Search for Public Policy,* 104, appendix B and passim. Also see Conniff, "Guayaquil Through Independence"; Estrada Ycaza, *Los bancos;* and L. A. Carbo, *Historia monetaria.*

16. MI, *Informe, 1887,* "Report of the Sub-director of Education of Guayas Province, May 3, 1887"; *Informe, 1903,* "Report on Public Works"; *Informe, 1885.*

17. See Patricio Martínez, *Las raíces del conflicto* (Guayaquil, 1979), 60–62, cited in Ayala Mora, *Epoca republicana,* 180.

18. MI, *Anexos al Informe, 1910,* xxi-xxiii.

19. PCC, *Informe, 1892,* 33; PCC, *Balance de la contabilidad municipal, 1910;* CC, *Gaceta municipal, 1908,* 207–8.

20. GG, *Informe, 1877,* 24; PCC, *Informe, 1887, 1889,* 17, 43–62, *1892,* 31, tables S-U, *1919,* 10, xxiii; CC, *Gaceta municipal, no.* 479, January 5, 1895, 529–43; PCC, *Balance de la contabilidad municipal, 1909;* TM, *Informe, 1915;* and L. A. Rodríguez, *Search for Public Policy,* appendix K.

21. Inflation did not become a factor until World War I. These figures were calculated from the sources cited in note 25. The budgets of other Guayas cities were always very small. For example, in 1877 Daule had a budget totaling 10,000 sucres, and Santa Elena's total budget was 9,000 sucres. In 1887 Yaguachi had a budget of 12,000 sucres, Santa Elena 9,000 sucres, and Daule 663 sucres. In 1903 Yaguachi had a budget of 20,000 sucres. In 1909 Yaguachi's budget was 32,000 sucres, Daule's was 38,000 sucres, Santa Elena's was 26,000 sucres, and Balzar's was 31,000 sucres. In 1917 Santa Elena had a budget of 34,000 sucres, and Yaguachi 15,000 sucres. GG, *Informe, 1877,* 27; MI, *Informe, 1887, 1903,* "Report of the President of Council of the Canton of Yaguachi," *1917,* "Report of the Governor," 610–25; *El Ecuador: guía,* 219–20.

22. This section is drawn from: MI, *Informe, 1887;* PCC, *Informe, 1887, 1889,* 43–53, *1892,* 31–37, tables P-U, *1916,* 8, *1919,* 10, xxiii; CC, *Gaceta municipal, no.* 479, January 5, 1895, 529–43; CC, *Gaceta municipal, 1908,* 207–8, 347; PCC, *Balance de la contabilidad municipal, 1909; El Ecuador: guía,* 228–29; TM, *Informe, 1915; América libre,* 131.

23. PCC, *Informe, 1895.*

24. MI, *Informe, 1903,* "Report of the Governor, Martín Aviles, June 30, 1903," *Anexos al informe, 1910,* "Report of the Governor, July 16, 1910," 7; PCC, *Informe, 1919,* 10.

25. GG, *Informe, 1877,* 24–25; PCC, *Informe, 1889, 1892,* table U; PCC, *Estado de la municipalidad de Guayaquil;* CC, *Gaceta municipal, 1908,* 208, 347; CC, *Gaceta municipal: actas de las sesiones efectuadas por el ilustre consejo municipal de Guayaquil, 1912,* 8, 9, 15–16; and L. A. Rodríguez, *Search for Public Policy,* 77, 116.

26. PCC, *Informe, 1889,* 50, *1892,* table U; CC, *Gaceta municipal, 1908,* 208, 347; PCC, *Balance de la contabilidad municipal, 1909.*

27. This section is drawn from MI, *Informe, 1887;* PCC, *Informe, 1887, 1889,* 43–53, *1892,* 31–37, tables P-U, *1916,* 8, *1919,* 10, xxiii; CC, *Gaceta municipal no.* 479, January 5, 1895, 529–43; CC, *Gaceta municipal, 1908,* 207–8, 347; PCC, *Balance de la contabilidad municipal, 1909; El Ecuador: guía,* 228–29; TM, *Informe, 1915; América libre,* 131.

28. PCC, *Informe, 1919,* "Informe del Tesorero Municipal, E. Aguirre Overweg," xxiii.

29. MI, *Informe, 1871.*

30. *El Ecuador: guía,* 105.

31. Guayas governor J. Sanchez Rubio, for example, denounced undue political centralization in his report for 1877. The governor felt that the push for excessive control from Quito was harming the educational system. GG, *Informe, 1877*, 8–9.

32. MI, *Informe, 1901*, 111–12, *Informe, 1903*, "Decretos Ejecutivos," and *Anexos al informe, 1910*, 42–45.

33. Kasza, "Regional Conflict," 4, 25, 31, 36. Even today the "conflictual issues caused by administrative centralization" generate regional political tensions. Guayaquil still feels that there is "regional discrimination in the administration of the law," that the central government tries "to control the autonomous institutions of Guayas Province," and that guayaquileños face "exorbitant amount[s] of red tape . . . when applying for government benefits or licenses." Branches of the national bureaucracy in Guayas have even been required to have the purchase of office supplies approved in Quito. Kasza, "Regional Conflict," 30, 31, 39.

## Chapter Five: The People of Guayaquil

1. Guayaquil enjoyed a situation of urban primacy in Guayas province, if not within Ecuador as a whole. Guayaquil represented 25 percent of the total population of Guayas province in the years 1857–58, 28 percent in 1877, 45 percent in the years 1886–87, 46 percent in the years 1889–90, 35 percent in 1894, 42 percent in 1905, 35 percent in the years 1908–9, and 25 percent in the years 1925–26. GG, *Informe, 1877*, 2–4, *1907*; PCC, *Informe, 1887*; Matamoros Jara, *Almanaque de Guayaquil*, 64; Linke, *Ecuador*, 4–8; Estrada Ycaza, *El hospital*, 58, 142; Gallegos Naranjo, *1883 almanaque de Guayaquil*, 201; IP, *Informe, 1890*, 8, 14–17, *1903*, 4, 16, *1904*, 64–65, *1905*, 133; Quintero López, *El mito del populismo*, 360; L. F. Carbo, *El Ecuador en Chicago*, 43–47; Estrada Ycaza, *Regionalismo y migración*, 265; MI, *Anexos al informe, 1910*, 16; Enock, *Ecuador*, 243; *América libre*; *1925 almanaque Guayaquil*, 6–10.

2. Boyer and Davies, *Urbanization in Latin America*, 62; Sanchez-Albornoz, *Population*, 172; DeShazo, *Urban Workers*, 4.

3. See McNeill, *Plagues and Peoples*; and Sanchez-Albornoz, *Population*.

4. MI, *Informe, 1903*.

5. MI, *Informe, 1912*; MIP, *Informe, 1921*, 137–38.

6. Such a pattern holds for most of Latin America in this era. See Sanchez-Albornoz, *Population*, 171.

7. Sanchez-Albornoz, *Population*, 153, 159; Hahner, *Poverty and Politics*, 47, 92; Blackwelder and Johnson, "Changing Criminal Patterns."

8. Conniff, "Guayaquil Through Independence," 391.

9. As Saunders notes in his study of Ecuadorian demographics, "long distance migration is selective of young males." In 1880 and 1890 male immigrants to Guayaquil outnumbered female ones about two to one. Immigrants were underrepresented in the death totals because few children made the trip. Immigrants tended to be adventuresome young men. See Saunders, *People of Ecuador*, 30. In 1911, 132 of 3,368, or 4 percent, of those who died in Guayaquil were foreign born, and in 1929 foreigners accounted for 1 percent of those who died in the city. SS, *Informe*,

*1911;* RC, *Informe, 1929–1930.* Other studies have also shown immigrants to be overrepresented in arrest totals. Blackwelder and Johnson noted that while immigrants totaled 49 percent of the population of Buenos Aires at the turn of the century, arrest records counted immigrants as 70 percent of all offenders. Blackwelder and Johnson, "Changing Criminal Patterns," 366. Census data on Guayaquil immigrants shows that in 1880 there were 930 adult immigrants in the city, 4,378 total immigrants in 1890, and 9,368 in 1899. PCC, *Informe, 1889, 1892;* IP, *Informe, 1890–1910;* JB, *Informe, 1893–1925.*

10. GG, *Informe, 1877,* 5–7; MI, *Informe, 1903,* "Births, Deaths, and Marriages in Ecuador in 1902"; MIP, *Informe, 1919,* cxiv, *Informe, 1921,* 138 and passim.

11. Other Latin American nations had more success with programs like this. On Brazil, for example, see Hahner, *Poverty and Politics,* 135. Sanchez-Albornoz, *Population,* 152. USCD, Owen McGarr, "Report," September 29, 1886.

12. Sanchez-Albornoz, *Population,* 154, 156–57.

13. See Le Gouhir y Rodas, *Historia de la república,* 1:117; and compare Martz, *Ecuador,* 36.

14. Compare Parlee, "Porfirio Diaz, Railroads, and Development," 282. The police contended that these Jamaicans were simply more prone to crime, but it is rather more likely that the immigrants were subject to police persecution. Police officials took a dim view of all working-class immigration; indeed, Police Commissioner Camilo Landin O. held that most of the immigrants were anarchists. Police officials generally blamed the city's small increase in crime on unwanted working-class foreigners. On the other hand, a few foreigners who arrived in Guayaquil were not there by choice. Sometimes whaling ships would desert sailors on the Ecuadorian coast in order to cheat the men out of their wages. These unfortunates would then wander into Guayaquil and beg for money to buy passage home. See, USCD, Horatio N. Beach, "Report," July 31, 1885; IP, *Informe, 1910,* 25.

15. Aviles, *Ecuador en el centenario,* 52; GBFO, Beauclerk, "Report of the British Minister on His visit to Ecuador," January 13, 1908, "Report," September 10, 1909; Gallegos Naranjo, *1900 almanaque; El Ecuador: guía,* 1143; USCD, William B. Sorsby, "Report," September 30, 1889; *La nación,* February 11, 1880, 2; *El grito del pueblo,* January 2, 4, and 7, 1912. The U.S. Consul reported in 1886 that 200 "coolies" had come from Peru since 1873, taking jobs as "tradesmen and cooks in Guayaquil . . . [or as] agricultural laborers on neighboring plantations." USCD, Owen McGarr, "Report," September 29, 1886.

16. Weinman, "Ecuador and Cacao," writes: "Foreigners outnumbered Ecuadoreans as importers, but they married the natives and their progeny quickly absorbed the local habits" (137; and see 196, 314). Also see the South American Development Company to the U.S. Department of State, May 21, 1918, in USGR, "Report," May 1918. See L. F. Carbo, *El Ecuador en Chicago,* 22–23. The photographs show that elite women were nearly always light-skinned. Ridings, in "Foreign Predominance," suggests that overseas traders who remained in Latin America, and many did not, "tended to be absorbed into the local landowning elite, often by way

of marriage" (11). Ridings suggests, however, that this social acceptance might have been shallow. "Much of the social and political acceptance of overseas merchants came because they were useful, not because they were admired" (17).

17. Hurtado, *Political Power*, 95, and 31; Rojas, *Novela*, 24; Estrada Ycaza, *Regionalismo y migración*, 265.

18. Hahner, *Poverty and Politics*, 92.

19. Blackwelder and Johnson, "Changing Criminal Patterns," 362; DeShazo, *Urban Workers*, xxi, 4.

20. Gallegos Naranjo, *1883 almanaque;* IP, *Informe, 1890;* PCC, *Census, 1919*. There is a paucity of information regarding population age and ethnicity in Guayaquil. There is, however, information on population flows in Guayaquil for the years 1890–1909. The number of families that moved within Guayaquil were as follows: 7,331 in 1891; 7,803 in 1897; 11,594 in 1898; an estimated 9,368 in 1901; an estimated 14,184 in 1903; 7,569 in 1908; and 12,382 in 1909. IP, *Informe, 1891, 1897, 1898, 1901, 1903,* and *1910*. Such urban fluidity has been noticed for other Latin American cities of this era. For example, McCreery notes in "'This Life of Misery and Shame,'" his study of Guatemala City from 1880 to 1920, that "a growing floating population of men lived at least part of the time in the city but remained without the economic conditions to sustain stable family life" (338). See also DeShazo, *Urban Workers*, 5.

21. IP, *Informe, 1890,* 17, *Memoria, 1898,* 11.

22. See Estrada Ycaza, *Regionalismo y migración;* L. A. Rodríguez, *Search for Public Policy,* 27. Regarding the modern-day urban squatters living in and around Guayaquil, Richard Moore, in "Urban Poor," writes that "rather than a sense of fatalism, there is a high sense of optimism, particularly with regard to aspirations for the educational improvement of their children" (199).

23. Gallegos Naranjo, *1883 almanaque;* IP, *Informe, 1890;* PCC, *Census, 1919*. Other Latin American cities of this era showed a similar imbalance. For instance, in Guatemala City from 1880 to 1921 females outnumbered males nearly six to four. McCreery, 337. Buenos Aires was a city fed by long-distance immigration, a process that tends to draw young men, and so an inverse gender ratio to that of Guayaquil applied. In 1914 there were three males for every two females in Buenos Aires. Sanchez-Albornoz, *Population,* 163; Saunders, *The People of Ecuador,* 28–31.

24. RC, *Informe, 1929–1930;* MI, *Informe, 1903,* "Informe de la dirección de la oficina central de estadística"; MIP, *Informe, 1916,* cxlii, *1919,* cxi-cxvi, *1921,* 138 and passim.

25. MI, *Informe, 1871*. And Kasza writes in "Regional Conflict," 19: "The Catholic Church of Ecuador has always been centered in Quito and has focused its proselytizing efforts on the Indians of the sierra, whose labor has maintained the religious institution throughout its history. By the early 17th century so many convents had been founded in the capital city that ecclesiastical authorities petitioned the Royal Council of the Indies to prohibit the establishment of any more. By contrast, no convent was built in Guayaquil until 1858. In 1780 there were only 20 clergymen in Guayaquil, and by the mid-19th century still only 71, many of these from Spain or the sierra. The priesthood has always been overwhelmingly recruited from the sierra."

26. RC, *Informe, 1929–1930;* MI, *Informe, 1903,* "Informe de la dirección de la oficina central de estadística," *1912,* 332 and passim; MIP, *Informe, 1919,* cix.

27. IP, *Informe, 1897, 1898;* MIP, *Informe, 1921,* 138 and passim; Kasza, "Regional Conflict," 19–20; DeShazo, *Urban Workers,* 72. This pattern of many births outside of marriage continues to be the case. One-third of children born in Ecuador are "illegitimate," most of these from the coast. The majority of children born in Guayas province are "illegitimate." E. Erickson et al., *Area Handbook,* 149.

28. Gallegos Naranjo, *1883 almanaque;* Franklin, *Ecuador,* 30; *El Ecuador: guía.*

29. Because most workers in Guayaquil found employment either on a loosely arranged daily basis or in jobs as itinerant vendors, it is difficult to get more than a general idea of the city's occupational structure. The most detailed source of occupational information is police arrest records. Police routinely asked those detained to state their type of work. The police records, while hardly a scientific sampling, do offer at least a general sense of the occupational make-up of Guayaquil. Moreover, police arrest records can be checked against other lists of occupations in Guayaquil. Comparison with limited available census data shows that the police arrest records present a reasonably fair estimate of the sorts of jobs that Guayaquil's workers performed. For instance, the 1890 census showed that male artisans were about one-fourth of the male working-age population. Police arrest records for the following two decades show that artisans were roughly one-third to one-fifth of the adult male population. Information for the years 1897 to 1909 indicates that service sector workers represented 54 to 61 percent of those arrested in Guayaquil; non–service sector workers totaled 19 to 41 percent of those arrested; and workers in other jobs or with unknown occupations equaled 5 to 20 percent of those arrested in Guayaquil. Further details are available. Unskilled workers represented from 49 to 52 percent of those arrested. Artisans were 41 percent in 1897, 38 percent in 1898, 22 percent in 1903, and 18 percent in 1909. Professionals totaled 3 percent in 1897, 5 percent in 1898, 5 percent in 1903, and 11 percent in 1909. People who gave their occupation as "businessmen" totaled 4 to 6 percent of those arrested in this era, 1897 to 1909. Police records throughout the late nineteenth and early twentieth centuries also repeatedly emphasized the steady rise in prostitution.

30. Guayaquil's 1919 census indicated the occupation of each person the census takers contacted. PCC, *Census, 1919.* However, there exists no tally for the 1919 citywide census. What does remain are some of the registers that field agents used in conducting the census, probably only about two-thirds to three-fourths of the original total. Most of these registers are in extremely bad condition, however. Also see Franklin, *Ecuador,* 25; IP, *Informe, 1889–1910.*

31. It would be both untrue and unfair to label this marginalized urban poor a "lumpenproletariate." (For an opposing view see Cueva, *Process of Political Domination,* 70.) These migrant men and women worked when they could; they were simply unable to find full employment.

32. DeShazo, *Urban Workers,* 6, 17; Hahner, *Poverty and Politics,* 17, 18, 205.

33. *Informe, 1890; El Ecuador: guía,* 745–62; *Guayaquil en la mano 1912,* 137–99.

34. IP, *Informe, 1897, 1898, 1903, 1910.*

35. *El Ecuador: guía,* 745–62; IP, *Informe, 1890, 1897, 1898, 1903, 1910;* Gallegos Naranjo, *1883 almanaque;* Gallegos Naranjo, *Almanaque 1884,* 73–74; Franklin, *Ecuador,* 22, 30.

36. Barbosa, *Almanaque 1907.*

37. *El grito del pueblo,* October 8, 1896.

38. CC, *Libro de ordenanzas o acuerdos municipales expedidos por el concejo cantonal de Guayaquil, 1895,* document no. 25; CC, *Peticiónes, 1893.*

39. This section on the Aspiazus is drawn from Phillips, "Gender, Class and Cultural Politics," 23, and from the appendix herein. See also Chiriboga, *Jornaleros.*

40. Until the 1920s the sucre remained stable in value, its purchasing power not eroded by inflation. See chapter 8.

41. IP, *Informe, 1897;* USCD, Alexander McLean, "Report for 1879," January 24, 1880; Ridings, "Foreign Predominance"; Hahner, *Poverty and Politics,* 23, 82, 140.

42. Ridings, "Foreign Predominance," 7; Hahner, *Poverty and Politics,* 23, 82.

43. Ridings, "Foreign Predominance," 3, 5, 9–11; Hahner, *Poverty and Politics,* 140.

44. *El Ecuador: guía,* 517–18, 545–46, 1303. Not all large cacao growers got deeply involved in commerce. The rich Puga, Acevedo, Aguire, Duran-Ballen, Buenaventura-Burgos, Gomez, and Robles families all had fewer ties to commerce in Guayaquil. On the other hand, some merchants purchased cacao land; Juan Kruger is a noteworthy example. However, such economic integration—through merchants buying cacao estates—was less typical. The city's diversified elite included some, but not all, of the littoral's important cacao producers. The largest growers, the Semenarios and the Aspiazus, did diversify.

45. Quintero López, *El mito del populismo,* holds that Guayaquil's emerging commercial elite split into two clearly identifiable and bitterly antagonistic class factions clustered around the city's major banks—importers at the Banco del Ecuador and exporters and growers at the Banco Comercial y Agrícola. In 1901 there were four major banks in Guayaquil: the Banco del Ecuador (BE) and its mortgage institution, the Banco Territorial (BT), on the one hand and the Banco Comercial y Agrícola (BCA) and its mortgage institution, the Banco de Crédito Hipotecario (BCH), on the other. Each bank had seventeen or eighteen top executives—directors, subdirectors, commissioners, subcommissioners, presidents, and managers—totaling sixty-nine posts in all, occupied by forty-seven men. Twenty of these men (43 percent) served as officials for one or more of the other banks. There was a great deal of overlapping. Counting together parent and offshoot banks, one-third of BCA and BCH officials were associated with the supposedly rival BE and BT grouping. Conversely, more than one-third of BE and BT executives served on the boards of directors of BCA or BCH. Therefore, one must conclude that there was simply far too much intermingling between the people involved with these supposedly rival bank groupings for distinct bourgeois class factions, as defined by Quintero, to have existed. This does not mean that the elites liked one another. Some were enemies; all were competitive. The point is that this economic jostling did not lead to the formation of clearly

identifiable rival class factions. Ordinarily we would presume that competing bourgeois class factions would have their contention rooted in something more substantial than banking at different locations. That is, for antagonistic bourgeois class factions to have existed, it would have been necessary for each to have been wedded to a distinctly different mode of surplus extraction, such as merchants versus industrialists or planters versus both. No such pattern emerges in Guayaquil. In fact the reverse is true. Of elites in the period 1909 to 1925, those with banking ties had interests in several economic pursuits: importing, exporting, retail sales, and light manufacturing. The Guayaquil elite—with the exception of the Chinese and Syrians—were a homogeneous group with overlapping economic interests. See GG, *Informe 1901*, 134–39.

46. Franklin, *Ecuador*, 7, 16, 21, 22, 24–27; *La nación*, April 21, 1880.

47. Estrada Ycaza, "Evolución urbana"; MI, *Informe, 1902*; PCC, *Informe, 1907*; *La nación*, February 4 and 14, 1880; *El guante*, January 5, 1925.

Police records can again be used to obtain a general idea of the literacy rate in Guayaquil. Among all lawbreakers, literacy rates ranged from just over half, in 1897, to about three-fourths, in 1908. Of course, Guayaquil police arrested far more men than women, and men were more likely than women to be literate.

Guayaquil's literacy rate was better than that of the countryside. The rural parish of Jesus María, near Guayaquil, offers an example of the situation in the hinterland. The 1871 census of Jesus María parish counted 431 people, of whom 290 were working age (twelve years or older). Of these people, 53 percent, all of them males, were employed as agricultural day laborers and 39 percent, all of them females, worked as seamstresses, cooks, or washerwomen. Of all adults, 68 percent were illiterate. Fully 78 percent of the adult women could neither read nor write. The overwhelming majority of adults in Jesus María parish held low-paying jobs and were illiterate. Even if it is impossible to know with certainty whether such numbers were typical for the Ecuadorian countryside, it does nevertheless seem likely. In many areas of Ecuador, rural schools did not even exist. MH, *Censo 1871 Samborondon, Jesus María, y Naranjal*; PCC, *Informe, 1889*, 19; Hurtado, *Political Power*, 141.

By way of comparison, in Tucumán province, Argentina, illiteracy rates ranged from 88 percent in 1869 to 73 percent in 1895. In Mexico in this era perhaps about 80 percent were illiterate. In Santiago, Chile, illiteracy decreased from 63.8 percent in 1885 to 38.2 percent in 1920, while in Valparaíso illiteracy fell from 59.3 percent in 1885 to 36.1 percent in 1920. In Rio de Janeiro, male illiteracy dropped from 58.5 percent to 33.5 percent from 1872 to 1920, while female illiteracy declined from 70.7 percent to 44.2 percent in the same period. In São Paulo, male illiteracy was 67.9 percent in 1872 but only 35.7 percent in 1920, and female illiteracy fell from 82.9 percent to but 47.9 percent in the same years. Guayaquil's 30 to 50 percent illiteracy rates compare favorably. See Lizardo, "Impact of the Sugar Industry," 44, 69–70; Knight, "Working Class," 53; Arellano, "Social Policies," 400; Hahner, *Poverty and Politics*, 89–90; and DeShazo, *Urban Workers*, 74. Also see A. Ferrin Weber, *Growth of Cities*, 397–98.

48. PCC, *Peticiónes, 1893,* February 3, 1893.

49. *El grito del pueblo,* January 1 and 6, 1912; *La nación,* February 5, 1880.

50. Franklin, *Ecuador,* 28; *Patria,* 1917–18.

51. *La nación,* March 11, 1880, February 5, 1880; *El grito del pueblo,* January 13, 1900; Franklin, *Ecuador,* 31, 33.

52. *El guante,* January 1, 1925; OP, *Correspondence,* January 23, 1894, nos. 455 and 456.

53. *La nación,* February 7 and 9, 1880; *Patria,* 1917–18; Franklin, *Ecuador,* 30, 45.

54. Weinman, "Ecuador and Cacao," 19, 76; Kasza, "Regional Conflict," 23, 38.

55. *El grito del pueblo,* January 2, 1900; *El guante,* January 1, 1925, 4.

56. *La nación,* January 17, 1880; *El grito del pueblo,* January 1, 1912; *El guante,* January 1, 1925.

57. *La nación,* March 31, 1880; *Los Andes* (Guayaquil), December 18, 1886, cited in unpublished research notes of Estrada Ycaza; *El grito del pueblo,* January 2, 1900; *El telégrafo,* October 3, 1916; *El guante,* January 2 and 3, 1925; Franklin, *Ecuador,* 22; *Patria,* 1917–18; *El Ecuador: guía,* 558.

58. *La nación,* February 1, 4, and 9, 1880; *El guante,* January 1, 1925; *Patria,* July 16, 1917, and 1917–18 passim; USCD, Martin Reinberg, "Report of Ecuador and Commerce of Guayaquil for the Year 1886," March 10, 1887, William Sorsby, "Report," January 20, 1890, "Report," May 31, 1890; *América libre,* 240; Paz Ayora, *Guía 1901,* 203; L. F. Carbo, *El Ecuador en Chicago,* 43–51; Milk, "Growth and Development," 21, 39.

Hahner, in *Poverty and Politics,* describes a somewhat similar practice among the elite of Santos and Rio de Janeiro, Brazil, where the affluent fled the summertime heat by migrating inland (160). In Brazil in the late nineteenth century, large landowners and their families took advantage of improved transportation in their nation to seek the attractions of the cities (6). Ecuador's coastal agricultural elites displayed another of the propensities shown by many Brazilian planters: the extremely rustic nature of country living drove some to avoid rural life. See Franklin, *Ecuador,* 50, 288. "The hacienda houses" he depicts as "simply larger copies of the bamboo huts."

59. See Weinman, "Ecuador and Cacao," 215–16, for a discussion of elite privileges; Hassaurek, *Four Years,* 202, 217.

60. Aviles, *Ecuador en el centenario,* 49; Hassaurek, *Four Years,* 216–17. For examples regarding impressments see: USMR, R. Wing, "Report," August 17, 1870, "Report," January 30, 1871, James Tillman, "Report," July 21, 1895, "Report," September 1, 1895; USCD, Horatio Beach, "Report," 2 December 1884; USGR, Herman Dietrich, "Report," January 5, 1912.

### Chapter Six: Life in Guayaquil

1. Niles, *Casual Wanderings,* 52; PCC, *Informe, 1879,* 13, 14; Gallegos Naranjo, *1883 almanaque,* 286.

2. Estrada Ycaza, "Desarrollo histórico," 20, 22; GG, *Informe, 1877,* 1; L. F. Carbo, *El Ecuador en Chicago,* 47.

3. Conniff, "Guayaquil Through Independence," 410.

4. Enock, *Ecuador*, 243; Parks and Nuermberger, "Sanitation of Guayaquil," 197–98, 212.

5. See: Barbosa, *Almanaque ilustrado 1907*, 34; *Guayaquil 1912: directorio*, 7; IP, *Informe, 1890*, 7; CC, *Peticiónes, 1893*, October 20, 1893; *La nación*, February 3, 4, 7, 9, and 16, 1880, and March 11 and 13, 1880; SS, *Informe, 1910; El grito del pueblo*, January 10, 1900, and January 6 and 7, 1912; PCC, *Informe, 1879, 1887, 1892*, 21, *1907;* USCD, William Sorsby, "Report," May 31, 1890; Estrada Ycaza, "Evolución," 49, 52; *El Ecuador: guía*, 697–99, 985; *América libre*, 136.

6. PCC, *Peticiónes, 1876*, February 17, 1876.

7. PCC, *Informe, 1919*, 7, v, *1916;* PCC, *Peticiónes, 1876*, March 10, 1876, May 10, 1876; *La nación*, May 1, 1880.

8. *El guante*, January 4, 1925.

9. Conniff, "Guayaquil Through Independence," 391; Gallegos Naranjo, *1900 almanaque*, 125–26.

10. See, for example, MI, *Informe, 1894; El grito del pueblo*, January 10, 1900.

11. IP, *Informe, 1891*, 44; Hassaurek, *Four Years*, 13.

12. USMR, Tillman, "Report On Visit to Guayaquil," October 12, 1896; *El grito del pueblo*, October 8 and 9, 1896; IP, *Informe, 1897.*

13. IP, *Informe, 1897, 1898*, 39; *El grito del pueblo*, October 9, 12, and 16, 1896.

14. *El guante*, January 1, 1925; *El grito del pueblo*, January 7, 1912; Estrada Ycaza, *El hospital*, 150; *Guía 1904/1905*, xxx; Barbosa, *Almanaque 1907*, 34.

15. Estrada Ycaza, "Evolución urbana," 54; Enock, *Ecuador*, 243; Barbosa, *Almanaque 1907*, 34; Paz Ayora, *Guía 1901*, 175; Ecuador, Consulate of Ecuador, New York, *The Republic of Ecuador* (December 1923), 31, cited in GBFO, "Report," January 1924.

16. MI, *Informe, 1903;* PCC, *Informe, 1887, 1889*, 13, *1892*, 10; GG, *Informe, 1916*, 6.

17. GBFO, Cartwright, "Report," January 16, 1909, "Samuel Wisdom to the British Home Secretary, September 8, 1909," included in "Report," October 10, 1909; PCC, *Informe, 1889*, 14. Even the new jail, completed in 1897, proved inadequate. See Estrada Ycaza, "Evolución urbana," 54.

18. MRE, *Informe, 1903; La nación*, February 25, 1880; MI, *Informe, 1899.*

19. IP, *Informe, 1890*, 53; MI, *Informe, 1906*, xiii.

20. PCC, *Informe, 1892*, 24; IP, *Informe, 1898*, 19, *1903, 1910*, 4; MI, *Informe, 1894.*

21. *El Ecuador: guía*, 549; IP, *Informe, 1890, 1898, 1910;* MI, *Informe, 1898, 1905*, 102–3, *1926–1928*, 70. Police salaries in Guayaquil rose during the years 1881–1910. The monthly salary in 1881 was 25 pesos; in 1890, 25.60 sucres; in 1896, 30 sucres; in 1898, 30 sucres; in 1901, 40 sucres; in 1903, 40 sucres; and in 1910, 50 sucres. PCC, *Memoria, 1881–1910;* CC, *Libro de ordenanzas o acuerdos municipales, 1895.* Compare Hahner, *Poverty and Politics*, 142.

22. For some examples see *La nación*, February 23, 1880, and May 1, 1880; OP, *Correspondence*, January 4, 1894, no. 432, January 6, 1894, 436; *El grito del pueblo*, January 9, 1900.

23. MI, *Informe, 1886.*

24. MI, *Informe, 1894*. Other Latin American cities similarly failed to attract enough qualified men to serve as police officers, largely because of the meager pay. In urban Brazil, "police ranks included too many vagabonds and 'bad elements.'" Hahner, *Poverty and Politics*, 56. In Chile, Sater found that "few men wished to become policemen. Chillan, for example, had twenty vacancies but applicants considered the pay of $112 per week inadequate to support a family. Those who enlisted often lacked education, or were delinquents or allies of the criminal they promised to pursue." Sater, *Chile and the War*, 166.

25. IP, *Informe, 1890*, 38, *1897, 1898*, 23, 18, *1901*, 7, *1903*, 5, *1910*, 18–20, 25; GBFO, Graham, "Summary by the British Consul in Guayaquil of President Tamayo's Speech," August 24, 1923; *Panama Herald*, February 10, 1871, reprinted in USMR, "Clip File," February 1871. In 1902, when the provinces of Pichincha and Guayas had roughly the same population of about 230,000, both experienced about the same number of petty crimes; Guayas had 28,888 and Pichincha had 24,969. Even though Guayas was more urbanized, it did not have a significantly higher crime rate. MI, *Informe, 1902*, 13. Zehr, *Crime and Development*. Blackwelder and Johnson, "Changing Criminal Patterns," 372.

26. IP, *Informe, 1891*, 27, *1898*, 8, 11, 14, 25–26, *1910*, 7.

27. IP, *Informe, 1890*, 42–45, *1891*, 38.

28. IP, *Memoria, 1898*, 12, 20.

29. Ibid., 23; GBFO, Graham, "Summary by British Consul in Guayaquil of President Tamayo's Speech," August 24, 1923; *Panama Herald*, February 10, 1871, reprinted in USMR, "Clip File." Blackwelder and Johnson, "Changing Criminal Patterns," 367–68.

30. For urban Argentina in the early nineteenth century, L. Johnson writes in *Problem of Order* that "those arrested by the police, . . . were usually young males from the working class" (xvi). "Younger, more masculine populations generally produce higher [crime] rates" (x).

31. Put another way, in Buenos Aires the ratio of arrests for property crimes to violent felonies was 261 to 100 in 1919 and 46 to 100 in 1926–30; in Guayaquil the ratio of property to violent crime was 129 to 100 in 1890, 53 to 100 in 1891, 62 to 100 in 1897, 27 to 100 in 1898, an estimated 30 to 100 in 1903, 60 to 100 in 1904, an estimated 68 to 100 in 1905, 57 to 100 in 1908, and 50 to 100 in 1909. L. Johnson, *Problem of Order*, 129; and adapted from table 6.2. Blackwelder and Johnson, "Changing Criminal Patterns," 363, 377.

32. Zehr's *Crime and Development*, an investigation into criminality in nineteenth-century Germany and France, also finds that theft gradually increased while violence slowly declined in European urban centers in this period.

33. IP, *Informe, 1910*, 18.

34. Wilson, *Development of Education*, 41, 43, 47. On education in Latin America during the nineteenth and early twentieth centuries, see Newland, "La educación elemental"; Yeager, "Elite Education"; Szuchman, "Childhood Education"; Vaughan, "Primary Education"; Jaksic, "Politics of Higher Education"; Spalding, "Edu-

cation in Argentina"; Loy, "Primary Education"; and Smith and Littell, *Education in Latin America*.

35. Wilson, *Development of Education*, 45; and Rojas, *La novela*, 39–40; Smith and Littell, *Education*, 145–62. Compare DeShazo, *Urban Workers*, 76.

36. Guayas had the following number of municipal primary schools in the years 1884 to 1921: in 1884 seven (11 percent of all Guayas provincial public elementary schools); in 1889 eighteen (20 percent); in 1894 twenty-seven (23 percent); in 1899 fourteen (11 percent); in 1900 fifteen (12 percent); in 1901 seventeen (13 percent); in 1902 thirteen (8 percent); in 1904 fourteen (10 percent); in 1908 twenty-seven (16 percent); in 1916 four (3 percent); in 1919 nine (7 percent); and in 1921 seven (5 percent). Guayas had the following number of national primary schools in the years 1884 to 1921: in 1877, 58; in 1884, 58; in 1889, 72; in 1894, 88; in 1899, 117; in 1900, 112; in 1901, 115; in 1902, 145; in 1904, 132; in 1908, 143; in 1911, 143; in 1916, 148; in 1919, 134; and in 1921, 148. Guayas had the following number of public primary schools, both national and municipal, in the years 1884 to 1921: in 1884, 65; in 1889, 90; in 1894, 115; in 1899, 131; in 1900, 127; in 1901, 132; in 1902, 158; in 1904, 146; in 1908, 170; in 1916, 152; in 1919, 143; and in 1921, 155. GG, *Informe, 1877*, 12; MIP, *Informe, 1885–1921*.

37. National funding for primary education in Guayas and all Ecuador in the years 1884 to 1920 was as follows: in 1884, 41,145 sucres to Guayas; 1887, 39,706 sucres to Guayas; in 1889, 45,948 sucres to Guayas; in 1892, 50,820 sucres to Guayas, 263,946 sucres in Ecuador (19 percent to Guayas); in 1893, 65,738 sucres to Guayas, 334,572 sucres in Ecuador (20 percent to Guayas); in 1898, 43,364 sucres to Guayas; in 1900, 223,690 sucres in Ecuador; in 1901, 82,968 sucres to Guayas, 292,972 sucres in Ecuador (28 percent to Guayas); in 1902, 145,524 sucres to Guayas, 491,327 sucres in Ecuador (30 percent to Guayas); in 1903, 132,880 sucres to Guayas, 496,632 sucres in Ecuador (27 percent to Guayas); in 1904, 124,092 sucres to Guayas, 498,170 (25 percent to Guayas); in 1911, 299,684 sucres to Guayas; in 1915, 787,444 sucres in Ecuador; in 1918, 360,375 sucres to Guayas, 1,406,359 sucres in Ecuador (26 percent to Guayas); and in 1920, 638,940 sucres to Guayas, 2,202,235 sucres in Ecuador (29 percent to Guayas). MIP, *Informe, 1885–1921*. Expenditures for construction, education-related and otherwise, fell under the budget for public works.

38. MIP, *Informe, 1909*, 7–8, *1911–1912*, 343, *1916*, xxiii.

39. MIP, *Informe, 1873, 1899*, 260; MI, *Informe, 1886, 1887*, 22. By 1899, the cacao and other customs taxes provided nearly all of the 39,800 sucres required to run the colegio.

40. MIP, *Informe, 1890*.

41. Figures selected from table 6.5. The role of the municipal government in funding public primary education in Guayas was not unique. For example, the various municipal governments of Ecuador provided 27 percent of all the revenues for public primary education in Ecuador in 1900; in 1901, they provided 38 percent; in 1902, 28 percent; in 1903, 30 percent; and in 1904, 32 percent. MIP, *Informe, 1901*, 14, *1905*.

42. MIP, *Informe, 1894*, 151. For example, in 1893 Guayaquil provided 3,978 sucres to support the fiscales in the city.

43. MIP, *Informe, 1909*, 7.

44. L. A. Rodríguez, *Search for Public Policy*, 85, 90.

45. By 1919 the Colegio Vicente Rocafuerte was the single largest nationally funded secondary school in Ecuador. MIP, *Informe, 1919*, lv, *1879*; MI, *Informe, 1871*, table 4.

46. The University of Guayaquil was one of four universities in Ecuador during this era. Quito and Cuenca had more students, while the very small facility in Loja had fewer. MIP, *Informe, 1919*, lvi; *El guante*, January 2, 1925. At El Colegio Nacional de San Vicente del Guayas, a public high school for young men, there were the following numbers of students in the years 1877–1909: in 1877, 146; in 1883, 155; in 1884, 168; in 1887, 159; in 1889, 134; in 1894, 275; in 1899, 222; in 1900, 249; in 1901, 330; in 1903, 324; in 1904, 300; in 1905, 340; in 1909, 296. At the Colegio de los Sagrados Corazones, a private school for young women, the numbers of students attended: in 1883, 115; in 1884, 122; in 1887, 94; in 1889, 165; in 1894, 154. At the Colegio Nacional Rita Lecumberry, a public high school for young women, there were 275 students in 1909. For all Guayas, the numbers of total colegio students were as follows: in 1884, 290; in 1887, 253; in 1889, 299; in 1894, 429; in 1903, 946; in 1904, 1,152; and in 1905, 1,731. At the Universidad de Guayaquil, the numbers of students attending, almost all of whom were males, were as follows: in 1884, 51; in 1887, 61; in 1889, 40; in 1894, 53; in 1903, 93; in 1904, 89; in 1905, 98; in 1909, 78; and in 1921, 151. See, GG, *Informe, 1877*, 10; Gallegos Naranjo, *1883 almanaque*, 229–65; MIP, *Informe, 1885–1921*; IP, *Informe, 1903, 1904*, 91–97, *1905*, 147–54; *El Ecuador: guía*, 330–31, 657, 661.

47. Available evidence places the numbers of pupils at charitable schools in Guayas as follows: 336 in 1884; 381 in 1886, 487 in 1887; 994 in 1889; and 580 in 1890. MIP, *Informe, 1885, 1890, 1894*, 151; MI, *Informe, 1887*; IP, *Informe, 1890*, 27, *1891*, 42–43.

48. Rodríguez J., *Historia de la sociedad filantrópica*.

49. It is only possible to get a rough idea of the numbers of students attending private or charitable schools. Few official records were kept regarding the many small private schools. MIP, *Informe, 1885*; *La nación*, March 15, 1880.

50. In 1873, of the 146 students attending particulares in Guayaquil, all but twenty were boys. In 1903, of the 815 students attending particulares in Guayas, 517 were boys. MIP, *Informe, 1873, 1904*.

51. MIP, *Informe, 1885, 1894*, 151, *1904, 1909, 1919*, viii, *1921*, 10–11; PCC, *Informe, 1887*; IP, *Informe, 1891*, 42–43, *1905*, 150.

52. MI, *Informe, 1900*; CC, *Informe, 1907*, 71–85, *1918*, 51–76; MIP, *Informe, 1909*, 341–55.

53. MIP, *Informe, 1909*, 341–55. Examples of private business schools include: the Instituto Mercantil of Guayaquil, present in the city by 1880; Colegio Francisco Campos, opened in 1916 or 1917; and the Escuela Nocturna María de Allieri. *La nación*, April 26, 1880, 1; *El guante*, January 1 and 3, 1925.

54. Gallegos Naranjo, *1883 almanaque*, 229.

55. In 1894, the colegio still received 6,120 sucres annually from the national government, while receiving 7,069 sucres in 1894 from student tuitions. MIP, *Informe, 1885, 1890, 1894*, 144–45; MI, *Informe, 1887*.

56. There were 165 pupils in the colegio in 1889. Another important private high school was the Colegio Rita Lecumberri, a school for young women. With typically 75 to 300 students, it was for a time the only secondary school for young women in the province. The school received some support from the national government. MIP, *Informe, 1890, 1906, 1916*, lii; *El Ecuador: guía*, 661. Even today Ecuador has few women attending universities when compared to other Latin American nations; it has more than Mexico but fewer than Argentina or Chile. Jaramillo, in *Family in Latin America*, 411.

57. *El guante*, January 2, 1925. Fee payment continues to be the practice. E. Erickson et al., *Area Handbook*, 165.

58. The number of public primary education teachers in Guayas province grew in the years 1884 to 1909. The numbers of teachers were as follows: in 1884, 95; in 1889, 108; in 1894, 158; in 1901, 217; in 1903, 178; in 1904, 224; and in 1909, 328. MI, *Informe, 1886*; MIP, *Informe, 1890, 1894*, 145–54, *1902*, 26, *1904*, x–xvii, *1905, 1909*; CC, *Informe, 1925*.

59. MIP, *Informe, 1873*.

60. *La nación*, April 10, 1880. In the 1890s and 1900s teachers received a salary of 24 to 60 sucres a month, when they were paid. MIP, *Informe, 1873, 1890, 1899*, 231, *1908*, 229; GG, *Informe, 1877*, 13; MI, *Informe, 1886*.

61. MIP, *Informe, 1899*, 236; *La nación*, April 10, 1880.

62. MIP, *Informe, 1873*.

63. MIP, *Informe, 1894*, 154.

64. MIP, *Informe, 1890, 1919*, xiii, *1921*, 15. Hahner, in *Poverty and Politics*, 24, finds that in Brazil "the replacement of men by lower paid women in the nation's primary school classrooms was well underway by the end of the nineteenth century. In Rio de Janeiro in 1872, women already comprised approximately a third of the city's teachers. By the early twentieth century, over two-thirds were women, and by 1920, over eighty percent."

65. MIP, *Informe, 1894*, 147.

66. MI, *Informe, 1886*, 17.

67. *La nación*, February 5, 7, and 12, 1880, and April 22, 1880; MIP, *Informe, 1885*.

68. MIP, *Informe, 1873*.

69. MIP, *Informe, 1879*.

70. USCD, Weile, "Commercial Report," January 17, 1872; Aviles, *Ecuador en el centenario*, 48, 49; MIP, *Informe, 1873, 1879, 1894*, 150–52; MI, *Informe, 1887*.

71. MIP, *Informe, 1873, 1894*, 150–51, *1890, 1916*, xx; MI, *Informe, 1886*.

72. MI, *Informe, 1887*; MIP, *Informe, 1873, 1916, 1908*; GG, *Informe, 1877*. The rural schools of Santa Elena canton were in especially bad condition. MIP, *Informe, 1885, 1908*, 231. As the city council president frankly admitted in his annual report for 1892, there were simply not nearly enough schools for the canton as a whole, the

level of instruction was very bad, and the teachers received low pay. PCC, *Informe,* *1892,* 16; MIP, *Informe, 1908,* 229.

73. *La nación,* March 6, 1880. Urban Chile exhibited some of the same characteristics noted in Guayaquil. In the cities of Chile the state built few schools but rented buildings for the purpose instead. DeShazo writes in *Urban Workers,* 74–75, that Chilean public primary schools were mainly attended by the children of the working class, and that secondary education remained a benefit reserved for middle and upper class youth. While it would be very useful to carefully compare education in Guayaquil to conditions in other Latin American cities, the existing evidence can only support impressionistic observations. Ecuadorian national regular budgetary allocations for education at first seem high when compared to those of Argentina. The Argentine numbers were: 1890, 6 percent; 1894, 5 percent; 1898, 3 percent; 1902, 4 percent; 1906, 6 percent; 1909, 7 percent; 1912, 10 percent; and 1914, 13 percent. Spalding, "Education in Argentina," 52. For comparison to Chile see Jaksic and Serrano, "In the Service of the Nation." In Chile the numbers were: 1870, 6 percent; 1871, 7 percent; 1872, 7 percent; 1873, 8 percent; 1874, 7 percent; 1875, 7 percent; 1876, 7 percent; 1877, 7 percent; 1878, 6 percent; and 1879, 6 percent. However, in Ecuador a large but unknown amount of national revenues went directly to local autonomous juntas not included in regular national expenditure totals. If these monies could be counted and then added into total government outlays (as indeed they should be), then education's share would appear smaller, probably considerably smaller. Literacy rate comparisons also would be very valuable. Sadly, existing data for Ecuador will yield up only the vaguest of guesses, for unlike other Latin American nations of this era, Ecuador made virtually no effort to determine its literacy rate. Police records can be used to obtain a general idea of the situation, for authorities routinely asked those arrested if they could read and write. Among all lawbreakers, literacy rates varied from just over half, in 1897, to about three-fourths, in 1908. However, Guayaquil police arrested far more men than women, and men were much more likely to be literate than women. As a result, police records overstate the amount of literacy that would have existed in the overall population. IP, *Informe, 1890, 1891, 1897, 1898, 1903, 1904, 1910.* Probably about one-third of Guayaquil's adult population was illiterate. MH, *Censo 1871 Samborondon, Jesus María, y Naranjal;* PCC, *Informe, 1889,* 19.

**Chapter Seven: Disease, Health Care, and Death in Guayaquil**

1. USCD, Charles Weile, "Report on the Death of Minister Thomas Biddle," May 8, 1875, "Report," October 24, 1875, "Report," March 3, 1876, Richard McAllister Jr., "Letter," August 2, 1876, Alexander McLean, "Report," May 31, 1880.

Another visitor to Guayaquil, physician Carlos Wiener, commented that it looked to him as if nearly everyone was observing a period of mourning. Paredes Borja, *Historia de la medicina,* 2:353.

Works that deal with nineteenth-and early twentieth-century health care in Ecuador include Madero, *Historia de la medicina;* Samaniego, *Cronología médica ecuatoriana;* and two works by Estrada Ycaza, *El hospital,* and "Apuntes para la historia."

Examples of studies on nineteenth-century Latin American health care include: Karasch, *Slave Life;* Cooper, "New 'Black Death': Cholera in Brazil," in Kiple, *African Exchange*, 235–56; Cooper, "Brazil's Long Fight"; and Adamo, "Broken Promise."

2. This section is drawn from: PCC, *Informe, 1881–1892;* IP, *Informe, 1890–1910;* GG, *Informe, 1901;* JB, *Memoria, 1893–1925;* SS, *Informe, 1913, 1914;* and *El Ecuador: guía*, 681–737.

3. SS, *Informe, 1913,* 13.

4. IP, *Informe, 1890,* 7, 54, *1903,* 18; PCC, *Informe, 1892,* 24, *1916,* 19; *El grito del pueblo*, September 16, 1896; Paz Ayora, *Guía 1901*, xiii; *Guía 1902/1903*, 21; MI, *Informe, 1902,* 43; Barbosa, *Almanaque 1907*, 34; *Guayaquil 1912: directorio*, 7; Parks and Nuermberger, "Sanitation of Guayaquil," 197–98, 212; Enock, *Ecuador*, 243; and Estrada Ycaza, "Evolución urbana."

5. PCC, *Peticiónes, 1876,* May 12, 1876, *1893,* August 30, 1892; *La nación*, 16 and 19 February 1880, and 1 April 1880; MRE, *Informe, 1903; El grito del pueblo*, January 7, 1912.

6. *La nación*, February 5, 1880, and May 1, 1880. Workers picked up trash every eight to thirty days or so. *El grito del pueblo*, January 3 and 8, 1900.

7. Enock, *Ecuador*, 247; SS, *Informe, 1913;* JB, *Memoria, 1914–1925; El grito del pueblo*, January 3, 5, and 8, 1900.

8. CC, *Peticiónes, 1893.*

9. *El grito del pueblo*, January 3, 6, and 7, 1900.

10. Estrada Ycaza, *El hospital*, 1–2; Barbosa, *Almanaque 1907*, 33; *América libre*, 155; *Los andes* (Guayaquil), June 23, 1866, cited in unpublished research notes of Estrada Ycaza; *La nación*, February 21 and 25, 1880, and April 15, 1880.

11. PCC, *Informe, 1892,* 3–6, 37; USCD, Martin Reinberg, "Report of Ecuador and Commerce of Guayaquil For the Year 1886," March 10, 1887; *América libre*, 155; *El Ecuador: guía*, 691; Parks and Nuermberger, "Sanitation of Guayaquil," 207, 212; *La nación*, April 7 and 17, 1880.

12. SS, *Informe, 1911;* see also *1910, 1912.*

13. Ecuador, Consulate of Ecuador, New York. *The Republic of Ecuador* (1921), 26, (December 1923), 32, cited in GBFO, "Report," January 1922, and "Report," January 1924; Aviles, *Ecuador en el centenario*, 64; *Patria*, December 10, 1918; CC, *Peticiónes, 1893,* *Jefatura Politica, 1890,* vol. 13, document no. 143, December 2, 1890; *El republicano* (Quito), April 1, 1893, cited in unpublished research notes of Estrada Ycaza. In January 1925 the city council could not pay the interest due on the 1.3 million sucre loan to buy more pipe. Into 1925 periodic interruptions of service continued, some of which lasted several days. *El guante*, January 4 and 8, 1925. The provisioning of potable water and the disposal of garbage and sewerage were key problems for most cities of South America at this time. In their study of Buenos Aires 1890 to 1914, Blackwelder and Johnson, in "Changing Criminal Patterns," 362, find that population growth severely strained urban services. "Housing deteriorated, public ways grew congested, garbage and debris littered the streets, noise levels escalated and transportation failed." DeShazo notes in *Urban Workers* that in Valparaíso, Chile, gullies "behind working class hills became the resting place for mountains of garbage and the subsequent breeding ground for swarms of rats" (7). In Santiago,

DeShazo writes, "during the heavy rainstorms, . . . sewer canals overflowed their banks and filthy water seeped onto streets and into homes" (69). Sater, in *Chile and the War*, 170, writes that "most Chilean cities looked and apparently smelled like cess pits. People defecated on the streets, irreverently urinated on the walls of Churches, and threw their garbage and offal everywhere." In the town of Lebu, "water drained from the cemetery into the . . . drinking supply." In São Paulo, "the city center reeks," the *Comercio de Sao Paulo* declared on October 5, 1910, as quoted in Greenfield, "Development of the Underdeveloped City," 113. Also see Greenfield, 108, 110; Boyer and Davies, *Urbanization*, 62; and Hahner, *Poverty and Politics*, 12, 159.

14. Sanitation director L. F. Cornejo Gomez correctly blamed the city's lack of sewers for the alarming rise in typhoid fever cases in 1910. SS, *Informe, 1910*.

15. Samaniego holds that yellow fever first came to Guayaquil in 1740, and perhaps even earlier, in *Cronología médica ecuatoriana*, 35, 102. Gallegos Naranjo, *1883 almanaque*, 169; Estrada Ycaza, *El hospital*, 138–42; Gallegos, *1900 almanaque*, 65; Parks and Nuermberger, "Sanitation of Guayaquil," 200. See Huerta, *Rocafuerte y la fiebre amarilla*.

16. Ward, *Yellow Fever*, 27. One lifetime resident of the city, noted Guayaquil historian Julio Estrada Ycaza, suggested to me another idea for explaining this finding. Estrada said he had long noticed a difference in the way that guayaquileño women and men respond to mosquitoes: women wave away and swat mosquitoes; men do not, and regard such behavior as markedly effeminate.

17. Madero, *Historia de la medicina*, 259; *La nación*, February 26 and 28, 1880, March 27, 1880, and April 1, 5, and 24, 1880.

18. SS *Informe, 1910*.

19. Ecuador, Consulate of Ecuador, New York. *The Republic of Ecuador* (1921), 25, 26–30, reprinted in GBFO, "Reports," January 1922; Parks and Nuermberger, "Sanitation of Guayaquil"; Niles, *Casual Wanderings*, 67–69; SS, *Informe, 1910*.

20. SS, *Informe, 1912*. "The measures we are actually taking in Guayaquil against malaria are very limited," said sanitation director L. F. Cornejo Gomez, SS, *Informe, 1910*.

21. Estrada Ycaza, in *Regionalismo y migración*, 265, finds that in 1899 about one-third of the people who lived in Guayaquil had migrated from elsewhere in Ecuador, and slightly more than half of these migrants had traveled down from the sierra.

22. SS, *Informe, 1910*.

23. SS, *Informe, 1910, 1912*.

24. Paredes Borja, *Historia de la medicina*, 448; GG, *Informe, 1907*; SS, *Informe, 1913*, 30, 36; Estrada Ycaza, *El hospital*, 144; Parks and Nuermberger, "Sanitation of Guayaquil," 220.

25. IP, *Informe, 1910*, 6, 42. On the Asian origins of this plague outbreak see Winslow, *Conquest of Epidemic Disease*, 356–57. An earlier Ecuadorian outbreak of bubonic plague may have occurred in 1825, according to Estrada Ycaza, *El hospital*, 108, 149, 159.

26. IP, *Informe, 1910*, 42.

27. Estrada Ycaza, *El hospital*, 144; Parks and Nuermberger, "Sanitation of Gua-

yaquil," 20. In 1911, 513 people entered Guayaquil's plague quarantine, of whom thirty-three came from the surrounding towns and countryside. SS, *Informe, 1911.*

28. Madero, *Historia de la medicina,* 261–62; SS, *Informe, 1913,* 27; PCC, *Gaceta municipal, 1908,* 124; IP, *Informe, 1890,* 55, *1898,* 39.

29. See for example, MIP, *Informe, 1879.*

30. SS, *Informe, 1910, 1912.*

31. IP, *Informe, 1910,* 21, *1904,* 42–45. Available evidence for other Latin American urban centers during this era suggests that digestive illnesses tended to be the most serious threat to the young, while respiratory ailments tended to prey more upon adults, as in Guayaquil. Karasch, *Slave Life,* 148, 157, 160–61, 176, 183; Hahner, *Poverty and Politics,* 32, 210; DeShazo, *Urban Workers,* 68, 73.

32. This section is drawn from: Duffy, *Healers;* Bordley and Harvey, *Two Centuries;* Rosen, *History of Public Health;* and Paredes Borja, *Historia de la medicina.*

33. Samaniego, *Cronología médica ecuatoriana,* 32, 89, 151, 162, 221–22, 366, 447–52, 457, 459–60, 466. In Guayaquil in 1895 there were thirty-five doctors for a population of over 50,000. Paredes Borja, *Historia de la medicina,* 322; *Los andes* (Guayaquil), June 29, 1867, cited in unpublished research notes of Estrada Ycaza.

34. The problem persisted. In 1925 the new dean of medicine, Dr. Teofilo N. Fuentes Robles, still pointed to the city's lack of adequate medical library facilities. *El guante,* January 6, 1925.

35. Paredes Borja, *Historia de la medicina,* 311–14; Madero, *Historia de la medicina,* 277.

36. This was clearly revealed in the blunt 1910 report by Abraham Flexner on the state of U.S. medical schools. That many Ecuadorian students nevertheless saw U.S. schools as an improvement over Ecuadorian ones spoke volumes on the slow pace of progress in Ecuadorian medical education. Bordley and Harvey, *Two Centuries,* 187, 327.

37. This section was drawn from Samaniego, *Cronología médica ecuatoriana.*

38. *La nación,* February 16, 1880; *El grito del pueblo,* January 3, 1900, and January 1, 4, and 6, 1912; *El guante,* January 1, 2, 4, and 5, 1925.

39. *La nación,* February 1880; *El grito del pueblo,* January 1, 6, 1900, and January 1, 1912; *El guante,* January 1 and 2, 1925; *El telégrafo,* October 1, 1916, and December 2, 1916.

40. This section is drawn from: MI, *Informe, 1903;* PCC, *Informe, 1881–1892;* IP, *Informe, 1890–1910;* JB, *Memoria, 1893–1925;* GG, *Informe, 1901;* SS, *Informe, 1913, 1914;* *El Ecuador: guía,* 681–737; Estrada Ycaza, *El hospital,* 149, 159; Samaniego, *Cronología médica ecuatoriana,* 346; Madero, *Historia de la medicina; Patria,* 1917–18. Elsewhere in Latin America, hospitals were also just for the underclass. Karasch, in *Slave Life,* 135, notes this situation in Rio de Janeiro, as does Adamo in "Broken Promise," 114, and DeShazo, for Santiago, Chile, in *Urban Workers,* 70.

41. The Sociedad de Beneficencia typically had about thirty-five members and operated under the ultimate authority of the provincial governor. The city usually allocated 7 to 17 percent of its budget in support of the Junta, and this money in var-

ious years accounted for 7 to 35 percent of all Junta funds. See table 4.1. *El Ecuador: guía*, 228; PCC, *Informe, 1892; América libre*, 149. Samaniego, *Cronología médica ecuatoriana*, 223, 248; Estrada Ycaza, *El hospital*, 146; Kasza, "Regional Conflict," 11; MI, *Anexos al informe, 1910*, lxiii–lxiv.

42. *El Ecuador: guía*, 699–721; Estrada Ycaza, *El hospital*, 145; *Gaceta municipal, 1908*, 124; *América libre*, 151–52.

43. PCC, *Memoria, 1881*, 5.

44. PCC, *Informe, 1889*, 23.

45. JB, *Informe, 1893*, 6, 7.

46. Samaniego, *Cronología médica ecuatoriana*, 344; *El Ecuador: guía*, 699; Estrada Ycaza, *El hospital*, 149–52; MI, *Informe, 1903*.

47. MRE, *Informe, 1903*.

48. *América libre*, 149; *El Ecuador: guía*, 681–737; JB, *Informe, 1893*, 7; Estrada Ycaza, *El hospital*, 149, 159.

49. JB, *Memoria, 1914, 1922*; Estrada Ycaza, *El hospital*, 150; MI, *Informe, 1903*.

50. *El Ecuador: guía*, 681–737; Estrada Ycaza, *El hospital*, 149, 159; MRE, *Informe, 1903*.

51. SS, *Informe, 1911*.

52. Madero, *Historia de la medicina*, 259.

53. In the yellow fever quarantine, of the 365 who entered in 1911, 287 came from Guayaquil and seventy-eight from surrounding towns and the countryside. SS, *Informe, 1912*.

54. SS, *Informe, 1912*.

55. Reform in the treatment of the insane dated from the 1790s in England. Soon the success of humane care spurred the creation of many small institutions in the 1820s and 1830s, write Bordley and Harvey in *Two Centuries*, 67. However, the momentum of the reform impulse was lost; after the 1850s public care for the insane failed to substantially improve again until well into the present century. Meanwhile, little was done anywhere to help the insane.

56. The city named the asylum after three-time city council president José Velez. In Quito, the insane were housed with elephantitis patients. *El Ecuador: guía*, 707; *América libre*, 147; PCC, *Memoria, 1881*, 7; GG, *Informe, 1877*, 18; IP, *Informe, 1891*, 59–60.

57. On Guayaquil philanthropy see Paredes Borja, *Historia de la medicina*, 343; *América libre*, 149; *El guante*, January 5, 1925; Uzcategui, *Apuntes para una historia*.

58. The private lab of pharmacist Ramon Flores Ontaneda dated from 1894. Samaniego, *Cronología médica ecuatoriana*, 287; Paredes Borja, *Historia de la medicina*, 447.

59. PCC, *Informe, 1907; El grito del pueblo* January 6 and 13, 1912.

60. SS, *Informe, 1910, 1911, 1912*. In 1911 the department circulated fliers stressing the link between mosquitoes and yellow fever and malaria and urging people to cover or screen water tanks and drain pools of standing water and put fish in water tanks. Fliers were also sent out on typhoid fever that discussed how to properly dispose of human waste from typhoid fever victims. The department urged people

to install special filters for their water, noting that the stone filters in common use did no good. It further recommended boiling all water used for drinking, bathing, preparing food and drinks, and washing dishes.

61. SS, *Informe, 1914*, 4; Parks and Nuermberger, "Sanitation of Guayaquil," 206–7; IP, *Boletín de información, 1904*, 60; *América libre*, 151; MI, *Informe, 1912*, 256.

62. There is not much comparative data for hospital death rates in other cities of this era. Limited available evidence does strongly suggest, however, that facilities in Guayaquil were as least as bad as or worse than others of the period. Between 1875 and 1889 the death rate at the Guayaquil city hospital fluctuated between 11 and 17 percent (see table 7.1). By way of comparison, in New York City in 1867 the six general hospitals treated 12,093 patients, and 9.28 percent died. In 1878 at New York City's Roosevelt Hospital, one of the city's most modern, 1,617 received treatment, and 9 percent died. On the other hand, at Bellevue, New York's hospital for the poor, the death rate for 1871 was much higher, 15 percent (1,102 of the 7,514 treated died), although in 1878 it fell to 12 percent. In Ecuador, Cuenca's hospital had an 8 percent death rate in 1869 (663 patients treated and 54 deaths), and Quito's hospital in 1886 had a 5 percent death rate (524 patients treated, and 27 died). Duffy, *History of Public Health*, 179; Bordley and Harvey, *Two Centuries*, 60, 277–78; Paredes Borja, *Historia de la medicina*, 330, 331.

63. This section is drawn from PCC, *Informe, 1881–1892, 1889*, 19; IP, *Informe, 1890–1910*; JB, *Memoria, 1893–1925*; SS, *Informe, 1913*; GG, *Informe, 1907*; USCD, Martin Reinberg, "Report for 1886," March 10, 1887; and adapted from table 7.3.

64. Sanchez-Albornoz, *Population*, 173.

65. Other death rate figures for comparison for the period 1908–11 are as follows: 13.8 per 1,000 in London, 17 in Paris, and 14.7 in Berlin. Rosario, Argentina, *Anuario estadístico de la ciudad del Rosario de Santa Fe (1908–1911)*, 12, cited in Query, "Private Interests," 120–23. Scobie notes a rate of 17 per 1,000 for Buenos Aires and 40 per 1,000 for Salta in 1900. Scobie, *Secondary Cities*, 98.

66. Dobyns and Doughty, *Peru*, 169, 187, 197, 212; Adamo, "Broken Promise," 87; DeShazo, *Urban Workers*, 68.

67. Karasch, *Slave Life*, 94, 109.

68. Weber, *Growth*, 314.

69. SS, *Informe, 1911*; Collver, *Birth Rates*, 67–170; Sanchez-Albornoz, *Population*, 171. The coast had compared unfavorably to the sierra for some time. In 1843 Guayaquil province had a death rate of 60.1 per 1,000, whereas Quito canton had a rate of 25.6. The coastal province of Esmeraldas also had a high rate that year, 86 per 1,000. The numbers for 1848 display the same pattern: 16.9 per 1,000 in all Ecuador; 15.7 in Pichincha province; and 22.6 in Guayaquil province. MIP, *Informe, 1910*.

70. Lima grew from 100,156 in 1876 to 143,000 by 1908, an annual population increase of 1.11 percent. Mexico City counted 225,000 residents in 1870, and 471,066 by 1910, for an annual increase of 1.85 percent. Santiago, Chile, grew from 177,271 in 1885 to 427,658 in 1920, a yearly growth rate of 2.52 percent. The population of

Rio de Janeiro increased from 274,972 in 1872 to 1,157,873 in 1920, an average rate of 3.0 percent annually. Buenos Aires grew from 186,320 in 1870 to 1,575,814 in 1914, or 4.85 percent a year. Sao Paulo, Brazil, grew from 31,385 people in 1872 to 579,093 in 1920, an average annual increase of 6.07 percent. Boyer and Davies, *Urbanization,* 7–129; DeShazo, *Urban Workers,* 4; Hahner, *Poverty and Politics,* 7.

71. Hahner, *Poverty and Politics,* 32, 160; Karasch, *Slave Life,* 156, 159; Cooper, "Brazil's Long Fight," 678, 679, 683; Henschen, *History of Diseases,* 36; Ward, *Yellow Fever,* 16; and Adamo, "Broken Promise," 113, 123. As early as 1847 the finance minister noted that Indian migrants to the coast were especially hard hit by illnesses due to the change of climate. MH, *Informe, 1847.*

72. USGR, The USS Maryland stationed off Santa Elena, Ecuador, "Report to the Dept. of State on Health Conditions and the Civil War in Ecuador," February 2, 1912.

73. USGR, Military Attaché of the U.S. Legation in Quito, Captain Cordier, "Report on Health Conditions and the Civil War," 22 March 1912; SS, *Informe, 1913,* 4–10, *1911.*

74. As Police Chief F. E. Ferrusola put it, "it is undeniable that many . . . illnesses come from the bad hygienic conditions that we live in." IP, *Informe, 1903,* 17; also, the comments of physician Carlos Wiener, cited in Paredes Borja, *Historia de la medicina,* 352–54; descriptions provided in Enock, *Ecuador;* and in Parks and Nuermberger, "Sanitation and Guayaquil."

75. IP, *Informe, 1879.*

76. Ibid.

77. MI, *Informe, 1886,* 21.

78. SS, *Informe, 1912.*

79. SS, *Informe, 1910.*

80. "The Second Annual Report of the Metropolitan Board of Health of the State of New York, 1867," quoted in Duffy, *History of Public Health,* 1.

81. Duffy, *History of Public Health,* passim, 643. Death rates in New York City were as follows: 1860–69, 31.68; 1870–79, 27.61; 1880–89, 26.82; 1890–99, 22.9; 1900–9, 18.3; 1910–19, 15.0; 1920–29, 11.5.

82. Hassaurek, *Four Years,* 326. Hellman, in her study of modern Mexico, *Mexico in Crisis,* 210, phrases it another way: "Attempts at reform fail . . . because the problems . . . [are] not incidental to the economic system, but rather . . . the logical and inevitable results of capitalist development."

### Chapter Eight: Collective Popular Action

1. USGR, "Quarterly Report no. 8," January 1, 1920; Maier, "Presidential Succession," 481.

2. Quintero López, *El mito del populismo,* 105; E. Erickson et al., *Area Handbook,* 243; USCD, Weile, "Report," June 24, 1875, "Report," September 9, 1875, "Report," March 12, 1888; *The South Pacific Times,* September 14, 1875, cited in USCD, Weile, "Clip File Report," September 5, 1875; GBFO, "Report," January 18, 1924, and "Annual Report for 1924," 30 January 1925; Naranjo Gallegos, *1900 almanaque,* 192; Ro-

jas, *La novela*, 16, 45; Weinman, "Ecuador and Cacao," 34; *La nación*, May 8, 1880; Niles, *Casual Wanderings*, 113; PCC, *Gaceta municipal*, January 5, 1895, 513.

3. GBFO, "Report," April 27, 1907, "Report," January 30, 1907; USGR, "Report," May 27, 1912; *South Pacific Times*, September 14, 1875, cited in, USCD, Weile, "Clip File Report," September 5, 1875; *El grito del pueblo*, September 20, 1896; Hassaurek, *Four Years*, 223–26; Rojas, *La novela*, 17–18.

Peasants did not have to learn about mass protest when they came to the city— they already knew. See Van Aken, "Lingering Death"; Tyrer, "Demographic and Economic History," 333; Browne, "Effects of Epidemic Disease," 127–28. Indian uprisings took place in highland Ecuador: from 1700 to 1711 in Pillaro, Ambato; 1706 in Angamarca, Latacunga; in 1730 in Pillaro, Ambato; in 1761 in Latacunga; in 1764 in Riobamba; in 1766 in Riobamba and Ambato; in the 1770s in Otavalo, Riobamba, and Ambato; in 1779 in Guamote, Columbe, and Chimbo; the 1893 peasant revolt in rural Chimborazo province; and the 1920s tax protest near Riobamba.

The arrival of political unrest could on occasion arouse acts of extreme violence from the population. See, USMR, James Tillman, "Report," June 22, 1895, and "Report," June 19, 1896; GBFO, Cartwright, "Report to the British Minister in Quito," April 9, 1910, included in the Minister's Report to the Foreign Office, April 16, 1910.

4. This is drawn from: Milk, "Growth and Development"; González Casanova, *Historia del movimiento obrero*, vol. 3; Plutarco Naranjo, *La I international en Latinoamérica;* Isabel Robalino Bolle, *El sindicalismo en el Ecuador;* and Patricio Ycaza, *Historia del movimiento obrero.*

5. For comparison to a similar pattern in Mexico see Ashby, *Organized Labor*, 4; Hart, *Anarchism and the Working Class*, 80. Milk, "Growth and Development," 18, 26.

6. Durán Barba, *Pensamiento*, 104; GG, *Informe, 1901*, 145; *América libre*, 157; MI, *Informe, 1900.* Also see Middleton, "Division and Cohesion," 176, 177.

7. Muñoz Vicuña, *El 15 de noviembre*, 17, 22; MI, *Informe, 1917*, 262; Peñaherrera and Costales, *Historia social.* Also see Middleton, "Division and Cohesion," 177.

8. *El telégrafo*, October 1, 3, and 4, 1916.

9. Guzmán, *La hora*, 16; PCC, *Informe, 1918.*

10. IP, *Boletín de informacion, 1904*, 55; *Almanaque 1914*, 71; Weinman, "Ecuador and Cacao," 13.

11. Muñoz Vicuña, *15 de noviembre*, 22; Guzmán, *La hora*, 1.

12. Bergquist, *Labor in Latin America.*

13. This section is drawn from L. A. Rodríguez, *Search for Public Policy*, passim, and L. A. Carbo, *Historia monetaria*, passim. Also see USCD, Shanon M. Eder, "Report for 1878," March 15, 1879; Gonzáles Bazo, *Compañía nacional de cacao;* CCm, *Report, 1900*, 5, *1904*, *1919*, 19–20; GG, *Informe, 1901*, 95–102; *El Ecuador: guía*, 897–98; AA, *Memoria, 1921;* V. E. Estrada, *Balanza económica*, 3; Weinman, "Ecuador and Cacao," 347; Chiriboga, *Jornaleros*, 365, 369–70, 377, 379.

14. By 1917, France and Great Britain had both imposed formal import restrictions and curtailed imports from Ecuador. L. A. Rodríguez, *Search for Public Policy*, 102. From 1903 through 1924 the leading world consumers of cacao were as follows:

the United States (36 percent); Germany (14 percent); Great Britain (14 percent); France (11 percent); and the Netherlands (8 percent). Gallegos Naranjo, *1900 almanaque*; AA, *Memoria, 1921*; Weinman, "Ecuador and Cacao," 348. Middleton notes in "Division and Cohesion," 179, that after World War I, Great Britain gave favored status to the Gold Coast.

15. Figures are adjusted to take into consideration exchange rate fluctuations. L. A. Rodríguez, *Search for Public Policy*, 120; Kenwood and Lougheed, *Growth*, 140–41, 145–46, 176–78, 201.

16. Decrease in cacao production was also a result of the swiftly dropping world price, for many growers chose to get out of cacao. Weinman, "Ecuador and Cacao," 202; *Bulletin of the Imperial Institute* 19 (1921), cited in Ecuador, Consulate of Ecuador, New York. *Republic of Ecuador* (July 1922), 22, reprinted in, GBFO, "Report," 1922; Hurtado, *Political Power*, 82, 324; L. A. Rodríguez, *Search for Public Policy*, 101; and Phillips, "Gender," 37.

17. L. A. Rodríguez writes in *Search for Public Policy*, 175: "Declines in export earnings rapidly translated into decreases in public revenues [for] public finances were at the mercy of fluctuations in world cacao markets."

18. N. Clemente Ponce Minister of Foreign Relations of Ecuador to the British Chargé d'Affaires in Quito, Mr. Graham, reprinted in, GBFO, "Report," January 24, 1922.

19. *El guante*, November 1922, cited in, Muñoz Vicuña, *15 de noviembre*, 18. Muñoz also cites Belisario Quevedo, *Sociología, política y moral* (Guayaquil, 1977), 85, 86. Also see GBFO, "Report on the President's Annual Message to Congress," August 11, 1923. President Tamayo discussed the general tripling of prices in this address. Weinman, "Ecuador and Cacao," 193. "The high cost of living is a heavy burden on the poor," reported the U.S. State Department, "and has produced anything but a friendly feeling among the poorer classes toward the Administration, which they hold responsible for all their trouble." USGR, "Quarterly Report no. 7," October 3, 1919.

20. GBFO, R. C. Mitchell, "Report on the Economic and Finacial Conditions in Ecuador September, 1923," September 25, 1923.

21. The railroad project was completed with foreign capital, both British and American. This discussion of the railroad strike is based upon the following: Muñoz Vicuña, *15 de noviembre*, 23, 24, 26, 27; Milk, "Growth and Development," 71–73; USGR, Badin, "Quarterly Report no. 20," December 30, 1922, 12, 13; GBFO, Mitchell, "Report," October 31, 1922; Niles, *Casual*, 80.

22. GBFO, Mitchell, "Report," 31 October 1922; Muñoz Vicuña, *15 de noviembre*, 24–42; USGR, Badin, "Quarterly Report no. 20," December 30, 1922, 12, 13; Milk, "Growth and Development," 73–77.

23. The following sources provided information on the beginnings of the strike: GBFO, W. S. Urguhart, "Report," November 29, 1922; USGR, F. W. Goding, "Subject: Insurrection at Guayaquil," November 25, 1922, quoted in Weinman, "Ecuador and Cacao," 365–70; Milk, "Growth and Development," 78; Guzmán, *La hora*, 2, 3;

*El universo*, November 10, 1922; *Para la historia: esposición de la Federación de Trabajadores Regional Ecuatoriana.*

24. *El universo*, November 10, 1922.

25. Muñoz Vicuña, *15 de noviembre*, 44, 49, 50, 54; Milk, "Growth and Development," 77, 80, 85; Naranjo, *La I international*, 209.

26. *El universo*, November 10 and 11, 1922; USGR, Goding, "Report on and Translation of 'Official Strike Report of the Governor of Guayas, J. Pareja, the Military Chief of the Zone, E. Barriga, and the Chief of Police, Alejo Mateus,'" December 1–6, 7, 1922.

27. *El universo*, November 11, 1922; Milk, "Growth and Development," 79–83.

28. *El universo*, November 10, 1922.

29. *El universo*, November 12, 1922.

30. *El universo*, November 11, 1922.

31. *El universo*, November 12, 1922; Muñoz Vicuña, *15 de noviembre*, 58.

32. *El universo*, November 13, 1922; Muñoz Vicuña, *15 de noviembre*, 59; USGR, Goding, "Report on and Translation of 'Official Strike Report,'" December 1, 7, 1922.

33. *El universo*, November 12 and 14, 1922; Muñoz Vicuña, *15 de noviembre*, 60; *El comercio* (Quito), quoted in *El universo*, November 12, 1922; Guzmán, *Hora*, 3, 4; Milk, "Growth and Development," 84; USGR, Goding, "Report on and Translation of 'Strike Report,'" December 1, 2, 7, 1922.

34. *El universo*, November 14, 1922.

35. During the general strike of 1916 in Mexico City, the issue of providing light for the city was a critical one, as it was in Guayaquil. See Hart, *Anarchism*, 154. In Mexico, "the restoration of electrical power . . . demoralized the workers, and . . . proved to be a major turning point in the defeat of the strike." In Guayaquil, the only lights in town came from the boats on the river that partially lit up the waterfront. *El universo*, November 14, 1922; Muñoz Vicuña, *15 de noviembre*, 64, 66; USGR, Goding, "Report on and Translation of 'Strike Report,'" December 1–3, 7, 1922.

36. *El universo*, November 14, 1922; USGR, Goding, "Report on and Translation of 'Strike Report,'" 2, 7; Milk, "Growth and Development," 83–85; L. E. Elliott, "Land of Equator," *Pan American Magazine* 36 (February 1923), 57–63; USGR, Goding, "Subject: Insurrection at Guayaquil," November 25, 1922, quoted in Weinman, "Ecuador and Cacao," 367; USGR, Badin, "Quarterly Report no. 20," December 30, 1922, 21–22.

37. Muñoz Vicuña, *15 de noviembre*, 67; USGR, Goding, "Subject: Insurrection at Guayaquil," November 25, 1922, quoted in Weinman, "Ecuador and Cacao," 366–67; Milk, "Growth and Development," 85–86; Untitled FTRE pamplet quoted in Muñoz Vicuña, *15 de noviembre*, 66–67. "La Aurora," a feminist group of some eighty-five women, also joined the movement.

38. USGR, Badin, "Quarterly Report no. 20," December 30, 1922, 21; Milk, "Growth and Development," 85–87.

39. USGR, Goding, "Report on and Translation of 'Official Strike Report,'" December 3, 4, 7, 1922.

40. Barrera, *Para la historia*, 10. This pamphlet presented the government's version of events. *El telégrafo*, November 17, 1922, 1; Guzmán, *Hora*, 2.

41. Guzmán, *Hora*, 5.

42. Barrera, *Para la historia*, 23; Muñoz Vicuña, *15 de noviembre*, 79–80.

43. Barrera, *Para la historia*, 23.

44. Capelo Coello, *El crimen*, 4.

45. Guzmán, *Hora*, 5, 6; USGR, Goding, "Subject: Insurrection at Guayaquil," November 25, 1922, quoted in Weinman, "Ecuador and Cacao," 365–70; USGR, Badin, "Quarterly Report no. 20," December 30, 1922, 21–22; Milk, "Growth and Development," 89–90; USGR, Goding, "Report on and Translation of 'Official Strike Report,'" December 5, 7, 1922; *New York Times*, November 19, 1922, December 5, 1922.

46. Barrera, *Para la historia*, 23.

47. Cited in Barrera, *Para la historia*, 24, and discussed in Capelo Coello, *El crimen*, 4.

48. "González Rubio & Co., (native), Enrique Ribas, (Spanish), Cassinelli Hnos., (Italian), Miguel Enrich, (Spanish) and González Hnos. (Italian) were the worst sufferers in the looting." GBFO, W. S. Urguhart, "Report," November 29, 1922.

49. Capelo Coello, *El crimen; El telégrafo*, November 18, 1922.

50. *El telégrafo*, November 20, 1922.

51. Guzmán, *Hora*, 6.

52. The British Foreign Office placed the number at 200, with 300 wounded. GBFO, W. S. Urguhart, "Report," November 29, 1922.

53. Weinman, "Ecuador and Cacao," 151; L. A. Rodríguez, *Search*, 124.

54. *El universo*, November 17 and 18, 1922; *El telégrafo*, November 17, 1922.

55. USGR, Badin, "Quarterly Report no. 20," December 30, 1922, 6.

56. *El guante*, quoted in Muñoz Vicuña, *15 de noviembre*, 82–83; *El telégrafo*, November 18 and 20, 1922.

57. USGR, Badin, "Quarterly Report no. 20," December 30, 1922, 22; Milk, "Growth and Development," 90–91.

58. The firms affected included Sola & Co., Leandro Carrera & Co., Wing Wo Tay & Co., Sociedad Continental S.A., and V. E. Illingworth & Co. GBFO, "Report," 4 January 1923, "Report," December 12, 1923, "Report," January 17, 1924, "Report," June 5, 1924, R. C. Mitchell, "Report," September 25, 1923.

59. GBFO, "Report," January 4, 1924, "Report," December 30, 1923, "Report."

60. GBFO, "Report," October 29, 1924, "Report,"; USGR, Badin, "Quarterly Report no. 20," December 30, 1922, 7–10.

61. GBFO, Mitchell, "Report on the President's Message to Congress," August 11, 1923.

62. GBFO, "Report," October 18, 1924; USGR, Badin, "Quarterly Report no. 20," December 30, 1922, 7–10.

63. Maram, in "Urban Labor," 220, notes that police repression discredited the general strike tactic in Brazil. To many workers, the strategy seemed too confrontational and yielded meager returns.

64. USGR, Badin, "Quarterly Report no. 20," December 30, 1922, 22.

65. Barrera, *Para la historia;* also see GBFO, Urguhart, "Report," November 29, 1922.

66. Barrera, *Para la historia,* 10, 12, 20, and *El comercio* (Quito), quoted in Barrera, 26–27.

67. GBFO, Mitchell, "Report on the President's Message to Congress," August 11, 1923, "Report." A British account of the bloodletting went along with this interpretation, claiming that the troops began firing only "when an overwhelming number of the strikers . . . assumed a threatening attitude," and that a "revolutionary movement" had been "nipped in the bud." "Since the 15th of November, 1922," wrote the Foreign Office, "there have been no further labour movements." GBFO, Mitchell, "Report," November 21, 1922, "Annual Report for 1923," December 31, 1923; USGR, Badin, "Quarterly Report no. 20," December 30, 1922, 13–14; Weinman, "Ecuador and Cacao," 242, 243; Milk, "Growth and Development," 2, 95–96; Middleton, "Division and Cohesion," 178. The railroad company management wrote, "After several days of rioting in Guayaquil the Governmental forces finally terminated the whole affair by killing and wounding several hundred persons. This drastic action had a very salutary effect and resulted in a distinct clearing of the atmosphere." *1922 Report of President to the Directors of the Guayaquil and Quito Railway Company for the year ended December 31, 1922* (Huigra, Ecuador, 1923), 7, reprinted in, GBFO, "Report," December 1923.

68. GBFO, "Report," October 29, 1924.

69. These thoughts on democratic insurgencies were inspired by Goodwyn, "Cooperative Commonwealth." See also Smelser's *Theory of Collective Behavior.*

## Chapter Nine: Reflections on the Possibilities of Urban Social Reform

1. Chiriboga, *Jornaleros.*

2. Ayala Mora, *Epoca republicana,* 135, 137.

3. The labor market in Latin American cities was segmented, and worker knowledge of job opportunities was imperfect. Shipley finds in "On the Outside Looking In" that unemployment was a serious problem even in thriving Buenos Aires.

4. São Paulo was like Guayaquil in this regard, producing great riches for Brazil, only to see its tax revenues drained off for use in other parts of the nation.

5. Lewis, *Evolution,* 23–24, notes some of the dilemmas of dependency that did pertain to Ecuador: "The points where profits were greatest (wholesaling, banking, shipping, insurance) tended to be foreign-controlled, and this certainly diminished the availability of funds and enterprise for investment in domestic manufacturing. . . . The fact is that the very success of the country in exporting created a vested interest of those who lived by primary production . . . and who opposed measures for industrialization."

6. J. Johnson, *Political Change,* finds that by 1900, the export economies helped create new commercial/industrial middle-ranking groups of "managers, applied scientists, and highly trained technicians" who were added to the existing middle-ranking groups—"members of the liberal professions, such as law and medicine;

they were writers, publishers, and artists; they were professors in secondary schools and institutions of higher learning; they were bureaucrats; they were members of the secular clergy of the Catholic Church, and of the lower and middle echelons of the officer corps" (1–2). "But the differences . . . [did] not prevent large and ordinarily major segments of the middle sectors from finding common ground for joint political action" (4).

7. Quoted in Rosen, *History of Public Health*, 464. As the chief of New York City's Health Department, Dr. Sigismund S. Goldwater said in 1915, "Public health is purchasable; within natural limitations a city can determine its own death rate." Quoted in Duffy, *History of Public Health*, 271.

8. L. Johnson, *Problem of Order*, xii: "by the 1890s . . . those nations that proved most successful in pursuing export-led development moved quickly to imitate the institutions and practices found in London, Paris, and New York."

9. As Lewis notes in *Evolution*, 40, urbanization is expensive. "Rural people do more for themselves with their own labor in such matters as building houses, or working communally on village roads or irrigation facilities." Argentina and other nations took steps to attract foreign capital, such as granting generous land concessions to the companies that built the railroads. Shipley, "On the Outside Looking In," 12, notes that "foreign capital poured into Argentina during these years. Foreign investment came in at such a rate that by 1913 almost one-half of the value of total fixed capital stock in the country was owned directly or indirectly by private foreign investors."

# Bibliography

**Unpublished Sources**

Great Britain. Foreign Office. Record Group 371.

United States. Department of State. Despatches from U.S. consuls in Guayaquil, 1826–1909. Record Group 59.

———. Department of State. Despatches from U.S ministers to Ecuador, 1848–1906. Record Group 59.

———. Department of State. General Records of the Department of State relating to the political affairs in Ecuador, 1910–1929. Record Group 59.

**Government Documents**

Ecuador. Gobernación de la Provincia del Guayas. *Informes* [Office of the Governor of the Province of Guayas. Reports]. Yearly; title varies.

———. Ministerio de Fomento. *Memoria, 1901* [Ministry of Development. Note].

———. Ministro de Hacienda. *Censo de Samborondón, Jesus María, y Naranjal, 1871* [Minister of Finance. Census for Samborondon, Jesus María, and Naranjal].

———. Ministro de Hacienda. *Informes* [Minister of Finance. Reports]. Yearly.

———. Ministerio de Instrucción Pública. *Informes* [Ministry of Public Education. Reports]. Yearly; title varies.

———. Ministro de lo Interior. *Informes* [Minister of the Interior. Reports]. Yearly; title varies.

———. Ministerio de Relaciones Exteriores. *Informes* [Ministry of Foreign Relations. Reports]. Yearly.

———. Registro Civil. *Informes* [Civil Registry. Reports]. Yearly.

———. Secretario de Instrucción Pública. *Memoria* [Secretary of Public Education. Note]. Yearly; title varies.

Guayaquil, Ecuador. Asociación de Agricultores del Ecuador. *Memorias* [Agriculturalists Association of Ecuador. Notes]. Yearly; title varies.

———. Cámara de Comercio. *Memorias* [Chamber of Commerce. Notes]. Yearly; title varies.

———. Concejo Cantonal de Guayaquil. *Jefatura política, 1890* [City Council of Guayaquil. Reports of the district political officers].

———. Concejo Cantonal de Guayaquil. *Libro de ordenanzas o acuerdos municipales expedidos por el concejo cantonal de Guayaquil, 1895* [City Council of Guayaquil. Book of ordinances and contracts issued by the council].

———. Concejo Cantonal de Guayaquil. *Peticiónes* [City Council of Guayaquil Petitions].

———. Dirección del Servicio de Sanidad Pública. *Informes* [Department of Sanitation. Reports]. Yearly.

———. Directorio de la Asociación de Agricultores del Ecuador. *Memorias* [Directorate of the Agriculturalists Association of Ecuador. Notes]. Yearly.

———. Documentos Oficiales. *Correspondencia* [Offical documents. Correspondence].

———. *Gaceta municipal* [Municipal Gazette]. Yearly.

———. Junta de Beneficencia de Guayaquil. *Informes* [Charity Council of Guayaquil. Reports]. Yearly.

———. Intendencia de Policía del Guayas. *Informes* [Guayas Police Department. Reports]. Yearly; title varies.

———. Oficina de Pesquisas, *Correspondencia* [Office of Investigations. Correspondence].

———. Presidente del Concejo Cantonal. *Actas de las sesiones efectuadas por el concejo municipal de Guayaquil, 1899* [President of the Guayaquil Regional Council. Acts approved by the city council].

———. Presidente del Concejo Cantonal. *Balanza de la contabilidad municipal* [President of the Guayaquil Regional Council. Budgets]. Yearly.

———. Presidente del Concejo Cantonal. *Censo, 1919* [President of the Guayaquil Regional Council. Census].

———. Presidente del Concejo Cantonal. *Informes* [President of the Guayaquil Regional Council. Reports]. Yearly; title varies.

———. Presidente del Directorio de la Empresa de Carros Urbanos. *Memoria, 1903* [President of the Streetcar Company. Note].

———. Tesorería Municipal. *Informe, 1915* [City Treasury. Report].

**Newspapers**

*El grito del pueblo* (Guayaquil).
*El guante* (Guayaquil).
*El telégrafo* (Guayaquil).
*El universo* (Guayaquil).
*La nación* (Guayaquil).
*New York Times.*
*Patria* (Guayaquil).

**Published Sources**

Adamo, Sam. "The Broken Promise: Race, Health, and Justice in Rio de Janeiro, 1890–1940." Ph.D. diss., University of New Mexico, 1983.

Alba, Victor. *Politics and the Labor Movement in Latin America.* Stanford: Stanford University Press, 1968.

Albornoz Peralta, Oswaldo. *Ecuador: luces y sombras del liberalismo* [Ecuador: lights and shadows of liberalism]. Quito: Editorial el Duende, 1989.

*Almanaque el mercurio, 1893* [Mercury almanac]. Guayaquil, 1893.

*Almanaque ilustrado ecuatoriano 1914* [Illustrated almanac of Ecuador]. Guayaquil: Imprenta la Reforma Casa Editorial Jouvin, 1914.

*Almanaque ilustrado 1884* [Illustrated almanac]. Guayaquil: Imprenta de Fidel Montoya, 1884.

*América libre: obra dedicada a conmemorar el centenario de la independencia de Guayaquil* [A free America: A work dedicated to commemorating the hundred-year anniversary of the independence of Guayaquil]. Guayaquil: Prensa Ecuatoriana, 1920.

Andrews, George Reid. "Latin American Urban History." *History Teacher* 19, no. 4 (August 1986): 499–515.

Arellano, José-Pablo. "Social Policies in Chile: An Historical Review." *Journal of Latin American Studies* 17 (November 1985): 397–418.

Ashby, Joe. *Organized Labor and the Mexican Revolution under Lázaro Cárdenas*. Chapel Hill: University of North Carolina Press, 1967.

Aviles, J. J. Jurado, ed. *El Ecuador en el centenario de la independencia de Guayaquil* [Ecuador at the hundred-year anniversary of the independence of Guayaquil]. Translated by Gustavo Carranza. New York: De Laisne and Carranza, 1920.

Ayala Mora, Enrique, ed. *Nueva historia del Ecuador: Epoca republicana* [New history of Ecuador: Republican era]. Vol. 1. Quito: Editora Nacional, 1983.

Baer, James. "Street, Block, and Neighborhood: Residency Patterns, Community Networks, and the 1895 Argentine Manuscript Census." *The Americas* 51, no. 1 (July 1994): 89–101.

———. "Tenant Mobilization and the 1907 Rent Strike in Buenos Aires." *The Americas* 49, no. 3 (January 1993): 343–68.

Barbosa, Jenardo, ed. *Almanaque ilustrado de Guayaquil, 1906* [Illustrated almanac of Guayaquil]. Guayaquil: Imprenta de El Telégrafo, 1906.

———. *Almanaque ilustrado de Guayaquil, 1907* [Illustrated almanac of Guayaquil]. Guayaquil: Imp. y Lit. del Comercio, [1907].

Barraclough, Geoffrey. *Main Trends in History*. New York: Holmes and Meier, 1978.

Barrera, J. R. *Para la historia* [For history]. Guayaquil: Imprenta el Ideal, 1922.

Bergquist, Charles. *Coffee and Conflict in Colombia, 1886–1910*. Durham: Duke University Press, 1978.

———. *Labor in Latin America: Comparative Essays on Chile, Argentina, Venezuela, and Colombia*. Stanford: Stanford University Press, 1986.

Beyer, Glenn H., ed. *The Urban Explosion in Latin America: A Continent in Process of Modernization*. Ithaca: Cornell University Press, 1967.

Blackwelder, Julis Kirk, and Lyman L. Johnson. "Changing Criminal Patterns in Buenos Aires, 1890 to 1914." *Journal of Latin American Studies* 14 (November 1982): 359–80.

Bordley, James, and A. McGehee Harvey. *Two Centuries of American Medicine, 1776–1976*. Philadelphia: Saunders, 1976.

Boyer, Richard E., and Keith A. Davies. *Urbanization in Nineteenth-Century Latin*

*America: Statistics and Sources.* Berkeley and Los Angeles: University of California Press, 1973.

Browne, Suzanne Austin. "The Effects of Epidemic Disease in Colonial Ecuador." Ph.D. diss., Duke University, 1984.

Browning, Harley L. "Some Problematics of the Tertiarization Process in Latin America." In *Urbanization in the Americas from its Beginnings to the Present,* edited by Richard P. Schaedel, Jorge E. Hardoy, and Nora Scott Kinzer. The Hague: Mouton, 1978.

Burns, E. Bradford, and Thomas E. Skidmore. *Elites, Masses, and Modernization in Latin America, 1850–1930.* Austin: University of Texas Press, 1979.

Capelo Coello, José Alejo. *El crimen del 15 noviembre 1922* [The crime of 15 November 1922]. Guayaquil: Imprenta el Ideal, 1922.

Carbo, Luís Alberto. *Historia monetaria y cambiaria del Ecuador* [Monetary and exchange history of Ecuador]. Quito: Imprenta del Banco Central del Ecuador, 1978.

Carbo, Luís F. *El Ecuador en Chicago* [Ecuador in Chicago]. New York: Imprenta de A. E. Chasmar y Cia., 1894.

Cardoso, Fernando Henrique and Enzo Falleto. *Dependency and Development in Latin America.* Translated by Marjory Mattingly Urquidi. Berkeley and Los Angeles: University of California Press, 1979.

Ceriola, Juan B. *Guayaquil a la vista: Colección de fototipias con sus explicaciónes históricas, artísticas y descriptivas* [Images of Guayaquil: a collection of photographs, with their historical, artistic, and descriptive explanations]. Barcelona: Vda. de Luis Tasso, 1910.

Chacon, Ramon D. "Rural Educational Reform in Yucatan: From the Porfiriato to the Era of Salvador Alvarado, 1910–1918." *The Americas* 42 (October 1985): 207–28.

Chance, John K. "Recent Trends in Latin American Urban Studies." *Latin American Research Review* 15 (1980): 183–88.

Chiriboga, Manuel. *Jornaleros y gran propietarios en 135 años de exportación cacaotera (1790–1925)* [Day laborers and large landowners in 135 years of cacao exportation]. Quito: Consejo Provincial Pichincha, 1980.

Cisneros Cisneros, César. "Indian Migrations from the Andean Zone of Ecuador to the Lowlands." *América Indígena* 19 (1959): 225–31.

Clayton, Lawrence A. *Caulkers and Carpenters in a New World: The Shipyards of Colonial Guayaquil.* Athens: Ohio University Center for International Studies, Latin American Program, 1980.

Collver, O. Andrew. *Birth Rates in Latin America: New Estimates of Historical Trends and Fluctuations.* Berkeley: Institute of International Studies, University of California, 1965.

Compañía Guía del Ecuador. *El Ecuador: Guía comercial, agrícola e industrial de la república* [Ecuador: Guide to commerce, agriculture and industry of the republic]. Guayaquil: Talleres de Artes Gráficas de E. Rodenas, 1909.

Cooper, Donald. "Brazil's Long Fight against Epidemic Disease, 1849–1917, with Special Emphasis on Yellow Fever." *Bulletin of the New York Academy of Medicine* 51, no. 5 (May 1975): 672–96.

Conniff, Michael. "Guayaquil Through Independence: Urban Development in a Colonial System." *The Americas* 33 (January 1977): 385–410.

Cortes-Conde, Roberto and Stanley J. Stein, *Latin America: A Guide to Economic History, 1830–1930.* Berkeley and Los Angeles: University of California Press, 1977.

Cross, Malcolm. *Urbanization and Urban Growth in the Caribbean.* Cambridge: Cambridge University Press, 1979.

Cueva, Agustín. *The Process of Political Domination in Ecuador.* Translated by Danielle Salti. New Brunswick: Transaction, 1982.

Dear, Michael, and Allen J. Scott. *Urbanization and Urban Planning in Capitalist Society.* London: Methuen, 1981.

Delavaud, Anne Collin. "From Colonization to Agricultural Development: The Case of Coastal Ecuador." In *Environment, Society, and Rural Change in Latin America: The Past, Present, and Future in the Countryside,* edited by David A. Preston. Chichester, N.Y.: John Wiley and Sons, 1980.

DeShazo, Peter. *Urban Workers and Labor Unions in Chile, 1920–1927.* Madison: University of Wisconsin Press, 1983.

Duffy, John. *The Healers: A History of American Medicine.* Urbana: University of Illinois Press, 1976.

Durán Barba, Jaime, ed. *Pensamiento popular ecuatoriano* [Ecuadorian popular thought]. Quito: Banco Central del Ecuador, 1981.

Elliott, L. E. "Land of Equator [sic]." *Pan American Magazine* 36 (February 1923): 57–63.

Enock, Charles Reginald. *Ecuador: Its Ancient and Modern History Topography and Natural Resources Industries and Social Developments.* London: Unwin, 1919.

Erickson, Edwin E., et al. *Area Handbook for Ecuador.* Washington, D.C.: U.S. Government Printing Office, 1966.

Erickson, Kenneth Paul, Patrick V. Peppe, and Hobart A. Spalding. "Dependency versus Working Class History." *Latin American Research Review* 15 (1980): 177–81.

———. "Research on the Urban Working Class and Organized Labor in Argentina, Brazil, and Chile: What Is Left to Be Done?" *Latin American Research Review* 9 (Summer 1974): 115–42.

Estrada, Victor Emilio. *Ensayo sobre la balanza económica del Ecuador* [Essay on Ecuador's economic balance]. Guayaquil: Tipografía y Papelería de Julio T. Foyain, 1922.

Estrada Ycaza, Julio. "Apuntes para la historia del Hospital Militar" [Notes toward a history of the military hospital]. *Revista del archivo histórico del Guayas* 1, no. 2 (December 1972): 42.

———. "Desarrollo histórico del suburbio guayaquileño" [Historical development of the Guayaquil suburbs]. *Revista del archivo histórico del Guayas* (June 1973): 14–26.

———. *El hospital de Guayaquil* [The Guayaquil hospital]. Guayaquil: Publicaciónes del Archivo Histórico del Guayas, 1974.

———. "Evolución urbana de Guayaquil" [Urban evolution of Guayaquil]. *Revista del archivo histórico del Guayas* (1972): 37–66.

———. *Los bancos del siglo XIX* [The banks of the nineteenth century]. Guayaquil: Publicaciónes del Archivo Histórico del Guayas, 1976.

———. *Regionalismo y migración* [Regionalism and migration]. Guayaquil: Publicaciónes del Archivo Histórico del Guayas, 1977.

———. Unpublished research notes.

Ferrer, Aldo. *The Argentine Economy.* Translation by Marjory Mattingly Urquidi. Berkeley and Los Angeles: University of California Press, 1967.

Franklin, Albert B. *Ecuador: Portrait of a People.* Garden City, N.Y.: Doubleday, 1944.

Furtado, Celso. *Economic Development of Latin America: A Survey from Colonial Times to the Cuban Revolution.* Translated by Suzette Macedo. Cambridge: Cambridge University Press, 1976.

Gallegos Naranjo, Manuel. *1883 almanaque ecuatoriano guía de Guayaquil* [Ecuadorian almanac and guide to Guayaquil]. Guayaquil: Tipografía de El Chimborazo, 1883.

———. *1900 fin de siglo almanaque de Guayaquil* [End-of-the-century Guayaquil almanac]. Guayaquil: Tipografía Gutenberg, 1900.

*General Regulations for Quarantine Service and Municipal Health of Guayaquil.* Guayaquil: Tipografía El Vigilante, 1900.

Glade, William P. *The Latin American Economies: A Study of Their Institutional Evolution.* New York: American Book Co., 1969.

Gonzáles Bazo, Vicente. *Compañía nacional de cacao: exposición del negociado* [National Cacao Company: business analysis] Quito: Imprenta de la Universidad Central, 1899.

González Casanova, Pablo, ed. *Historia del movimiento obrero en América Latina: Colombia, Venezuela, Ecuador, Peru, Bolivia, Paraguay.* [History of the labor movement in Latin America]. 3 vols. Mexico City: Siglo Veintiuno Editores, 1984.

Goodwyn, Lawrence. "The Cooperative Commonwealth and Other Abstractions: In Search of a Democratic Premise." *Marxist Perspectives* (Summer 1980): 8–39.

Graham, Richard. *Great Britain and Modernization in Brazil 1850–1914.* Cambridge: Cambridge University Press, 1972.

Greenfield, Gerald Michael. "The Development of the Underdeveloped City: Public Sanitation in São Paulo, Brazil, 1885–1913." *Luso-Brazilian Review* 17 (Summer 1980): 107–18.

———. "New Perspectives on Latin American Cities." *Journal of Urban History* 15, no. 2 (February 1989): 205–14.

*Guayaquil en la mano 1912: directorio del Guayaquil, Ecuador* [Guayaquil handbook and city directory]. Guayaquil: Imprenta la Reforma Casa Editorial, 1912.

Guerrero, Andres. *Los oligarcas del cacao* [The cacao oligarchies]. Quito: Editorial el Conejo, 1980.

*Guía de Guayaquil y almanaque de La Nación 1902/1903* [Guayaquil guide and almanac of *La Nación*]. Guayaquil: Imprenta de La Nación, [1902, 1903].

*Guía de Guayaquil y almanaque de La Nación 1904/1905* [Guayaquil guide and almanac of *La Nación*]. Guayaquil: Imprenta de La Nación, [1905].

Guzmán, José I. *La hora trágica* [The tragic hour]. Guayaquil: Lópes-Quisuis, 1974.

Hahner, June E. *Poverty and Politics: The Urban Poor in Brazil, 1870–1920.* Albuquerque: University of New Mexico Press, 1986.

Hall, Michael M. "Approaches to Immigration History." In *New Approaches to Latin American History*. Austin: University of Texas Press, 1974.

Hamerly, Michael. *Historia social y económica de la antigua provincia de Guayaquil 1763–1842* [Social and economic history of the old province of Guayaquil]. Guayaquil: Archivo Histórico del Guayas, 1973.

———. "Quantifying the Nineteenth Century." *Latin American Research Review* 13 (Summer 1978): 138–56.

———. "A Social and Economic History of the City and District of Guayaquil during the Late Colonial & Independence Periods." Ph.D. diss., University of Florida, 1974.

Hardoy, Jorge E., ed. *Urbanization in Latin America: Approaches and Issues.* Garden City, N.Y.: Anchor, 1975.

Harris, Walter D. Jr., *The Growth of Latin American Cities.* Athens: Ohio University Press, 1971.

Hart, John. *Anarchism and the Mexican Working Class, 1860–1931.* Austin: University of Texas Press, 1978.

Hassaurek, Friedrich. *Four Years among Spanish Americans.* New York: Hurd and Houghton, 1867.

Henschen, Folke. *The History of Diseases.* Translated by Joan Tate. London: Longmans, Green, 1966.

Hobsbawm, Eric J. *Industry and Empire.* Harmondsworth, U.K.: Penguin, 1978.

Huerta, Pedro José. *Rocafuerte y la fiebre amarilla de 1842* [Rocafuerte and the yellow fever of 1842]. Guayaquil: Universidad de Guayaquil, 1947.

Hurtado, Osvaldo. *Political Power in Ecuador.* Translated by Nick D. Mills, Jr. Boulder, Colo.: Westview Press, 1985.

Icaza, Jorge. *The Villagers.* Translated by B. Dulsey. Carbondale: Southern Illinois University Press, 1973.

Jaksic, Ivan. "The Politics of Higher Education in Latin America." *Latin American Research Review* 20, no. 1 (1985): 209–21.

Jaksic, Ivan and Sol Serrano. "In the Service of the Nation: The Establishment and Consolidation of the Universidad de Chile, 1842–1879." *Hispanic American Historical Review* 70, no. 1 (February 1990): 139–71.

Jaramillo, Alfredo. "The Ecuadorian Family." In *The Family in Latin America*, edited by Man Singh Das and Clinton J. Jesser. New Delhi: Vikas Publishing House, 1980.

Joll, James. *The Anarchists.* Boston: Little, Brown, 1964.

Johnson, John J. "One Hundred Years of Historical Writing on Modern Latin America by United States Historians." *Hispanic American Historical Review* 65, no. 4 (1985): 745–65.

———. *Political Change in Latin America: The Emergence of the Middle Sectors.* Stanford: Stanford University Press, 1958.

Johnson, Lyman L., ed. *The Problem of Order in Changing Societies: Essays on Crime and Policing in Argentina and Uruguay.* Albuquerque: University of New Mexico Press, 1990.

Karasch, Mary C. *Slave Life in Rio de Janeiro, 1808–1850.* Princeton: Princeton University Press, 1986.

Kasza, Gregory J. "Regional Conflict in Ecuador: Quito and Guayaquil." *Inter-American Economic Affairs* 35 (Autumn 1981): 3–41.

Kemper, Robert. *Migration and Adaptation.* Beverly Hills: Sage, 1977.

Kenwood, A. G. and A. L. Lougheed, *The Growth of the International Economy, 1820–1960.* Albany: State University of New York Press, n.d.

King, William Martin. "Ecuadorian Church and State Relations under García Moreno, 1859–1963." Ph.D. diss., University of Texas, 1974.

Kiple, Kenneth. "Cholera and Race in the Caribbean." *Journal of Latin American Studies* 17 (1985): 157–77.

———, ed. *The African Exchange: Toward a Biological History of Black People.* Durham: Duke University Press, 1988.

———, ed. *The Cambridge World History of Human Disease.* Cambridge: Cambridge University Press, 1993.

Kiple, Kenneth F., and Virginia H. Kiple. "Deficiency Diseases in the Caribbean." *Journal of Interdisciplinary History* 11 (Autumn 1980): 197–215.

Knight, Alan. "The Working Class and the Mexican Revolution, c. 1900–1920." *Journal of Latin American Studies* 16 (May 1984): 51–79.

Le Gouhir y Rodas, José. *Historia de la República del Ecuador* [History of the Republic of Ecuador]. Vol. 1. Quito: Tipografía y Encuadarción de la Prensa Católica, 1920.

Lewis, W. Arthur. *The Evolution of the International Economic Order.* Princeton: Princeton University Press, 1978.

Linke, Lilo. *Ecuador: Country of Contrasts.* London: Oxford University Press, 1962.

Lizardo, Mary Ann. "The Impact of the Sugar Industry on the Middle Class of an Argentine City: San Miguel de Tucumán, 1869–1895." Ph.D. diss., George Washington University, 1982.

Loy, Jane Meyer. "Primary Education during the Colombian Federation: The School Reform of 1870." *Hispanic American Historical Review* 51, no. 2 (May 1971): 275–94.

Madero, Mauro. *Historia de la medicina en la provincia del Guayas* [History of medicine in the Province of Guayas]. Guayaquil: Imprenta de la Casa de la Cultura, Nucleo del Guayas, 1955.

Maier, Georg. "Presidential Succession in Ecuador: 1860–1968." *Journal of Inter-American Studies and World Affairs* 13 (July–October 1971): 475–509.

Maram, Sheldon. "Urban Labor and Social Change in the 1920s." *Luso-Brazilian Review* 16 (Winter 1979): 215–23.

Martz, John D. *Ecuador: Conflicting Political Culture and the Quest for Progress.* Boston: Allyn and Bacon, 1972.

Mason, Keith. "Demography, Disease and Medical Care in Caribbean Slave Societies." *Bulletin of Latin American Research* 5 (1986): 109–19.

Matamoros Jara, Carlos. *Almanaque de Guayaquil del diario de avisos #1* [Guayaquil almanac from the record of public notices]. Guayaquil: Imprenta Comercial, 1892.

McCreery, David. "'This Life of Misery and Shame': Female Prostitution in Guatemala City, 1880–1920." *Journal of Latin American Studies* 18 (November 1986): 333–52.

McKeown, Thomas. *The Origins of Human Disease.* Oxford: Basil Blackwell, 1988.

McNeill, William H. *Plagues and Peoples.* Garden City, N.Y.: Anchor, 1976.

Middleton, Alan. "Division and Cohesion the the Working Class: Artisans and Wage Labourers in Ecuador." *Journal of Latin American Studies* 14 (1982): 171–94.

Milk, Richard Lee. "Growth and Development of Ecuador's Worker Organizations." Ph.D. diss., Indiana University, 1979.

Mills, Nick Jr. "Liberal Opposition in Ecuadorean Politics." Ph.D. diss., University of New Mexico, 1972.

Minchom, Martin. *The People of Quito, 1690–1810: Change and Unrest in the Underclass.* Boulder, Colo.: Westview Press, 1994.

Moore, Richard J. "The Urban Poor in Guayaquil, Ecuador: Modes, Correlates, and the Context of Political Participation." In *Political Participation in Latin America: Politics and the Poor,* edited by John A. Booth and Mitchell A. Seligman. Vol. 2. New York: Holmes and Meier, 1979.

Morawaska, Ewa. "The Sociology and Historiography of Immigration." In *Immigration Reconsidered: History, Sociology, and Politics.* New York: Oxford University Press, 1990.

Mörner, Magnus. *The Andean Past: Land, Societies, and Conflicts.* New York: Columbia University Press, 1985.

Mörner, Magnus, with Harold Sims. *Adventurers and Proletarians: The Story of Migrants in Latin America.* Pittsburgh: University of Pittsburgh Press, 1985.

Morrill, Richard L. and Juan J. Angulo. "Spatial Aspects of a Smallpox Epidemic in a Small Brazilian City." *Geographical Review* 69 (July 1979): 319–30.

Morse, Richard M. *From Community to Metropolis: A Biography of Sao Paulo, Brazil.* New York: Octagon, 1974.

———. "Recent Research on Latin American Urbanization: A Selective Survey with Commentary." *Latin American Research Review* 1 (1965): 35–74.

———. "Trends and Issues in Latin American Urban Research, 1965–1970 (Part II)." *Latin American Research Review* 6 (Summer 1971): 19–75.

———. "Trends and Patterns in Latin American Urbanization, 1750–1920." *Comparative Studies in Society and History* 16, no. 4 (September 1974): 416–47.

———, ed. *The Urban Development of Latin America 1750–1920.* Stanford: Stanford University Press, 1971.

Muñoz Vicuña, Elías. *El 15 de noviembre de 1922* [15 November 1922]. Guayaquil: Departamento de Publicaciónes de la Facultad de Ciencias Económicas de la Universidad de Guayaquil, 1978.

Newland, Carlos. "La educación elemental in hispanoamérica: desde la independencia hasta la centralización de los sistemas educativos nacionales" [Elementary education in Hispanic America: From independence to the centralization of the national educational systems]. *Hispanic American Historical Review* 71, no. 2 (1991): 335–64.

Naranjo, Plutarco. *La I international en Latinoamérica* [The first international in Latin America]. Quito: Editorial Universitaria, 1977.

Niles, Blair. *Casual Wanderings in Ecuador.* New York: Century, 1923.

*1925 almanaque nacional Guayaquil, Ecuador* [National almanac for Guayaquil, Ecuador]. Guayaquil: Imprenta El Porvenir, 1925.

Palacios, Marco. *Coffee in Colombia, 1850–1970: An Economic, Social, and Political History.* Cambridge: Cambridge University Press, 1980.

Palmer, David Scott. *Peru: The Authoritarian Tradition.* New York: Praeger, 1980.

*Para la historia: esposición de la federación de trabajadores regional ecuatoriana sobre la actitud obrera en los meses de octubre y noviembre de mil novecientos veintidos* [For history: report of the Regional Federation of Ecuadorian Workers on the attitude of labor in the months of October and November 1922]. Guayaquil: Imprenta Guayaquil, 1923.

Paredes Borja, Virgilio. *Historia de la medicina en el Ecuador. 2 Vols.* [History of medicine in Ecuador]. Quito: Editorial Casa de la Cultura Ecuatoriana, 1963.

Paredes Ramirez, Willington. "Económica y sociedad en la costa: siglo XIX" [Economics and society on the coast: nineteenth century]. In *Nueva historia del Ecuador: epoca repúblicana* [New history of Ecuador: Republican era]. Quito: Editora Nacional, 1983.

Parks, Lois F., and Gustave A. Nuermberger. "The Sanitation of Guayaquil." *Hispanic American Historical Review* 23 (1943): 197–221.

Parlee, Lorena M. "Porfirio Diaz, Railroads, and Development in Northern Mexico." Ph.D. diss., University of California, 1981.

Payne, James L. *Labor and Politics in Peru: The System of Political Bargaining.* New Haven: Yale University Press, 1965.

Paz Ayora, Vicente. *Guía de Guayaquil y almanaque del comercio ecuatoriano* [Guayaquil guide and commercial almanac for Ecuador]. Guayaquil: Imprenta de El Grito del Pueblo, 1901.

Peñaherrera de Costales, Piedad, and Alfredo Costales Samaniego. *Historia social del Ecuador.* 4 vols. [Social history of Ecuador]. Quito: Editorial Casa de la Cultura Ecuatoriana, 1964–71.

Perez Brignoli, Hector. "The Economic Cycle in Latin American Agricultural Export Economies (1880–1930): A Hypothesis for Investigation." Translated by John Gitlitz. *Latin American Research Review* 15 (1980): 3–33.

Phillips, Lynne P. "Gender, Class and Cultural Politics: A Case Study of Rural Vinces, Ecuador." Ph.D. diss., University of Toronto, 1985.

Pike, Fredrick B. *The United States and the Andean Republics: Peru, Bolivia, and Ecuador.* Cambridge, Mass.: Harvard University Press, 1977.

Pineo, Ronn F. "Recent Contributions to Ecuadorian Political History." *Latin American Perspectives,* forthcoming.

Platt, Desmond Christopher Martin. *Latin America and British Trade 1806–1914.* London: Adams and Charles Black, 1972.

Query, Lance D. "Private Interests and Public Welfare: Rails, Sewers and Open Spaces in Urban Rosario, Argentina (1865–1914)." Ph.D. diss., Indiana University, 1981.

Quintero López, Rafael. *El mito del populismo en el Ecuador: analisis de los fundamentos del estado ecuatoriano moderno (1895–1934)* [The myth of populism in Ecuador: Analysis of the foundation of the modern Ecuadorian state]. Quito: Universidad Central del Ecuador, 1983.

Ramos-Escandon, Carmen. "Working Class Formation and the Mexican Textile Industry: 1880–1912." Ph.D. diss., State University of New York, 1981.

Redclift, Michael R. *Agrarian Reform and Peasant Organization on the Ecuadorian Coast.* London: Athlone Press, 1978.

Ridings, Eugene W. "Foreign Predominance among Overseas Traders in Nineteenth-Century Latin America." *Latin American Research Review* 20 (1985): 3–27.

Robalino Bolle, Isabel. *El sindicalismo en el Ecuador* [Syndicalism in Ecuador]. Quito: Instituto Ecuatoriano para el Desarrollo Social, 1981.

Robalino Davila, Luis. *Orígines de Ecuador de hoy.* [Origins of Ecuador of today]. 7 vols. Puebla: Editorial Cajica, 1967–70.

Rodríguez-O., Jaime. *Down from Colonialism.* Los Angeles: Chicano Studies Research Center Publications, University of California, 1983.

———. "New Research Opportunities in Ecuador." *Latin American Research Review* 8 (1973): 95–100.

———. "Research into the National Period." In *Research Guide to Andean History.* Durham: Duke University Press, 1981.

Rodríguez J., C. E. *Historia de la sociedad filantrópica* [History of the Philanthropic Society]. Guayaquil: Talleres Tipo-Litográficos de la Sociedad Filantrópica del Guayas, 1926.

Rodríguez, Linda Alexander. *The Search for Public Policy: Regional Politics and Government Finances in Ecuador, 1830–1940.* Berkeley and Los Angeles: University of California Press, 1984.

Rojas, Angel F. *La novela ecuatoriana* [The Ecuadorian novel]. Mexico City: Fondo de Cultura Económica, 1948.

Rosen, George. *A History of Public Health.* New York: MD Publications, 1958.

Roweis, Shoukry T. "Urban Planning in Early and Late Capitalist Societies: Outline of a Theoretical Perspective." In *Urbanization and Urban Planning in Captialist Society.* London: Methuen, 1981.

Samaniego, Juan José. *Cronologia médica ecuatoriana* [Chronology of Ecuadorian medicine]. Quito: Editorial Casa de la Cultura Ecuatoriana, 1957.

Sanchez-Albornoz, Nicolas. *The Population of Latin America: A History.* Translated by W. A. R. Richardson. Berkeley and Los Angeles: University of California Press, 1974.

Sater, William F. *Chile and the War of the Pacific.* Lincoln: University of Nebraska Press, 1986.

Saunders, John Van Dyke. "Man-Land Relations in Ecuador." *Rural Sociology* 26 (March 1961): 57–69.

———. *The People of Ecuador: A Demographic Analysis.* Gainesville: University of Florida Press, 1961.

Schaedel, Richard. "The Anthropological Study of Latin American Cities in Intra and Interdisciplinary Perspective." *Urban Anthropology* 3 (1974): 139–70.

Schaedel, Richard P., Jorge E. Hardoy, and Nora Scott Kinzer, eds. *Urbanization in the Americas from its Beginnings to the Present*. The Hague: Mouton, 1978.

Schodt, David W. *Ecuador: An Andean Enigma*. Boulder, Colo.: Westview Press, 1987.

Scobie, James. *Buenos Aires*. New York: Oxford University Press, 1974.

————. "The Growth of Latin American Cities, 1870–1930." In *Cambridge History of Latin America*, Vol. 4. Cambridge: Cambridge University Press, 1986.

————. *Secondary Cities of Argentina: The Social History of Corrientes, Salta, and Mendoza, 1850–1910*. Compiled and edited by Samuel L. Baily. Stanford: Stanford University Press, 1988.

Shipley, Robert Edward. "On the Outside Looking in: A Social History of the 'Porteno' Worker During the 'Golden Age' of Argentine Development, 1914–1930." Ph.D. diss., Rutgers University, 1977.

Simon, S. Fanny. "Anarchism and Anarcho-Syndicalism in South America." *Hispanic American Historical Review* 26 (1946): 38–59.

Smelser, Neil J. *Theory of Collective Behavior*. New York: Free Press, 1962.

Smith, Henry Lester and Harold Littell. *Education in Latin America*. New York: American Books, 1934.

Socolow, Susan. "Three Contributions to Latin American Social History." *Latin American Research Review* 13, no. 3 (1978): 233–37.

Sofer, Eugene. "Recent Trends in Latin American Labor Historiography." *Latin American Research Review* 15, no. 1 (1980): 167–76.

Sofer, Eugene F. and Mark D. Szuchman, "City and Society: Their Connection in Latin American Historical Research." *Latin American Research Review* 14, no. 2 (1979): 113–29.

Solberg, Carl. *Immigration and Nationalism: Argentina and Chile, 1890–1914*. Austin: University of Texas Press, 1970.

Spalding, Hobart A. Jr., "Education in Argentina, 1890–1914: The Limits of Oligarchical Reform." *Journal of Interdisciplinary History* 3, no. 1 (Summer 1972): 31–61.

————. *Organized Labor in Latin America*. New York: University Press, 1977.

————. "The Parameters of Labor in Hispanic America." *Science and Society* 36 (Summer 1972): 202–16.

Spindler, Frank MacDonald. *Nineteenth Century Ecuador: An Historical Introduction*. Fairfax, Va.: George Mason University Press, 1987.

Szaszdi, Adam. "The Historiography of the Republic of Ecuador." *Hispanic American Historical Review* 44 (November 1964): 503–50.

Szuchman, Mark D. "Childhood Education and Politics in Nineteenth-Century Argentina: The Case of Buenos Aires." *Hispanic American Historical Review* 70, no. 1 (1990): 109–38.

Taber, Clarence Wilbur. *Taber's Cyclopedic Medical Dictionary*. Philadelphia: F. A. Davis, 1970.

TePaske, John J., et al., *Research Guide to Andean History*. Durham: Duke University Press, 1981.

Tilly, Charles; Louise Tilly; and Richard Tilly. *The Rebellious Century*. Cambridge, Mass.: Harvard University Press, 1975.

Townsend, Camilia. "The Guayaquileña and Guayaquil: Early Republican Women and City Life in Nineteenth-Century Ecuador." Paper presented at the annual meeting of the South Eastern Council on Latin American Studies, Charleston, S.C., April 1992.

Tyrer, Robson. "The Demographic and Economic History of the *Audiencia* of Quito." Ph.D. diss., University of California, 1976.

Urquidi, Victor L. "The Underdeveloped City." In *Urbanization in Latin America: Approaches and Issues*. Garden City, N.Y.: Anchor, 1975.

Uzcategui, Maruja de. *Apuntes para una historia de la protección y de los servicios sociales en el Ecuador* [Notes toward a history of support and social services in Ecuador]. Quito: Imprenta de la Universidad, 1952.

Van Aken, Mark. *King of the Night: Juan José Flores and Ecuador, 1824–1864*. Berkeley and Los Angeles: University of California Press, 1989.

———. "The Lingering Death of Indian Tribute in Ecuador." *Hispanic American Historical Review* 61 (1981): 429–59.

Vaughan, Mary Kay. "Primary Education and Literacy in Nineteenth-Century Mexico: Research Trends, 1968–1988." *Latin American Research Review* 25, no. 1 (1990): 31–66.

———. *The State, Education, and Social Class in Mexico, 1880–1928*. De Kalb: Northern Illinois University Press, 1982.

Wallerstein, Immanuel. *The Modern World System*. 2 vols. New York: Academic Press, 1974–80.

Walter, Richard J. "Recent Works on Latin American Urban History." *Journal of Urban History* 16, no. 2 (February 1990): 205–14.

Ward, James S. *Yellow Fever in Latin America: A Geographical Study*. Liverpool: Centre for Latin-American Studies, University of Liverpool, 1972.

Weber, Adna Ferrin. *The Growth of Cities in the Nineteenth Century: A Study in Statistics*. Ithaca: Cornell University Press, 1963.

Weinman, Lois Johnson. "Ecuador and Cacao: Domestic Responses to the Boom-Collapse Monoexport Cycle." Ph.D. diss., University of California, 1970.

Whitbeck, R. H., et al. *Economic Geography of South America*. New York: McGraw-Hill, 1940.

Whitten, Norman E. Jr., ed. *Cultural Transformation and Ethnicity in Modern Ecuador*. Urbana: University of Illinois Press, 1981.

Wiles, Dawn Ann. "Land Transportation within Ecuador, 1822–1954." Ph.D. diss., Louisiana State University, 1971.

Wilson, Jacques M. P. *The Development of Education in Ecuador*. Coral Gables: University of Miami Press, 1970.

Winslow, Charles-Edward Amory. *The Conquest of Epidemic Disease: A Chapter in the History of Ideas*. Princeton: Princeton University Press, 1943.

Wolf, Theodore. *Geography and Geology of Ecuador*. Translated by James W. Flanagan. Toronto: Grand and Toy, 1933.

Yans-McLaughlin, Virginia, ed. *Immigration Reconsidered: History, Sociology, and Politics.* New York: Oxford University Press, 1990.

Ycaza, Patricio. *Historia del movimiento obrero ecuatoriano* [History of the Ecuadorian labor movement]. Quito: CEDIME, 1984.

Yeager, Gertrude M. "Elite Education in Nineteenth-Century Chile." *Hispanic American Historical Review* 71, no. 1 (1991): 73–105.

Zehr, Howard. *Crime and the Development of Modern Society: Patterns of Criminality in 19th Century Germany and France.* Guildford, Surrey, England: Croom, Helm, Rowman, and Littlefield, 1976.

Zschock, Dieter K. "Health Care Financing in Central America and the Andean Region." *Latin American Research Review* 15 (1980): 149–68.

# Index

Page numbers in italics refer to figures and tables.